Ultra in the West

THE NORMANDY CAMPAIGN 1944-45

Ralph Bennett

Ultra in the West
THE NORMANDY CAMPAIGN 1944-45

CHARLES SCRIBNER'S SONS • NEW YORK

To Daphne
who put up with so much

Contents

Maps and Figures

Maps

Figures

The Figures are based on Ellis i. 501, 552, ii. 401–2, and Schramm iv. 1757–9 and 1870–2.

Preface

The book sets out to do something which has not been attempted before: to portray the Anglo–American campaign of 1944–5 for the liberation of Europe solely through the intelligence supplied by a single source, Ultra, to demonstrate how reliable forecasts of enemy action were composed out of separate items from the source, and to deduce Ultra's contribution to victory by comparing in detail the contemporary flow of information from it with the whole course of events as now understood. For by often revealing the enemy's plans to them before they decided their own, Ultra gave the Allied commanders an unprecedented advantage in battle: since Ultra was derived from decodes of the Wehrmacht's wireless communications, there could be no doubt about its authenticity, and action based upon it could be taken with the greatest confidence.

So prolific was the source that at many points the Ultra account of the campaign is almost indistinguishable from the 'total' account. On other occasions there are discrepancies between them, because there were gaps in Ultra which it was impossible to prevent or fill. This is therefore not the complete story of the Allies' progress from the invasion beaches to the river Elbe, closely as it may sometimes approach completeness.

Nor is it either a history of Ultra or a history of that part of Bletchley Park where Ultra was produced. Several accounts of the cryptographic assault upon the Enigma machine have been published. None of them is exhaustive, and they do not always agree on important matters of fact; however, I have drawn upon them as well as upon my own memory for the sketch with which chapter 1 begins. The greater part of that chapter describes at first hand the work of the intelligence department—I was a member of it for more than four years—which received decodes of army and air Enigma from the cryptographers, translated and annotated them, and distributed the resulting intelligence to those best capable of using it to further the conduct of the war. Less has been written about this department ('Hut 3'), but here again I have deliberately confined myself to a brief outline. The need to keep safe the secret that Enigma was being broken regularly and to ensure that maximum value was extracted from every decode imposed an ordered discipline upon the way we performed a number of intricately related tasks with the accuracy and speed required, but this discipline was in truth little more than common sense tempered by experience; it is therefore of small interest now, and only a summary of it is necessary. Again, security regulations and shift-working combined to create an inward-looking habit of mind and to build up tensions which affected the behaviour of individuals and groups and made for a vivid social life both on and off duty; but this too is irrelevant to an estimate of what our material enabled us to achieve.

My subject is the intelligence it produced, not Bletchley Park or its inhabitants, but a few preliminary remarks about them are nevertheless required. Most of the leading figures in the early days of Hut 3 were academics, and the exactingly precise standards of meaning and phraseology which their predominantly intellectual approach to military intelligence evolved in response to the demands of the first twelve or eighteen months were strictly preserved throughout the war and became the foundation upon which Ultra's reputation rested. The population of the Hut at that time was small and fairly homogeneous, and this made it easy for decisions to be improvised swiftly to meet the unforeseeable requirements of an age of discovery; it also ensured that most of the decisions were so sound that there was seldom much need to modify them later on. But progressive cryptographic successes soon led to the recruitment of a larger intelligence staff with more varied backgrounds and a wider range of abilities at about the same time as the introduction of direct signalling to Mediterranean commands made it essential to familiarize these headquarters with Hut 3's product and its uses by a stricter adherence to precedent and routine than hitherto. Changes of such magnitude posed problems of administration, organization and authority on a scale not previously encountered. More professional skills were now needed, not to supersede the intellectual but to give them freedom to do their work without distraction, and so to protect and preserve the standards of the past in a new situation when horizons were becoming wider and responsibilities heavier and more complex. The steadying temperament and business experience of Squadron Leader E. M. (later Group Captain Sir Eric) Jones, who became head of Hut 3 at this juncture, ensured that the process of adaptation was smooth, and guided Hut 3 calmly and wisely until the end of the war. Even the briefest account would be seriously incomplete if it did not recognize how much he did for Ultra. Lastly, the comparatively few intelligence officers through whose hands the decodes and signals passed could have achieved nothing without the support of a far larger ancillary staff (part WAAFs, part civilian girls) who manned the teleprinters, encoded our signals, kept the indexes up to date and performed a number of other tasks without which Ultra could not have been produced. Their work was far less interesting than ours, but they were invariably cheerful and devoted to duty.

It is unusual to have the opportunity, when young, of sharing in the creation of an archive and then to be able to use it in later life for the purpose of historical research. I am conscious of my good fortune, but also of the hazards it brings. Writing 'from the inside', I have the advantage of knowing exactly how Ultra was handled. Re-reading the 1944–5 signals, although after so long an interval, has even brought back surprisingly vivid recollections of the particular circumstances in which some of the thousands which bear my initials[1] were drafted. But this advantage has demanded the counterbalance of a deliberate will to

---

1. The three sets of initials which each signal bears identify respectively the Air, Military or Naval Adviser who drafted it, the Duty Officer who approved it for transmission, and the typist.

write objectively; I have tried, for instance, to be as quick to point out what Ultra did not or could not do as to draw attention to its triumphs. It has also enlarged the historian's familiar problem, the avoidance of hindsight, not least because in this instance it has an unfamiliar twist.

Hut 3's job was to process with meticulous care a stream of intelligence items as they came in, and to publish them, under appropriate safeguards, to those who could use them. Our function was to elucidate each item, not to assess the broad significance of them all or to issue periodical commentaries upon the intelligence as a whole. It was not for us to write position papers or propose action, scarcely even to suggest that a certain interpretation might be placed upon a number of apparently unrelated items if they were viewed together in a particular light, unless the reason for doing so derived from our specialized technical knowledge. These things were the province of command staffs and service ministries; we were neither an operational headquarters nor an aloof body of strategists. But since we did not issue appreciations or forecasts, we could hardly make mistakes on the grand scale, although we might err in translating or interpreting single items. There is nothing, for instance, to record what Hut 3 thought at the time about the evidence for an offensive in the Ardennes assembled in chapter 7, or even that it had a collective opinion at all. Awareness of this immunity from past error has made me very cautious before expressing my conviction that the field commanders more than once seriously mistook the true meaning of the Ultra intelligence with which we supplied them.

Just how well was the value of Ultra appreciated by those to whom our signals were sent, and how much use did they make of it? No general or air marshal seems to have left an account of the influence Ultra had on his actions, how much he relied on it, or when and why he disregarded it. The few published statements—like that of Eisenhower (printed in Winterbotham, *The Ultra Secret*)—are so general as to be platitudinous, and Mr Lewin's inquiries (described in *Ultra Goes to War*) did not get very near to a precise and documented answer to the question 'How was Ultra used in the field?' The area left open to speculation is therefore inconveniently large, and is likely to remain so unless the archives in London or Washington still contain unpublished memoranda composed at the time by senior officers which list specific instances of the use of Ultra.[1] It would probably be a great mistake to assume that because its value is now evident Ultra 'must have been' always rated as highly then, or to imagine that it could be used regularly in the field in a way corresponding at all closely to the intellectual care lavished upon each signal at Bletchley. There is, for instance, good reason to think that some commanders viewed it more favourably than others, and that the range of difference between them was wide.

Nevertheless, it is important historically to determine the relation between military intelligence and military action as far as possible. In the absence of contemporary statements, my approach has necessarily been from the opposite direction: by a close comparison between the times of Ultra signals and the times of related events to show what information was in commanders' hands before they took decisions which Ultra could affect, and to assume that they always took account of everything from so important a source if they received it in time. This method cannot, of course, provide an absolutely certain answer to the question 'How was Ultra used?' but it ought to produce a close approximation in most cases.

The exhaustive study of western Ultra in 1944–5 thus involved has gradually forced me to the unexpected conclusion that there is a striking difference between the heed paid to Ultra before and after the great August advance from Falaise. During the landings, round Caen, along the Odon, on the road to Avranches and at Mortain, the operational use of Ultra is written plainly in the record of events: knowledge of what was in their enemy's mind manifestly brought military advantages to the Allied commanders and saved many lives. Unhappily, there is a different story to tell between early September and Christmas. Ultra's warnings were disregarded over the capture of Antwerp docks and before Arnhem and the Ardennes offensive, with unfortunate consequences on each occasion. At a loss for

1. A few instances are quoted, but in rather general terms, in the reports of some American Ultra officers: PRO 31/20.

a better explanation (for of course Ultra itself suggests none) I have accepted one that has been advanced before—the dulling effect on tired minds of the heady scents of victory carried by the warm breezes of late summer, and the over-confidence that resulted. But although this may serve over Antwerp (where success was sudden and unforeseen) it wears thin for Arnhem and is threadbare by mid-December. The new Ultra evidence drives home the avoidable nature of the mistakes which were made during the autumn of 1944, and sharpens criticism of the Allied command. The three real though transient victories which were Hitler's reply to his defeat at Mortain and Falaise could have been prevented. To say this, however, is not to forget that intelligence about the enemy is only one (and not necessarily the chief) among the many considerations which determine a general's actions, nor (to return to an earlier point) does it arise out of any desire on my part to prove that Bletchley always knew best—for I do not believe that the residual loyalties of the former intelligence officer have clouded the judgement of the present-day historian.

About 25,000 signals[1] were sent from Hut 3 to western commands between the opening of the service to Eisenhower's headquarters in January 1944 and the end of hostilities. They form the evidence upon which this book is based, but it should be realized that they were only a small part of Hut 3's output. The most urgent and important translated decodes were teleprinted to London at once, signals derived from some of them having been dispatched already; the rest were prepared in the form of typewritten reports. Although by the autumn we were signalling troop movements in the Baltic lands to General Eisenhower and news of the fighting in the Danube valley to Field Marshal Alexander in Italy, some teleprinted and most re-

1. Signals to western and Mediterranean commands were included in the same numerical series, so that it is impossible to determine accurately how many went to each theatre without counting them individually. The combined total for the period January 1944–May 1945 is well over 45,000. The figure of 25,000 in the text rests on my impression that the Italian signals I merely glanced at in the Public Record Office were rather less numerous than the western signals I studied.

ported items went unsignalled, and they must together have
been at least four or five times more numerous. The evidence
used here—for neither teleprints nor reports have been released
—is therefore but the tip of an iceberg for volume, although of
course it includes everything deemed at the time to be of any
operational significance.

Every Ultra-based statement in the following pages is supported by one or more signals, but all references to the signals
have been placed at the end of the book (pp. 292–322) save
when it was desirable to draw attention to the speed with which
a particular piece of information was passed to commands in
the field. Such references appear in the margin, opposite the
statement they support, in the form 0221/6 KV 6573 0530/6
(the example comes from p. 65). This means that signal number KV 6573 was derived from an Enigma message originating
at 0221 hours on the sixth day of the month (the month is usually self-evident from the context) and was dispatched from
Hut 3 at 0530 hours the same day—i.e. that only three hours
and nine minutes separated German and British times of origin;
if the exact German time of origin is not stated in the signal,
the figures 0221/6 are replaced by a phrase like 'early/6' or '6
June'.[1] Where no such reference appears in the margin, it may
be assumed that in most cases the relevant signal was passed
between six and twelve hours after German time of origin, but
that it did not seem necessary to record here either time-lag or
time of Ultra delivery. The vast majority of Ultra signals fell
into this category, and the text should be read with this in
mind. There was also a small third class, mainly derived from
the frequently recalcitrant army keys: decodes delayed by cryptographic difficulties which would have had greater value if they
had been available sooner. They were only a minority of cases,
and I hope that my scrupulousness in drawing attention to them
has not given undue prominence to these occasional delays.
It has sometimes been necessary to refer to non-Ultra
sources, whether contemporary or subsequent, to fill in a gap or

1. An asterisk after the marginal note indicates that this signal is reproduced
in the section on pp. 276–91.

reinforce an argument. I have endeavoured always to frame my sentences so that the distinction between Ultra and non-Ultra is immediately apparent, but cannot hope that I have always succeeded. In order to avoid another unintentional ambiguity of language, I have always referred to communications between Germans in Enigma as 'messages' and communications from Hut 3 to field commands as 'signals'.

Each chapter begins with a short section sketching the outline, from standard sources, of the events to be covered in that chapter.

Among the many who have given me valuable help and advice were several former wartime colleagues: Dr D. W. Babbage, Mr T. R. Leathem, Sir Herbert Marchant, Sir Stuart Milner-Barry, Mrs Mary Pain and Professor F. P. Pickering. I am grateful to them all, but must emphasize that none has read my text and that I alone am responsible for any errors in it. The greatest kindness has been shown me at the Public Record Office by Miss P. M. Barnes, Mr E. M. Denham and Mr F. F. Lambert, all of whom have put themselves to much trouble to assist me on many occasions. I owe a debt of gratitude to my editor, Mrs Sue Hogg, whose watchful eye spotted several inconsistencies in my text and helped me to remove accidental traces of unfamiliar intelligence jargon. My regular typist, Mrs Joanna Sanders, has enthusiastically adapted herself to the unfamiliar vocabulary of war, and Mrs Janet Webb has deputized for her several times: I thank them both.

Special thanks are due to my publisher, Charles Clark, who has borne with equanimity a series of frustrating delays in the release of my material to the Public Record Office, and to his former colleague, my elder son Francis, who—perhaps because he was born at Bletchley—first suggested that his father should write this book.

Bletchley wives with young children had a miserable war: not permitted to know until thirty years later what it was that took their husbands away at all hours of the day or night with the rotation of shift-work and returned them tired, uncommunicative and irritable, they bore their lot as cheerfully as they could.

I have dedicated this book to my wife in recognition of her for-bearance then and her encouragement now.

Cambridge   *Ralph Bennett*
May 1979

Note: My manuscript was already in the printer's hands before the first volume of the official British Intelligence history (F. H. Hinsley, E. E. Thomas, C. F. G. Ransom and R. C. Knight, *British Intelligence in the Second World War,* Volume 1, HMSO, 1979) was published. The two books appear to agree on all material points concerning the breaking of Enigma, but otherwise cover completely different ground.

1

How it was done

The secret that during almost the whole of the Second World War the radio communications of the German armed forces were decoded at Bletchley Park was kept for thirty years. The feats of cryptography, mathematics and electrical engineering which made the decoding possible were marvels without parallel. In consequence, the 1939–45 war was the first in which one side was regularly privy to the thoughts of the other and could shape its own actions in the light of that knowledge so far as its resources permitted and its strategic objectives made desirable. But there is a third, almost equally remarkable side to the story. Known in 1939–40 only by a handful of British Intelligence personnel, the astonishing secret was shared in 1944–5 by several thousand British and American men and women of all types, and yet it was as safely kept at the end as at the beginning. Ultra undoubtedly brought new dimensions into strategic planning and battlefield generalship, and it has been somewhat loosely said that the Allies might not have won the war without it. To measure the new dimensions with any precision is difficult enough, without indulging in unprovable speculations like this; what is certain, however, is that ill-considered action by commanders or careless talk by any of those who handled Ultra at home or abroad might have betrayed the secret, thus drying up the invaluable source by causing the enemy to change his cipher-system, and so have cost countless lives by denying the Supreme Command the benefit of Ultra during the 1944–5 campaign. The great marvel was the opportunity to see into the enemy's mind, but several scarcely lesser marvels flowed from it.

The success of the Government Code and Cipher School at Bletchley in defeating the supposedly invulnerable Enigma machine and reading the signals encoded with it was not officially admitted until October 1977, when a batch of Ultra material was deposited in the Public Record Office. Unofficially, the cat had been out of the bag since the publication of F. W. Winterbotham's *The Ultra Secret* in 1974, and several books as well as radio and television programmes followed in the course of the next four years. As one of the founders of the party working on Enigma, Group Captain Winterbotham had inside knowledge, and so had some others who have written or spoken since. With three partial[1] exceptions, however, all these authors were writing from memory and not from documents. The present book is the first to reconstruct the Ultra story of a campaign directly from the signals which were sent from Bletchley to the Allied commanders.

Decoding Enigma

Because victory is seldom won by force alone, German rearmament in the 1930s was not simply a matter of building enough aircraft, tanks and pocket battleships to impose the Führer's will. These weapons would lose half their stunning power unless there were swift, secret and reliable means of directing them so that, for instance, the armoured spearheads could be told their next objective even when far ahead of the rest of the army, or Stuka attacks be laid on at a moment's notice to clear their path. Effective control called for a vast radio network—existing civilian telephone cables could not carry all the extra traffic, nor could new lines be laid with sufficient speed—and for signals equipment robust enough to stand up to service conditions. Radio communications can always be intercepted: how,

1. Part of Patrick Beesly's *Very Special Intelligence* (1977) is based on naval decodes which were placed in the Public Record Office in 1975. R. V. Jones, *Most Secret War* (1978), draws on reports he wrote at the time; the reports were in many cases based on Enigma material. There are some references to Ultra signals in Ronald Lewin, *Ultra Goes to War* (1978).

then, find a code which would prevent an enemy from understanding what he heard and yet at the same time be swift enough in use to meet the requirements of *Blitzkrieg?* The cryptographic successes of the British in particular during the 1914–18 war showed that the only really secure code was the one-time pad system,[1] but this was unsuited to the task in hand: it requires skilled operators, and there was not time to train so many (the Luftwaffe communications system in the West alone employed 50,000 men in 1944); it demands an impossible foresight in printing and distributing millions of pads in advance; and it is slow in operation.

The solution of the problem was to use machine-encipherment—still a novelty at that time—to perform the intricate part of the process. The Enigma machine had been patented in 1919 and marketed without much success during the 1920s by a German firm as a means of safeguarding commercial secrets. It used a system of wheels or drums to complicate the path followed by an electric current when a key on its keyboard was depressed, thus making the relationship between the letters of the plain-text and the encoded version so erratic as to be undiscoverable by any decoding process then known. Soon after they seized power, the Nazis bought up the patent and improved the machine, and by the late 1930s it was in use by all branches of the Wehrmacht. It looked like a rather large and clumsy portable typewriter, but it was compact and sturdy enough to stand up to rough treatment. The electrical circuits it contained were immensely complicated, but anyone could learn to use it. Thus it was ideal for its purpose—simple in operation, yet it could make radio signals secure against the eavesdropper. Its only drawback was that it did not print out the encoded text; in-

1. A military vocabulary is constructed, and each word or phrase represented by a group of figures. To the groups representing the words of the message which is to be sent are added other random figure-groups taken from one page of a pad supplied for the purpose. The receiver, who holds another copy of the same pad, subtracts the random numbers and recovers the vocabulary figure-groups. Both sender and receiver then destroy that page of the pad. Provided the random numbers are used only once, the hostile cryptographer is defeated because he can never collect enough evidence to enable him to discover the underlying vocabulary-groups (if he succeeded in doing this, there would be no insuperable problem in finding out their meaning, given a sufficiency of signals-traffic).

stead, each letter was lit up in turn on a display-screen, so that two or more operators were needed—one to type out the plain-text, another to copy down the code-letters as they appeared. The three wheels or drums could be chosen from a set of five, and were interchangeable; each had an outer metal rim which could be locked to it in twenty-six different positions, one for each letter of the alphabet. Each time a key was depressed the right-hand wheel moved on one place (i.e. made one twenty-sixth of a revolution), once in every twenty-six times the middle wheel also moved, and all three moved together when the middle wheel had made a complete revolution—just in the way a car's mileometer does. The current passed through all three wheels and a fixed drum (the *Umkehrwalze*) which sent it back again by a different route. Later on, another complication was introduced: after leaving the wheels, the current was made to pass along loose wires ending in *Stecker* (plugs) which could be plugged in pairs into the machine in any order. The positions of the wheels and the order of the plugs were frequently changed in accordance with standard instructions; there was usually one major rearrangement every twenty-four hours, with minor adjustments at shorter intervals. In addition, the sender chose different settings of the wheels for every message, telling the receiver what he had done by means of an 'indicator'—two groups of three letters with which every message began. (The receiver would set his wheels to the position shown by the first group and by decoding the letters of the second group discover the setting at which the body of the text could be decoded.) In order to decode a given group of traffic, it was necessary (and sufficient) to know the choice and order of the three wheels, the positions of their outer rims, and the *Stecker* pairings. Wheels and rims together could provide something over a million possible arrangements, and the introduction of the *Stecker* pairings multiplied this to a total of approximately 150 million million million possible but unpredictably different code versions of a single original text. It might take months—perhaps years—of unremitting application by a roomful of expert mathematicians to find the right solution to even a single day's key, and the Germans therefore believed that an Enigma message could safely be transmitted by wireless in ordinary Morse code, for although it was sure to be intercepted it would certainly be unintelligible. They never seriously questioned this belief.

The Polish Government, fearful that it was to be Hitler's next victim and anxious for warning of his army's moves, trained a party of mathematicians and set them to work to break the Enigma code; they devised a machine to test possible solutions, and read many signals until the Germans introduced new complications into their procedure in 1939. France and England were also tackling the problem and the three countries began to concert measures, most notably when the Poles handed over a reconstructed Enigma machine to the British shortly before the outbreak of war. Anglo–French co-operation continued until the fall of France in 1940, after which all the work was concentrated at Bletchley Park.[1]

Possession of an Enigma machine gave indispensable familiarity with its circuits, but otherwise did not help towards decoding its messages; for this, it was essential to discover the settings used, and the mathematical problem thereby posed was formidable indeed. Only a machine could consistently defeat the machine; certainly, nothing else would do if the messages were to be read in time to be useful. A young Cambridge mathematician, Alan Turing, who had worked on the theory of a universal calculating machine, was brought together with cryptographers skilled in all the tricks of their trade, and they had the benefit of the Poles' experience with the decoding machine they had constructed. By the early summer of 1940 an electro-mechanical engine (always referred to as the 'bombe') had been built at Bletchley and had proved its designers' genius by decoding several days' traffic.

Human ingenuity had to give the machine a start, however. In theory the bombe could try out all the millions of possible solutions to a day's key, but it would take an immensely long time to do this. And how was it to tell its attendants that it had come upon the right solution, because it had found one that was in German not gibberish? Before starting the bombe, it was necessary to make a correct guess at the decoded version of a

---

1. Somewhat differing accounts of all this are given by Winterbotham, Calvocoressi, Cave Brown, Jones, Johnson and Lewin.

bit of the text. In the early days it was sometimes possible, because of the slack cipher discipline of some of the GAF (German Air Force) signalling staff, to guess the initial settings of some messages, and this provided decodes of the last three letters of their indicator-groups. The first breaks were achieved during the spring of 1940 in this way—that is, by hand and without the help of the bombe. Before long the Germans tightened up their cipher discipline, but by that time the damage had been done. For as soon as a few days' traffic had been decoded, a second careless habit[1] was discovered, one which the GAF signallers never abandoned. The tightening-up of cipher discipline had made future breaks by hand impossible or hopelessly laborious, but the second bad habit was enough to start the bombe off and to give it a good chance of finding the right solution to the day's key.

Success came just in time for the Battle of France and the Battle of Britain, though as yet it was by no means always possible to break a given day's key while it was still current. If the bombe occasionally faltered, however, it never failed: the flow of decoded messages was already regular and remunerative enough when I arrived at Bletchley in February 1941 for shift-working round the clock to be necessary for the intelligence staff which translated and appraised them. From then on, the output of decodes showed a constant tendency to rise, except for rare and fortunately brief intervals. A temporary decline in the volume of traffic accounted for one or two of these intervals, and progressive improvements in the Enigma machine for others. But although these improvements eventually raised the number of possible versions of a given plain-text to over 10^{33}, none of them caused more than transient inconvenience to the Bletchley codebreakers.

1. Military operations call for regular reports from the front line back to headquarters: they are likely to be rendered at much the same time each day and may be of much the same length. Thus there is a reasonable chance of identifying them on external evidence alone. The first few days' traffic to be decoded showed that—contrary to the rule that all cipher staff are taught—the GAF frequently began these routine reports with the same formula each time ('Evening report from Fliegerkorps II', for instance). If the probable evening report in a new day's undecoded traffic could be identified from external evidence, and if these words were set against its opening code-groups, then the bombe could get to work with good prospects of success.

This brief and entirely second-hand description of Enigma, the cryptographic problems it presented and how they were solved may end with an account of the way in which Enigma served the Wehrmacht's ends and how it consequently presented itself to Bletchley Park. All three services used Enigma, but differently, and within each service different forms of it were used for different purposes. Thus by 1945 there were more than a dozen 'species' (so to speak) of naval Enigma—one for surface ships in the North Sea and Atlantic and another for U-boats in the same area, a third for Mediterranean surface vessels and a fourth for Mediterranean U-boats and so on. Naval Enigma proved difficult to break and the first successes were not gained until early in 1941. German Air Force Enigma was easier game—partly because there was much more of it, so that the cryptanalysts' foundations were laid sooner, partly because of the slack signals discipline resulting from hasty expansion and low-grade operators[1]—and it was the first to be broken in late spring 1940. Again, there were several 'species'—one for general GAF use in north-western Europe, another for the Mediterranean (respectively 'Red' and 'Light Blue' in Bletchley jargon), several for aerial reconnaissance and army co-operation in particular theatres of war. A great deal of ground information was thus transmitted over GAF links (the Flivos—*Fliegerverbindungsoffiziere,* air liaison officers—were one of our most prolific sources of information about the Panzer divisions or corps to which they were attached) and it therefore did not matter so much that army signals discipline was good enough to delay regular decoding until 1942. All told, there were not less than thirty different army and air Enigma keys, several of which might, in the last two years of the war at any rate, be 'running' at the same time, at least one of them currently.

Signalling Ultra

Popular accounts of Bletchley Park have hitherto concentrated on the decoding miracle, and indeed some of the foregoing has

---

1. See the complaint of General Martini, head of GAF Signals, in Jones 244.

been drawn from these accounts. But as soon as decoded signals were plentifully available a new requirement promptly became evident. Cryptographic skill and mathematical insight were no longer enough; an exact and fluent knowledge of German and an aptitude for intelligence work were now also needed if the miracle was to be exploited to the full. The two sets of qualities complemented each other; the latter was only called for because of the success gained by the former, of course, but henceforth it was just as essential.

Inescapable differences between the best methods of handling intelligence by the three British services now imposed organizational distinctions. Evidence about the movements of German surface vessels and U-boats could be properly appraised and acted on only by those who knew where British ships and convoys were—that is to say, by the Admiralty, which was an operational command headquarters as well as a government ministry. Naval decodes were therefore translated at Bletchley Park and teleprinted, almost without annotation, to the Admiralty, who re-routed convoys or took other necessary action. Similar considerations scarcely applied to army and air intelligence. Except for advance news of German bombing raids (for which the Air Ministry acted in the same way as the Admiralty did for all naval intelligence), very little of it could be immediate and operational in the circumstances prevailing during the winter of 1940–41. War Office and Air Ministry had much in common with each other (for the moment the former was very much the junior partner, since army Enigma was at first so much more recalcitrant than air), and many things distinguished the attitude of both towards Ultra from that of the Admiralty. A common intelligence organization for these two services was therefore set up at Bletchley Park. It was always known as Hut 3,[1] even after it moved into more convenient brick premises; it was this organization which I joined in February 1941, and it is only Hut 3 and its output with which the rest of this book is concerned.

As soon as the Germans invaded Yugoslavia and Greece and

---

1. Decodes were supplied to Hut 3 by Hut 6. In a similar pairing, Hut 8 supplied Hut 4 (the Naval Section).

began to intervene in Africa in the spring of 1941 a further common characteristic of army and air Ultra became evident, and this too shaped our organization in a fundamental way. Like the Naval Section, Hut 3 teleprinted its hottest information to ministries in London (less urgent material was typed and sent up by bag), but in addition it had already begun to annotate and elucidate each item from background information derived from previous decodes and accumulated in its card-indexes. The swift movement of events in Greece and Cyrenaica, and the direct bearing of Ultra evidence on the fate of British troops there, soon made it plain that much would be gained if the decodes were fully processed in Hut 3 and if signals based on them were immediately sent to commands in the field. Many perhaps vital hours would thus be saved. The first signals were sent to Cairo in March 1941. Other receiving stations were established as need arose—the air and naval headquarters in Malta and Alexandria were the first—until by the time the Allied armies broke out of the Normandy bridgehead in July 1944 Hut 3 must have been serving forty or fifty subscribers in north-west Europe, Italy and the Mediterranean. Each of these subscribers was serviced by a Special Liaison Unit, a signals link established for this sole purpose and operating under stringent security rules; the SLUs have been described by Group Captain Winterbotham, who set them up and was responsible for their activities.

The veil of official secrecy which had hidden Ultra was lifted in October 1977 when some 25,000 of these signals, covering the period November 1943 to August 1944, were placed in the Public Record Office.[1] Later, the series was carried down to the end of the war. These signals are the evidence upon which this book is based. Each signal drew its authority from one or more decodes, which were themselves translated and teleprinted *in extenso* to the service ministries along with copies of the Hut 3 signals derived from them. The teleprints, if they still exist, have not been released. Because the Hut 3 signals were not only checked meticulously at the time of drafting for accurate

---

1. A larger number of the (far shorter) naval teleprints was also released. These covered rather different dates.

statement of fact and appropriately qualified comment but also
re-checked later on both in the Hut and in London, it is safe to
assume that their wording fairly represents the information received, though usually in summary form. Moreover, nothing
which was regarded, either at the moment of receipt or during
subsequent re-scrutiny, as being important for the conduct of
Allied operations was left unsignalled. Even unsupported by
the teleprinted translations, therefore, the signals represent all
the Ultra that was sent to field commands and all that was
thought worth sending. The evidence used here is the same as
that which was in the hands of the chief intelligence officers on
the staffs of Eisenhower, Montgomery and Bradley.

What most of the signals lack, however, is more than a hint
of the considerable intelligence servicing which almost every
decode needed and received. The full meaning of the information conveyed by a message was only rarely self-evident from
the translation alone, and it was usually necessary to draw out
its significance by providing it with a context and setting it
against a background as like as possible to that which would
have been in the minds of the German sender and receiver.
With the aid of Hut 3's extensive indexes, built up from previous messages, this could nearly always be done in considerable
detail, and the teleprint annotated accordingly. An order for a
Panzer division to move from one part of the front to another,
for instance, obviously gained added significance if a note
pointed out that we already knew that several others were going
in the same direction or that the new message countermanded
previous orders. Little of all this intelligence work appears in
the signals, however; partly in order to save scarce signalling
time, and partly because recipients would draw the same deductions from the same evidence; these annotations—always introduced by the word 'Comment', to distinguish them clearly from
the text of the German message—were much scantier in the signals than in the teleprints. This is now occasionally an obstacle
to understanding all the implications of the intelligence conveyed in a given signal, and since I have been able neither to
see the teleprint footnotes nor to attempt to reconstruct them
by consulting the card-index, I may have slightly misjudged the
significance of some items.

By early in 1941 a convenient flow of work and a suitable division of labour had been discovered by experience; it remained substantially unchanged for the rest of the war.

At whatever hour of the day or night a key was broken by Hut 6, word was immediately passed to Hut 3 and decodes soon began to reach the No. 1 of the Watch. Partly for historical reasons dating back to pre-war recruitment, partly by chance, the translating watch was largely composed of civilians, although almost all the rest of the Hut's personnel were in uniform. From mid-1942 onwards an ever-growing number of Americans joined us. So interdependent was every phase of the work and so enthusiastic everyone to play his part to the best of his or her ability that Hut 3 was from the start, and always remained, a good example of that inter-service and inter-Allied co-operation which kept the wheels of the Anglo–American Supreme Command turning smoothly, but which completely eluded the Germans although they possessed the formal framework for it in the OKW (Supreme Command of the Armed Forces). This spirit of co-operation had to withstand quite severe strains, particularly when an essential expansion of staff brought some overcrowding. On days when Red and Light Blue were both current at once—and very likely other keys as well—and critical operations were on hand in both theatres, an eight-hour tour of duty could be very tiring, because it required repeated shifts of attention from Normandy to Italy and back again and because it called incessantly for absolute accuracy and continual alertness against errors of judgement while at the same time demanding that everything be done as quickly as possible.

Work reached the No. 1 of the Watch in the form of printouts from the intercept stations with lengths of paper-tape from the decoding machine (Hut 6 was better off than the German operators in this respect) pasted on to the back of each sheet. Intercept and decode alike were in the five-figure groups of the original transmission. Weather conditions or static might have caused some letters to be missed at the moment of intercept and others to be taken down wrongly, but in most cases an experienced No. 1 had only to glance at a message to decide its urgency. The first task of the watchkeeper who dealt with it was to supply the missing letters and correct the corruptions, dividing the five-letter groups up into words and expanding the many abbreviations used. The work of emendation could be quite straightforward with a clean text in continuous German prose, but when unfamiliar technical terms were used, or when missed or corrupt letters occurred at critical points, considerable difficulty could be encountered before the German text could be plausibly reconstructed and an acceptable translation made. Where it proved impossible to eliminate all doubt from a word or phrase, the degree of uncertainty was shown in the translation by one of several typographical conventions devised for the purpose.

When he was satisfied that the English version fairly represented the sense of the German, the No. 1 handed text and translation to the Air and Military Advisers, service officers who sat opposite each other at the next table in the production-line. One or other, as the case required, would use the resources of the huge card-indexes maintained by his section to explore the significance of the text before him—for a correct and lucid translation could still present severe intelligence problems. Valuable information was often squeezed out of unpromising material by persistent investigation of such unlikely detail as the previous employment of a corporal (if he were known to have been engaged on radar work, for instance, his present movements might suggest those of his unit, or the opening of a new tracking station). There was also a Naval Adviser ready to deal with such messages (they were rare in the western campaign) as might have naval interest—e.g. orders for GAF cover to be provided for German shipping movements; the Naval Adviser was also the channel by which such Hut 4 productions as concerned the ground fighting (for instance, reports to the German Admiralty from the naval base at Brest, when it was isolated and besieged, about the morale of the garrison) were routed through Hut 3 and signalled to Allied ground commands. Having solved his problems as best he could, the Adviser annotated the translation accordingly, decided whether the item merited a signal to commands abroad, drafted the signal if he so decided, and then handed everything over to the Duty Officer for final approval before it passed to the Signals Officer and his staff of teleprinter operators and coding clerks. Over two hundred such signals were sent on D-Day, and an average of more than a thousand a week was maintained for the next fcw months.

Duty Officers knew German and the intelligence background well, but their prime function was to be responsible for everything rather than to be as expert as their colleagues in any single field; my own qualifications for the post (I was appointed when the system began early in 1942 and served until the end of the war) did not include a degree in modern languages, for instance. Theirs was a twofold responsibility: first, to see that translation and signal both faithfully represented the sense of the original, looking for misconceptions which incautious wording might accidentally convey to recipients of a signal, and asking for appropriate changes if necessary. A partially corrupt text, a translation unavoidably loose because of the imprecision of the German original, difficulty in drawing confident conclusions from a perhaps incomplete intercept—all these might lead to uncertainties, the exact nature and degree of which it was essential to make clear to recipients, who in some instances might possess evidence capable of resolving them provided they were told exactly what was certain and what doubtful. After discovering the unavoidable ambiguities of 'probably' and 'possibly', we settled on 'strong', 'fair' and 'slight indications' to represent descending degrees of confidence, placing the doubtful words in brackets.[1] This convention will be noticed in some of the signals reproduced.

1. For example, suppose a message to concern the movement of a division the number of which is partly corrupt and reads NEUND-EA. Clearly, the division's number is somewhere in the nineties. Either ZWEI, DREI or VIER will fit the second figure: DREI is the most likely, for two of its letters are correct; but a fifty-fifty probability falls far short of certainty, and there might be one or two corrupt letters as well as the missed letter. The Hut 3 signal should read '. . . nine (fair indications three) division . . .'. If the 93rd division has been identified at the front through prisoners, say, the recipient will probably disregard our doubt, but he is also warned of the possibility that the enemy has been reinforced by another division whose number is in the nineties, because the signal has left the second numeral uncertain. (The next day might produce an intercept or a prisoner from the 92nd or the 94th division.)

Single brackets were used, as above, to define the area of doubt. The double brackets which occur in every signal are merely a device indicating how the address was buried for transmission purposes, in order to avoid the same dangerous error as that noted on p. 6.

As well as overseeing the observance of standard conventions like these, the Duty Officer was responsible for ensuring that strict security was maintained. Nothing must be signalled which openly revealed the source, nothing sent to a recipient which did not directly concern him—the criterion was his 'need to know' its content, which must be of 'value not interest' to him—and various groups of recipients had to be kept informed on an all-or-none basis lest consultation between them be frustrated.

Behind the sometimes hectic activity of these front-line troops lay several research departments whose specialized knowledge was indispensable. One of them combined a rigorously academic understanding of grammatical niceties and precise shades of meaning and a knack of divining the correct expansion of novel German abbreviations with a trained mechanic's repertory of the technical terms: it invited the Duty Officer to veto inspired guesses at baffling texts if they did not meet its exacting standards, and it knew the meaning of the long German names for the working parts of radar sets and rockets, tank-tracks and self-propelled guns (without which the significance of repair-shop reports and supply returns could not be grasped). Another section took on longer-term research projects where only the careful sifting of accumulated evidence could solve a problem. Supply returns for both services were normally rendered according to a pro-forma, for instance, but the pro-forma was unintelligible without a key to the numbered paragraphs. Given enough examples and the dexterous juxtaposition of scraps of information and plausible hypotheses, the key could almost always be found in the end—and commands informed how many tanks and guns a Panzer division possessed, or how many serviceable aircraft there were in a bomber squadron and how many under repair in the workshops. When the Enigma used by the German State Railways (first broken in the summer of 1940) was found to contain little more than strings of six-figure consignment numbers, it was this department which painstakingly distilled a meaning from the mass of superficially uninteresting and unrewarding detail, managed to associate some of the consignment numbers with army or air force units, noted how destinations and the timing of movements converged on Germany's eastern frontier in the spring of 1941—and forecast the invasion of Russia. A third section concentrated on the inscrutable but tremendously important traffic which carried instructions about navigational beams to the long-range bomber Gruppen and (later on) provided valuable clues to the research going on at Peenemünde and to the construction of V-weapon sites for the bombardment of London.[1] A fourth undertook to assemble and collate German identifications (mainly derived from the German Y-Service, which studied the external features of undecoded wireless traffic and located transmitters by direction-finding techniques) of British and American formations and their ideas about the Allied order of battle. Its studies were of immense value, particularly in the weeks immediately before and after D-Day, because they showed the success of the Allied deception plan in creating the impression that the Normandy landings were only secondary and that the main invasion would come in the Calais area. Ultra showed how well Fortitude (as the deception plan was code-named) was working; some of the evidence will be examined later on.

These research departments had some contact with the world of non-Ultra intelligence outside Bletchley Park and were able to utilize information thus gained to assist and accelerate their work. But they were alone in this. Hut 3 existed to purvey pure Ultra, not to adulterate it with anything else. No teleprint or signal ever bore footnote or comment derived from anything except Hut 3's own card-indexes, save that map-references were interpolated into front-line reports, etc., as an aid to quick understanding. No hint of forthcoming Allied operations normally reached the Hut, so that we remained 'pure'. It was an exception to this rule when a few of us were given details of Overlord a day or two before the landings in order that we might keep an eye open for anything bearing on them, but a fortnight later we had no more idea than the general public that Montgomery planned to attract as many German tanks as he

1. Because of the peculiarly complex and technical nature of this material, it was early removed from the normal flow of work and diverted to a special section in Hut 3 which was in direct contact about it with the Air Ministry. The use made of it is fully described in R. V. Jones, *Most Secret War*.

could towards Caen in order to facilitate the American break-
out farther west. This 'purity' was in some respects a hindrance,
and no doubt meant that we sometimes sent information need-
lessly or when it was already out of date; but it ruled out all
possibility that we might unconsciously read our evidence in the
light of extraneous knowledge, and left it entirely to intelligence
staffs in the field to assimilate Ultra to other sources, judge between them if there were discrepancies and present their commander with a single picture.

This 'purity' had one unforeseen consequence. It meant that
we followed the fighting from the German point of view exclu-
sively, and knew much more about most German divisions and
some German generals than we did about any on our own side.
Rommel, Westphal and Bayerlein were familiar figures long before they came to France, 90 Light Division so daily an ac-
quaintance during the African campaign that there was even a
sort of temptation to rejoice when it scored a success. Although
9 and 10 SS Panzer Divisions became as familiar in the west,
because of their repeated appearances in crucial roles, they
never acquired the same almost friendly aspect. No doubt the
mood belonged, as with the general public, to the desert war.

Is it possible to discover how much Ultra contributed to the
whole intelligence picture? The chapters which follow are an
attempt to answer this question, but several points must be
made first, lest false impressions be given.

(i) Because Hut 3 was told nothing about Allied intentions,
nothing in the signals themselves indicates their relative value
(save, of course, in so far as the priority given to each is a
guide to the opinion of those who drafted it[1]). In order to try to
estimate this fairly, I have always compared the signals with the
actual course of events as it is now known from official histories and from the memoirs of leading participants, setting what
we knew in Hut 3—and the time at which we knew it—beside
what happened (so far as this can be reconstructed) and point-

---

1. Its relative priority was shown by one, two, three, four or five zs at the
head of each signal, zzzzz indicating maximum urgency.

ing out the similarities and—where necessary—the contrasts and discrepancies. Essential though it was, in order to ensure a sound frame of reference, this has meant risking unconscious hindsight, and I have tried to be continuously on my guard against it. For Ultra, in common with all other military intelligence, became available piece by piece in no very logical order as a pattern of largely unforeseeable events gradually unfolded itself, while a historian writing thirty years later cannot entirely obliterate from his mind an awareness of their outcome. Yet this awareness must make it harder for him to assess objectively the importance which may have seemed to belong to each item of information at the time it was received and to see that its place in the jigsaw of interpretation may then have appeared quite different from what it really was.

In one form or another, this risk is inseparable from all history-writing; but it is particularly acute in this case, where the value attached to a piece of information could often depend directly upon whether it was received before or after the events it foretold. Further, it is necessary to recognize that historians often discover an unbridgeable gap between information and action; even when the former is known to have been available in time to influence the latter, we may not be quite positive that it did, and the exact reason why Caesar crossed the Rubicon or Cardigan ordered the charge of the Light Brigade may elude inquiry. In many cases, no doubt, there never was any written record of how a commander arrived at a decision and of the part Ultra played in making up his mind; in the heat of battle it was necessary for him to issue orders, not to spend time recording why he did so. 'From the standpoint of the soldiers, everything else was more important than what the future would eventually read', ruefully wrote the distinguished medievalist Percy Ernst Schramm when he edited the War Diary of the OKW which, as a major in the Reserve, he had kept throughout the western campaigns; he remembered how hard it had been to persuade the generals to give him copies of their orders for inclusion in the diary. Much of the evidence which would be needed for a precise estimate of the importance of Ultra may in fact never have existed.

(ii) Since every Ultra item carried weight because of its un-impeachable authenticity, however, common sense suggests that a very close approximation can be obtained through a careful study of the timing of Ultra intelligence. For where an Ultra item can be shown to have arrived in time, it is not likely to have been disregarded. The history of most Enigma messages can still be traced from German time of origin to the moment at which the Ultra signal derived from it was sent off. Reasonable allowance must then be made for transmission time, for decoding upon receipt, and for consideration by the intelligence officer who received it and by the commander who might act upon it. Where this still leaves an interval before the action described in, or consequent upon, the signal, it may be presumed that the Allied commander's measures were taken in the light of the Ultra information. Thus Ultra gave ample warning of Hitler's foolhardy attempt to cut off the spearhead of the American advance by attacking from Mortain towards Avranches in August 1944, and so enabled Montgomery and Bradley to make preparations to meet it and to take full advantage of the confusion into which its failure threw the German armies.[1] Few cases are as simple or as obviously important as this, but I have been at pains to give full evidence about timing so that the probable bearing of information upon decisions may be estimated as exactly as possible. This evidence does not support the claim that decoded information was sometimes passed 'within the hour'. Granted the number of operations to be performed—decoding, translating, intelligence servicing, encoding the new signal—it would scarcely have been possible to do this. The shortest interval I have noticed between Enigma and Ultra times of origin is just over two hours,[2] and this is surely remarkable enough.

(iii) A still more serious danger in this line of thought is the assumption that Ultra's chief value lay in the realm of battlefield tactics. This was almost certainly not the case. Even in the most favourable circumstances, three or four hours might

1. See pp. 114–19 below.
2. xls 3877, 6234 (pp. 109 and 122 respectively), 5111 and 5119 (neither quoted in text) were all passed in two and a quarter hours. A three-hour interval was comparatively common: there are examples on pp. 107 and 108.

still be too long, and tactical information might consequently arrive too late to be useful. The unspectacular accumulation of evidence about the Germans' supply situation, which Ultra made possible, may in the long run have proved more valuable because it enabled long-term trends to be analysed and pressure to be brought to bear on tender spots. This type of information did not depend for its value on being up to the minute; it could be almost equally useful even when a week old. It first came into prominence in Africa, when Ultra enabled a close watch to be kept on Rommel's petrol and ammunition supplies and gave foreknowledge of the restrictions on tank movements and air-craft sorties which the sinking of even a single cargo could bring, as well as providing tactical targets in the shape of con-voy-routes. In the west, comparable information was most often put out by Luftgauen (GAF administrative areas) and Flak commands, with the result that stocks of fuel for fighters and shells for anti-aircraft guns were kept under constant ob-servation. Somewhat more intermittent, but of even greater in-terest, were the long statements of the number of their battle-worthy tanks and guns periodically rendered by army corps and divisions, for they permitted the regular monitoring of the en-emy's supply situation in a way no other source could have made possible. The evident importance of Ultra's almost daily advance warnings of GAF operations, even that of the rare and outstanding item like Hitler's order for the Mortain attack, must not take too much of the limelight away from material of a quite different and less glamorous kind which, recurring at regular intervals, acquired a value all the greater because it was cumulative.

(iv) Since it was the secret operational communication of one German headquarters with another, every Enigma message was authentic and reliable. There was no need, as with agents, to wonder about the good faith of the source or the soundness of his judgement. But no message had more authority than that of the officer who sent it, nor more reliability as a guide to his superiors' intentions than the extent of the knowledge they al-lowed him to have or the initiative to which his rank entitled him. It was perhaps easier for the Hut 3 intelligence officers then than it is for the reader of today to keep constantly in mind the caution this imposed. Every Ultra signal had to be suitably attributed (for instance, 'Fliegerkorps II's intentions at 1045 hours ninth were . . .') so that it carried within itself an indication of the credence it deserved as a forewarning of events to come, and it was not uncommon—to take a very simple case—for a signal stating the operations proposed by a Fliegerkorps to be followed within the hour by another announcing that the parent Luftflotte had countermanded them in favour of a different target.

Delicate problems of interpretation and judgement could arise in the drafting of a signal and—no doubt still more anxiously—in the assessment and utilization of it by commanders in the field. For by no means the majority of Enigma messages originated with officers of high rank possessed of strategic or even tactical foreknowledge. These, and still more their superiors at OB West[1] or in Berlin, used telephones and teleprinters in preference to wireless, and their communications with each other were therefore normally inaccessible to radio intercept services. In something like the same way in which, as has already been shown, a picture of the combat effectiveness of German divisions could be built up by the painstaking study of their supply returns, so the likelihood of an attack by corps or army had often to be inferred from separate scraps of information suggesting that several units were assembling in the same area or that a large number of aircraft was under orders to support ground troops at a certain time and place. Explicit operation orders for the attack were relatively much rarer, particularly at the higher levels. In that sense it is not true to call Hut 3 a 'shadow OKW', as Group Captain Winterbotham more than once does. For months on end, Hut 3 handled several thousand decodes a day, seven or eight hundred of which might be of first-rate importance, but comparatively few were signed by Keitel or Hitler. We could not always look directly over the shoulders of the supreme command, but we could often reconstruct its plans by observing the execution of its orders by sub-

1. Commander-in-Chief West; see Figure 2.

ordinates and by studying the conduct of operations at Army Group or Luftflotte level and below.

(v) This restriction of scope was imposed in the first place by the natural preference of rearward headquarters for telephone or teleprinter over radio, as already indicated. A large number of very secret and very important messages, the content of which it would have been extremely useful to know, were for this reason never received at all. But as instructions had to be disseminated nearer and nearer to the front, so the chance that all or part of the original order would become accessible through transmission over the ether began to rise: thus details of the Mortain attack became known through a communication to 7 Army and General Eberbach, who was to lead it. Again, it could be tantalizing to intercept the answer to a question which had evidently been asked by land-line (destruction of the line by sabotage or bombing could prevent the answer going by the same route), for the one was unlikely to be fully comprehensible without the other, and once more laborious analysis and comparison with parallel evidence was necessary before a plausible conclusion could be drawn and useful intelligence extracted.

For although Ultra was absolutely reliable when it appeared, it could not be relied on always to appear when needed or to answer every question explicitly. Deliberate wireless silence, which Hitler imposed for security reasons along with a special oath on those he entrusted with planning it, was one reason why Ultra had no precise foreknowledge of the Ardennes offensive of December 1944.[1] An intercept might be missed perhaps because weather conditions or fading temporarily blotted out a radio link while it was carrying an important message; this, or the accident that the land-lines in its area survived the pre-D-Day bombing undamaged, perhaps explains another of the tiny handful of alleged 'failures' by Ultra—the absence of explicit warning that 352 Division was so near Omaha Beach on 6 June 1944.[2] Another possibility, of course, was prolonged delay in

1. See pp. 191–204 below.
2. See p. 45 below.

the breaking of an occasional day's key, but so far as can now be seen this was very unusual in 1944–5.

(vi) From a totally different angle, there was the necessary restriction imposed by our own security regulations upon the use of Ultra. The number of those allowed to know about it was strictly limited both at home and in the field. Commanders were strictly forbidden to order any action which might imperil the source by seeming to be ascribable only to the reading of Enigma traffic—thus, for example, ship movements and concentrations of tanks had to be confirmed by aerial reconnaissance, and seen to be observed, before they could be bombed. Ultra was too strong a medicine to be taken neat; unless it was diluted from less secret sources, the consequences might be disastrous—it might be compromised and so lost for the future. For similar reasons, no Ultra signals were sent direct to commands below the level of an army headquarters or the equivalent, and anything passed to corps or division had to be disguised in the form of an operational order.[1] The number of those in the secret was kept to the minimum compatible with effective use. How severe these limitations were in practice, Hut 3 never knew; its duty was done when it had dispatched its signal.

(vii) Lastly, it has to be remembered that Ultra was not the only source of military intelligence. It did not replace the traditional sources, but was a superb addition to them because it provided what they could not and because it came straight from the horse's mouth. The traditional sources remained of great value in their own way. Agents might hear things which had not been signalled, low-grade ciphers used in the front line carried tactical details of immediate (if also ephemeral) value if broken at once, prisoner interrogation and aerial reconnaissance could confirm that the orders conveyed by Ultra were actually being carried out. Thus the old and the new were complementary, each yielding information beyond the reach of the

1. For an account of the security regulations, see Winterbotham 88–9.

other. To say this is in no way to diminish the importance of
Ultra, but to see it in its proper light; to recognize that Ultra
could not do everything is to appreciate the complexity of the
intelligence puzzle as it was painfully put together when there
were battles to be fought and a war to be won. The consensus
of opinion among intelligence officers attached to field commands whose after-action views are known is that blending of
all sources was vital, but that Ultra almost always took the
lead.[1] And here again, of course, the question 'How much Ultra,
how much the rest?' cannot be answered from Hut 3's signals
alone—except by observing how little of what is thought worth
recording by the operational histories they failed to reveal.

Ultra's successes were in fact in some respects its own worst
enemies at the time, and it is essential that the occasional and
temporary mistakes of the past should not be repeated now nor
false beliefs become engrained. Ultra was not omniscient, and
could not be, for the reasons already given. But because it was
so nearly omniscient so often, there were a few occasions when
something like the opinion 'If it's not in Ultra, it can't be true'
seems to have prevailed in some quarters. It is no part of my
purpose to inquire whether this led to errors by Allied commanders, but at the risk of repetition it is worth making two
points, both of which are illustrated in the subsequently notori-
ous case of the surprise the Germans achieved in the Ardennes.
Bletchley's bombes could not decode what had never been encoded in Enigma nor sent over the air, and so deliberate wireless silence could make vital information totally inaccessible to
Ultra. Because of the consequently unavoidable gaps in the
story told by Hut 3's signals, these had to be very carefully interpreted before being either made the basis of command decisions or discarded as unhelpful. The fact that they were for
once mistakenly interpreted (as is suggested in chapter 7)
throws into sharp relief the predicament of generals thrust back
upon traditional methods of intelligence-gathering alone, and

1. To quote two of the Americans: 'Dire results follow from the notion that
Ultra is the only intelligence agency which need be studied and believed.' 'The
two easy errors, isolation from other sources and the conviction that Ultra will
produce all needed intelligence, are the Scylla and Charybdis of the recipient.'

by contrast highlights the service Ultra was able to render on nearly every other occasion.

To return to the original question: how far can Ultra's contribution be measured? Churchill, Eisenhower, Alexander and others paid such handsome tributes at the end of the war that there is no doubting its incalculable value. It put the Allied general into the position of a chess-player whose opponent announces his moves in advance and explains why he makes them. None of the generals, unfortunately, seems to have left a considered account of his opinion of Ultra, or to have compiled detailed examples of the use he made of it. But it is a fair presumption that the possession of Ultra did not dispense generals from any of their traditional responsibilities. They still had to plan their attacks and carry them out; Ultra simply helped them to apply force most economically and with maximum effect. In so far as one of the novelties which distinguished Ultra from older forms of intelligence-gathering was that it was not the monopoly of the battlefield general because it was produced far behind the front, Ultra may indeed have somewhat increased a general's burdens; for he must always have been aware that his political chiefs were in the secret too, saw the same decodes as he, and were therefore in a good position to breathe down his neck should they choose to do so (as Churchill evidently often did during the desert campaigns of 1941–2 although scarcely at all in 1944–5).

Sweeping suggestions have been made that the revelation of Ultra would make it necessary to rewrite the history of the war. The evidence presented here does not altogether bear them out. On the other hand, neither the frequency with which Ultra was able to give Allied commanders forewarning of exceptional strokes planned by their enemies, nor the tremendously detailed day-to-day information about the German army and air force (only a comparatively small proportion of which could be included here without overloading the pages that follow) have been known until now. If knowledge of these things will probably not lead to a wholesale revision of prevailing views about those commanders' actions, it must surely modify them by showing that vital decisions were, or ought to have been, taken against an intelligence background which was sometimes markedly different from what has hitherto been supposed.

2

Before the landings

After Hitler's first victories (Poland, September 1939; France, May 1940; the invasion of Russia, June 1941), the tide of battle began to turn at Alamein (October 1942) and Stalingrad (January 1943). Hastened on by Anglo–American landings in their rear (November 1942), the Germans retreated non-stop from Alamein to Tunis; when they could go no farther, 330,000 of them surrendered on Cape Bon in May 1943. On their eastern front, German armies were in the Caucasus and the Crimea at the beginning of 1943, but after Stalingrad (where 100,000 surrendered) they were steadily pushed back until most of Russia was free by the end of the year.

An assault on 'Fortress Europe' by the British and Americans (allies since Pearl Harbor in December 1941) was not practicable during 1942, although Stalin called for it to bring relief to his hard-pressed country, and although Roosevelt at first favoured it. Instead, the Allies adopted Churchill's plan and landed in north-west Africa. But even before victory was won there, the question of a 'Second Front' in Europe had again been raised at the Casablanca Conference of January 1943; once more American opinion, at first favourable, gave way before British warnings (amply justified by later events) that to attempt so tremendous an enterprise with inexperienced troops would be to court disaster. It was agreed to attack Germany in 1943 through Sicily (July) and Italy (September) rather than by direct assault. Only when the Italian front had advanced to about halfway between Naples and Rome shortly before Christmas were Eisenhower, Montgomery and some of their now battle-trained divisions withdrawn for a decisive assault on Europe in 1944.

Command structure

Both sides set up a command structure for the invasion during the winter of 1943–4. General Eisenhower was appointed Supreme Allied Commander on 6 December and arrived in England on 15 January, by which time General Montgomery, commanding 21 Army Group (which was to control the invading armies), was already at work examining and criticizing the draft plans for the operation. Special Liaison Units (SLUs) were established at both headquarters (which until now had been kept abreast of Ultra information by the three service ministries), and the first signal was dispatched to Supreme Headquarters Allied Expeditionary Force (SHAEF) on 26 January; VL 4789[1] gave the not very momentous news that IKG 30 had flown from Istres to Piacenza on the previous day, i.e. that some thirty-five German bombers had moved from the south of France to the Italian front.

On the other side, Rundstedt had been Oberbefehlshaber West[2] since May 1942. Rommel was transferred from the command of Army Group B in Italy on 5 November 1943 to examine the state of the western defences and report directly to Hitler on them. He was assigned a special staff for the purpose, and Ultra identified it on 2 March when a situation report on the Russian front was sent to 'Staff Rommel' via OB West. Six

1. The Ultra signals series are explained in the Bibliography, p. 273.
2. Commander-in-Chief West. The title was regularly abbreviated to OB West and the abbreviation was often used, like SHAEF, to signify the headquarters rather than the man.

weeks earlier this special staff had already been formally
rechristened with the name of Rommel's old Italian command
and put in charge of coastal defence, but Ultra's first glimpses
of Army Group B in the west did not come until mid-March; in
VL 8693 the Senior Signals Officer of Army Group B was asked
to say where one of his subordinates was to be posted, and the
extremely cautious comment which was agreed with MI 14[1]
and appended to the signal reads oddly today: 'No mention of
Army Group B since December and no location since it left
North Italy. But suggest former connection with Rommel may
have been maintained.' By 21 March Army Group B's headquarters had been tentatively located in the St Quentin area.
The armoured striking force, Panzergruppe West, turned up for
the first time in a mention of its signals section on 6 March.
The four armies in Rundstedt's command were well known. In
the north, Army Group B controlled 7 Army on the western
sector of the Channel coast and 15 Army on the eastern (15
Army's jurisdiction extended as far east as the Dutch–German
frontier). Farther south, Army Group G was established in
May to control 1 Army on the Atlantic coast and 19 Army on
the Mediterranean.

Behind these arrangements for assaulting and defending German-occupied Europe lay the organization of the High Command on both sides. The two systems are set out for comparison in Figures 1, 2 and 3. The German was the neater and the
more logical—or, rather, it had been so until December 1941,
when Hitler dismissed von Brauchitsch from the post of Supreme Commander of the Army and appointed himself instead
(thus giving himself two places in the hierarchy of command at
different levels) and deprived OKH (Supreme Command of the
Army) of strategic control over all theatres but the Russian.
The apparently superior merits of the German system were
enough to convince Hitler even as late as September 1944 that
the whole world envied Germany her OKW, but in fact the Allied system worked far more smoothly and far more efficiently.
Just because they depended on an overriding compulsion to
consult and co-operate if victory was to be won for the com-

1. The War Office department in charge of German intelligence.

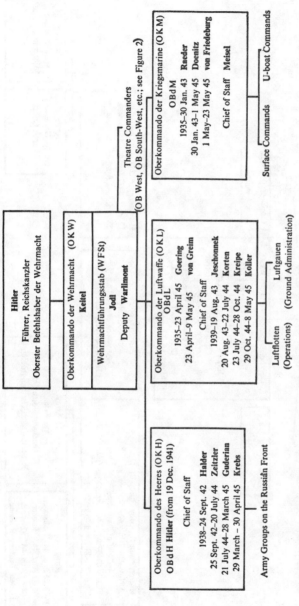

Figure 1 The command of the German Armed Forces

Hitler
Führer, Reichskanzler
Oberster Befehlshaber der Wehrmacht

Oberkommando der Wehrmacht (O K W)
Keitel

Wehrmachtführungsstab (WFSt)
Jodl   Deputy **Warlimont**

Theatre Commanders
(OB West, OB South-West, etc.; see Figure 2)

Oberkommando des Heeres (O K H)
O B d H **Hitler** (from 19 Dec. 1941)

Chief of Staff

1938–24 Sept. 42   **Halder**
25 Sept. 42–20 July 44   **Zeitzler**
21 July 44–28 March 45   **Guderian**
29 March – 30 April 45   **Krebs**

Army Groups on the Russian Front

Oberkommando der Luftwaffe (O K L)
O B d L

1935–23 April 45   **Goering**
23 April–9 May 45   **von Greim**

Chief of Staff

1939–19 Aug. 43   **Jeschonnek**
20 Aug. 43–22 July 44   **Korten**
23 July 44–28 Oct. 44   **Kreipe**
29 Oct. 44–8 May 45   **Koller**

Luftflotten   Luftgauen
(Operations)   (Ground Administration)

Oberkommando der Kriegsmarine (O K M)

O B d M

1935–30 Jan. 43   **Raeder**
30 Jan. 43–1 May 45   **Doenitz**
1 May–23 May 45   **von Friedeburg**

Chief of Staff **Meisel**

Surface Commands   U-boat Commands

Notes: Oberster Befehlshaber der Wehrmacht = Supreme Commander of the Armed Forces.
Oberkommando der Wehrmacht, des Heeres, der Luftwaffe, der Kriegsmarine = Supreme Command of the Armed Forces, the Army, the Air Force, the Navy.
Wehrmachtführungsstab = Armed Forces Operations Staff.
OBdH, OBdL, OBdM = Oberbefehlshaber = Supreme Commander of the Army, the Air Force, the Navy.

Figure 2 The German command in the west, January–August 1944

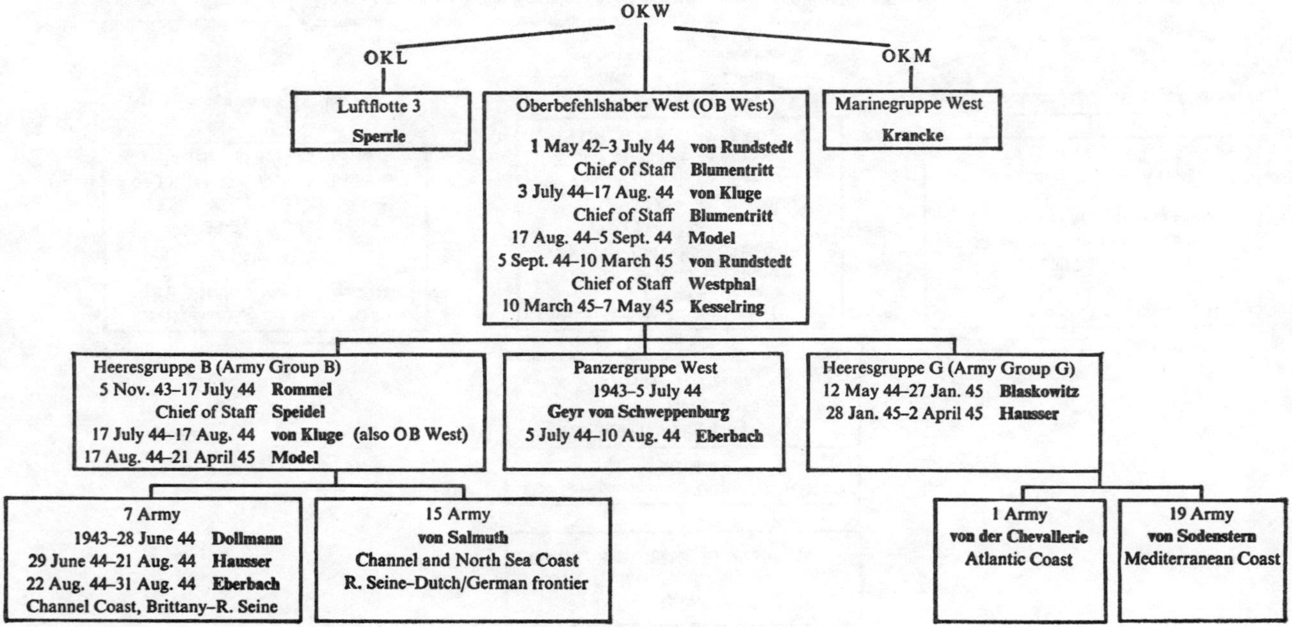

OKW

OKL — Luftflotte 3 — Sperrle

OKM — Marinegruppe West — Krancke

Oberbefehlshaber West (OB West)

1 May 42–3 July 44   von Rundstedt
Chief of Staff   Blumentritt
3 July 44–17 Aug. 44   von Kluge
Chief of Staff   Blumentritt
17 Aug. 44–5 Sept. 44   Model
5 Sept. 44–10 March 45   von Rundstedt
Chief of Staff   Westphal
10 March 45–7 May 45   Kesselring

Heeresgruppe B (Army Group B)
5 Nov. 43–17 July 44   Rommel
Chief of Staff   Speidel
17 July 44–17 Aug. 44   von Kluge (also OB West)
17 Aug. 44–21 April 45   Model

Panzergruppe West
1943–5 July 44   Geyr von Schweppenburg
5 July 44–10 Aug. 44   Eberbach

Heeresgruppe G (Army Group G)
12 May 44–27 Jan. 45   Blaskowitz
28 Jan. 45–2 April 45   Hausser

7 Army
1943–28 June 44   Dollmann
29 June 44–21 Aug. 44   Hausser
22 Aug. 44–31 Aug. 44   Eberbach
Channel Coast, Brittany–R. Seine

15 Army
von Salmuth
Channel and North Sea Coast
R. Seine–Dutch/German frontier

1 Army
von der Chevallerie
Atlantic Coast

19 Army
von Sodenstern
Mediterranean Coast

Figure 3 The Allied command in the west, January–August 1944

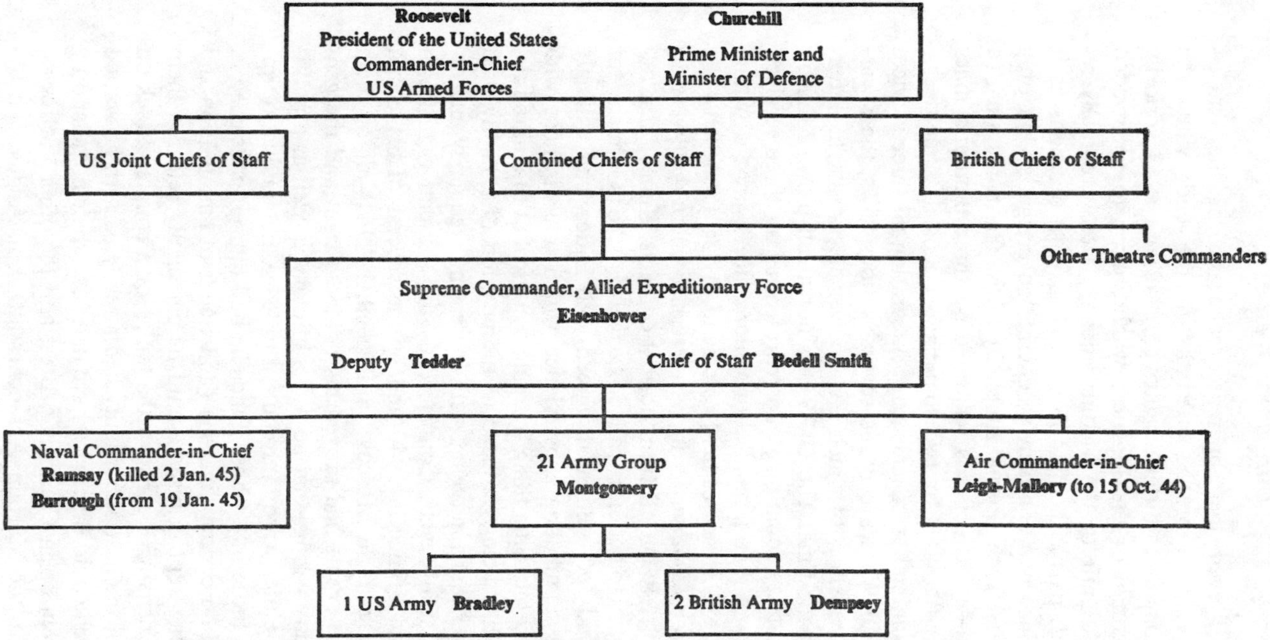

Roosevelt	Churchill
President of the United States	Prime Minister and
Commander-in-Chief	Minister of Defence
US Armed Forces	

US Joint Chiefs of Staff

Combined Chiefs of Staff

British Chiefs of Staff

Other Theatre Commanders

Supreme Commander, Allied Expeditionary Force
Eisenhower

Deputy   Tedder   Chief of Staff   Bedell Smith

Naval Commander-in-Chief
Ramsay (killed 2 Jan. 45)
Burrough (from 19 Jan. 45)

21 Army Group
Montgomery

Air Commander-in-Chief
Leigh-Mallory (to 15 Oct. 44)

1 US Army   Bradley

2 British Army   Dempsey

Notes: The arrangement of the land command was altered on 1 August 1944.
See Figure 4.

mon cause, even the apparent weaknesses of the Anglo–
American scheme proved strengths in the end; when the
long and sometimes bitter disputes of 1942 and 1943 (priority
for the German or the Japanese war? Europe to be invaded
from the Atlantic or the Mediterranean?) were eventually resolved, both parties held as firmly to the joint decisions as if
they were not two completely separate sovereignties but only
one. Conversely, the formal simplicity of the German system (a
single head—not two heads separated by three thousand miles
of ocean and advised by two sometimes opposed committees—
and a streamlined arrangement for integrating all three services
under the OKW) scarcely hid several serious flaws, the devas-
tating consequences of which it was nevertheless easy to under-
estimate at the time. The OKW was not a full-blown Ministry
of Defence truly combining and representing all three services,
but little more than a handful of senior officers, none of whom
had recent experience of field command, living an artificial life
at the *Führerhauptquartier* in East Prussia, where they were almost completely cut off from normal contacts. Keitel ('Lackei-
tel' he was sometimes called—*Lackei* is the German for
'lackey') and Jodl seldom disagreed with Hitler, and willingly
accepted a humiliating subservience which one of those who
had suffered the same thing by remote control at Stalingrad described as like being 'reduced to the position of a highly paid
NCO.' For Hitler intervened with increasing frequency and ar-
bitrariness at all levels. Convinced by the German victories in
Norway and France in 1940 and by the success of his 'Stand
fast' policy outside Moscow in December 1941—all of them
cases where events had proved his boldness right and the generals' timidity wrong—that he was a military as well as a political genius, Hitler was never content to leave the conduct of operations to those into whose hands he had himself consigned it.
He insisted on certain divisions (and stocks of ammunition and
petrol) being kept in reserve until he personally released them
for action, denying Rundstedt the tanks for a counter-attack on
6 June until the best opportunity had already passed; he wasted
troops which could otherwise have defended their homeland by
shutting them up in Cherbourg, Brest and the other 'fortresses'
he ordained; the Mortain–Avranches attack in August and the

Ardennes offensive in December were his alone, planned and persisted in against the advice of those best qualified to judge their feasibility.

Hitler's interference wrecked the very real advantages which the German system might have possessed. But even on paper the simplicity and comprehensiveness of the OKW was never reproduced in the command arrangements for the western or any other theatre of war—whereas, paradoxically, the Allies secured to themselves the benefits of unified command in every theatre although, in the nature of the case, they could not attain it in Washington or London. Eisenhower was given authority over all three services of both nations, but Rundstedt had none over the navy or the air force in the west, and only limited power over the SS troops in his armies, and he had to tolerate the occasional interference of Doenitz, Goering and Himmler as well as Hitler's control over his strategic reserve. Finally, the demands of a war on three fronts, and the severe industrial damage inflicted by the RAF and USAAF, kept Rundstedt short of men and equipment.

All this may easily give the impression that the odds were very heavily on an Allied victory and a German defeat right from the moment of the landings, and it has become a familiar feature of historical writing in both English and German to take this line. It is no doubt true that the disparity in resources was so great, and the application of them so well organized on the Allied side by 1944, that there could be only one end in the long run. But this is not how it appeared to most people at the time, nor is this an appropriate starting-point for an appraisal of the Ultra evidence. There was certainly confidence in ultimate victory, but the campaign of 1940 had etched the habit of considering German armies invincible so deeply into the western consciousness that neither Alamein nor Cape Bon nor the Russian advances could yet erase it.

The Ultra evidence itself still warns against too complacent a hindsight, just as in early 1944 it seemed to lift but a corner of the veil hiding a still-mighty Nazi war machine. Many of the SS Panzer divisions were only being raised and trained in the spring of 1944, it was plain, but their expected fanaticism and their enormous size (20,000 men) would probably more than compensate for the reduction of some infantry divisions to only 8000 men apiece, and they were to be equipped with large numbers of the dangerous Mark V (Panther) and Mark VI (Tiger) tanks.[1] Shortages of ammunition and fuel were reported, but maldistribution might account for them and there was always the suspicion that units might be exaggerating their own shortages in order to ensure that they, and not others, got the lion's share of whatever supplies were available. New types of aircraft, like the jet-propelled Me 262, would probably outpace and outgun the Allies' piston-driven machines—and such fears were justified to the extent that it is now widely held that one of Hitler's most serious mistakes was to give priority to his 'secret weapons' and not to manned jet fighters. The secret weapons themselves, the V1s and V2s, seemed the more menacing in the first months of 1944 because so little was known about them and because none had yet landed in England.[2] The first U-boats fitted with the Schnorkel[3] appeared in January 1944 and for a short time threatened to reverse the ascendancy over the U-boats which the Allies had so suddenly and so completely secured during the previous spring.

Nothing that came through on Ultra before mid-September ever hinted at despair or the expectation of defeat, but rather at a continuation of the dogged resistance under pressure which prolonged the battle of Normandy; there were even signs of skilful improvisation in the escape of some divisions from the threat of encirclement in the Falaise pocket. Ultra reported nothing of Keitel's and Jodl's alarm after only ten days' fighting in the bridgehead, nor of Rundstedt's and Rommel's disagreement with Hitler at the Berchtesgaden conference of 29 June, still less of Rundstedt's irritated 'Make peace, you fools'[4] on the telephone to Keitel two days later, just before he was dismissed. It was only when Paris fell on 25 August, British

1. See p. 48 below.
2. The first V1s fell on 13 June, the first V2s on 8 September.
3. Tubes which enabled them to take in air and use their diesel engines when submerged, thus avoiding the dangerous necessity to surface in order to recharge electric batteries.
4. In answer to Keitel's querulous 'What shall we do?' after the British attack across the river Odon. On the other hand, Ultra succeeded in piecing together most of the evidence which led to this outburst, and this is a good example of the point made on p. 20. See also p. 92.

tanks advanced from the Seine to Brussels and Antwerp in four days (30 August–3 September) and Bradley at Chartres was poising 12 Army Group for an American drive to Frankfurt and the Rhine (2 September) that Ultra began to show unmistakable evidence of large gaps in the German front and thereby offered some encouragement (by no means unqualified, however) to the dangerously exaggerated optimism about an imminent German collapse which seems to have pervaded the Allied command in the first days of September when the Veghel–Nijmegen–Arnhem operation was being planned.

Until then—that is to say from early 1944 until three months after the landings—Ultra intelligence, like all other intelligence, was seen at the time against a sombre background. Particularly during the last weeks before D-Day, there was an anxious awareness of the magnitude of the task ahead and an urgent need for every scrap of information about the state of German preparedness and the disposition of German troops. There was no inclination to expect that victory would be quick and easy or to under-rate the opposition. It is in this light that the intelligence provided by Ultra during the first six months of 1944 must be seen.

German preparations and Allied deception

'Where will they land, and in what strength?' 'How strong will the opposition be, and where are its resources concentrated?'— these were the questions uppermost in the minds of the rival leaders during the spring and early summer. Ultra provided a good deal of information under both heads, but it could not draw a complete picture either of what the Germans expected or of how they had disposed their troops. It could do neither of these things, so long as the enemy relied—as he could until the middle of June—on telephones and teleprinters in preference to the slower business of encoding and decoding wireless messages. But there was a compensating advantage, and it went some way towards levelling the balance. During these same months, the cryptographers managed to break a number of isolated days' traffic in hitherto impregnable army keys. It was so difficult to do this that they were sometimes held up for a week

or more, but the effort was abundantly worthwhile. Most of the
late decodes quoted in this chapter were obtained in this way;
they conveyed information of immense value, and their lateness
seldom detracted much from it.

In an appreciation of invasion prospects, drawn up on 28
October 1943, Rundstedt pointed to the Channel coast, the
French Riviera and the Bay of Biscay as the probable assault
areas, perhaps in some combination. This was quickly followed
on 3 November by Hitler's Directive 51, which laid it down
that Germany was now in more danger from the west than from
the east, and added that the forces stationed there should not
be reduced but that more tanks and guns should be allotted to
the western theatre of war; however, the directive was quite
unspecific about the point at which the blow to be expected 'at
latest in the spring' would fall. Both of these, it has been asserted, became known through Ultra: the evidence to confirm
this cannot be consulted, since both date back to a time before
signals were sent to field commanders in the west.

The first invasion news to appear in these signals was a rhetorical order promulgated to the troops in Italy by Hitler on 28
January: the Allies' invasion year, he said, had already begun
at Anzio,[1] the landings at which were designed to tie down German troops as far away from the Channel as possible, and the
battle for Rome would soon flare up. 'Fanatical determination
therefore required . . . holy hatred of enemy conducting a mer-
ciless campaign of extermination . . . destruction of European
civilization . . . enemy to be made to realise that German
fighting spirit was unbroken and that the great invasion of 1944
would be stifled in the blood of its soldiers.' (This bombast, of
little value as either intelligence or propaganda, happened to be
accompanied on the same day by a signal in which Kesselring
explained his plan for a counter-attack south of Rome in great
detail: a lot would soon depend on whether this sort of thing,
long familiar in Africa and Italy, appeared in western Ultra as
well.) After this, there was silence on the subject until March,
when a succession of reports showed how difficult the German
command was finding it to determine whether any one point on

1. The landings at Anzio, south of Rome, took place on 22 January.

the European coastline from Norway to Spain was more threatened than another, and to decide where the Mediterranean
figured in Allied plans. (Jodl had in fact already begun to plot
agents' reports of possible landing areas on a large-scale map,
only to find that there was hardly a mile of this whole coastline
which was not threatened by one or another of them.) OKM
(Supreme Command of the Navy) believed on 5 March that
there might be as many as six British divisions in Scotland
ready for an operation 'of limited scope' in central or southern
Norway, and clung to its opinion well into May. (Fortitude
North, the deception plan, was in fact suggesting this, and the
heavy-water plant at Rjukan in Norway had been blown up on
20 February.) Foreign Armies West[1] could not be more precise
about the assault area than 'somewhere between the Pas de
Calais and the Loire valley' (that is, more than half the northern
and western coasts of France!) on 20 March, but Rundstedt received from Kesselring on the same day a description of the Allies' assault procedures and their use of new types of landing-
craft. A long appreciation from OB West next day said that
preparations were complete but that agents reported that the invasion had been postponed; an attack on the south-west of
France was possible and this, OKH concluded a week later,
might be synchronized with landings from England.

April brought nothing but a proclamation from Doenitz on
the 17th along much the same lines as Hitler's of 28 January. A
large-scale landing was to be expected at any moment; its success or failure would decide the issue of the war and the fate of
the German people. 'Throw yourselves recklessly into the fight
. . . any man who fails to do so will be destroyed in shame and
ignominy.' The absence of any reference to the interception of
Exercise Tiger[2] off Slapton Sands ten days later, however,
suggested that Doenitz 'at any moment' might be generalized

1. The Intelligence department of OKH responsible for estimating the
strength and order of battle of the British and American armies.
2. One of several practice landings carried out by Allied troops during the
spring on the south coast of England. A flotilla of German motor torpedo
boats encountered it by chance and sank two landing ships. A later German
radio broadcast seemed not to connect the exercise with preparations for invasion.

alarm rather than rational deduction, and that the Germans could do little but guess at the date of D-Day.

The fullest information yet came in a lengthy appreciation from Rundstedt on 8 May decoded a week later. Agents had forecast a number of different landing dates, he said, but most of them were in the first half of May; Allied preparations were complete and more than twenty divisions would be landed in the first wave. This was four times the number of divisions then preparing for the first day of the assault, and was therefore a valuable indication of the state of German intelligence. Rundstedt was nearer the mark when locating the main concentration between Southampton and Portsmouth, but could not narrow the assault area down more closely than somewhere between the Scheldt and the tip of Brittany, most probably 'between Boulogne and Normandy'. It would be essential for the Allies to capture large ports like Le Havre and Cherbourg; they were modifying their landing techniques to cope with the new outer beach obstacles and would attack 'not only on the incoming tide before dawn' but also later. The main assault would take place as soon as there was a series of fine days, but commando raids on the southern French coast might occur at any time.[1] On the same day Luftflotte 3, the senior air command in the west, made the best forecast so far picked up by Ultra—the landings would be between Le Havre and Cherbourg—and this was decoded at once; three weeks later Luftflotte 3 wrongly thought they might be as far east as Dieppe. Practice anti-invasion exercises were held at various points along the coast from Bruges to the mouth of the Loire; one assumed a bridgehead 50 km long between Ouistreham and Isigny (just where the assault forces landed on 6 June), but no particular importance was assigned to this over other areas. Foreign Armies West's last appreciation before the invasion was dated 1 June but was not decoded for ten days. It forecast 12 June as the beginning of the next danger period and deduced that a landing might take place in south France because Montgomery and

---

1. Two evidently similar appreciations, dated 24 April and 15 May, are quoted in Ellis i. 129, but not the one mentioned above. Cave Brown 491 has Blumentritt, Rundstedt's Chief of Staff, sending an appreciation on 8 May, but gives it a different content.

Wilson were said to have met in North Africa (perhaps one of the very few known repercussions of Operation Copperhead, the visit of an actor disguised as Montgomery to Gibraltar and Algiers on 26 and 27 May?), adding that there was evidence of preparation for a landing in the Balkans as well.

It looks as if Ultra gave a fair sample of the confused ideas about the probable landing place which competed for the attention of senior German officers all through the spring, but did not manage to pick up a hint of Hitler's conviction that Normandy and Brittany were the likely target area. Since neither Rundstedt nor anyone else seems to have agreed with him or acted upon his conviction much more than obvious geographical logic compelled, however, Ultra may have given something like the right impression, although of course this could not be realized at the time. Nor was anything revealed by Ultra about the bitter disagreements between Rundstedt, Rommel and Geyr von Schweppenburg over the relative merits of beach defences and mobile armoured reserves. Ultra, it would seem, was useful but was not able to give either full reassurance or clear warning either about the enemy's efforts to identify the landing area or about his probable counter-measures.

It was just as important to deceive the enemy about date as about place. Here Ultra's evidence was slender. On 8 May Rundstedt was clearly quite uncertain when the attack would come, and he seems still to have suspected nothing on the 27th, since he was prepared to review progress with the building of fortifications (he complained of being allotted too little concrete, and of inadequate rail transport) after 10 June; but confirmation that Berlin believed that nothing would happen before 12 June was, as has been seen, not available until after the event. However, this slender evidence was sufficient to suggest that in all probability no inkling of the truth had dawned on the German command. More could hardly be expected of a source which was still denied access to nearly all communications at the highest level.

Somewhat better results seem to have been achieved with the more negative aspect of the deception plan. Analyses of the radio networks of British and American formations in the

United Kingdom and deductions therefrom were distributed to German headquarters in Enigma code and intercepted from January 1944 onwards. A threefold comparison between these deductions, the actual distribution of troops in England, and the fictitious distribution which it was hoped to induce the enemy to believe could, if made at intervals of (say) a month between February and August 1944, show the various stages of the Fortitude deception plan and the extent of their success. The Ultra evidence for what the Germans believed is now available. But evidence for the other two limbs of the comparison—the true and the false Allied order of battle and locations—is hard to discover and would be laborious to compile into a form in which it could usefully be set beside Ultra. By early autumn the disparity in force between the two sides was so great that it probably mattered very little—save perhaps, during the Ardennes offensive—whether the Germans did or did not know where the Allied troops were and what their strength was, but until then it was important to deceive them in order to prevent undue interference with the build-up of this disparity and with the break-out from the original bridgehead. Ultra gave regular information about the German assessment of Allied dispositions all through the vital months, and this was presumably of considerable value both to the deception planners (as confirmation that their deceit was a success) and to the operational staffs (because it showed them why some divisions were being kept away from the Normandy battle, and consequently enabled them to forecast with some confidence how long they would remain uselessly aloof from the fighting). But without a strict and detailed comparison between the three types of information, no precise assessment of the extent to which Ultra revealed the success of the deception plan can be made. To seek the evidence (mostly unpublished) essential for such a comparison and to set it out in parallel with Ultra would have been a major undertaking and would have entailed a long digression from an account of Ultra's part in operations. What follows is therefore not this strict comparison; it aims only at outlining the way in which Ultra helped the deception planners and makes no claim to completeness.

Fortitude[1] sought to persuade the enemy that the First United States Army Group (FUSAG—which had no real existence at all) under General Patton would land in the Pas de Calais during July and that this, not the Normandy landing, would be the chief invasion effort. The object, of course, was to ensure that German troops and armour were retained north of the Seine for as long as possible, and so to prevent the reinforcement of the German forces in Normandy until the invaders were too strong to be dislodged. Some indication that the deception was proving successful came when FUSAG first appeared in Enigma traffic on 9 January 1944 and again on 23 March, and when Patton was mentioned in this context in late March; evidence that its (entirely imaginary) threat to 15 Army in Calais and the Netherlands was still being taken seriously persisted until late July. Apart from Rundstedt's expectation that more than twenty divisions would be landed in the first wave, which has already been quoted, there does not seem to have been any direct confirmation of the over-estimate of Allied strength which it was hoped to implant in the enemy's mind, save for such false or inaccurate identifications as may have been revealed to the deception planners by lists of Allied units like that in κv 5792 of 27 May. The best evidence that the bait was being swallowed was that the largest single category of pre-invasion Ultra evidence concerned the location of German army and air formations, that a great deal of it suggested that the enemy was taking the threat from Kent and Sussex to the Calais–Boulogne area seriously enough to keep this part of the Channel coast strongly manned, and that none of it gave any hint to the contrary.

Divisions located

Some twenty-eight German divisions manned the coast between Amsterdam and Brest on 6 June; Ultra had mentioned fifteen of them at least once in a French context (not always very precise) by the end of May. From Brest along the Biscay coast to

---

1. For an outline of the plan, see Masterman, *The Double Cross System* 145–63.

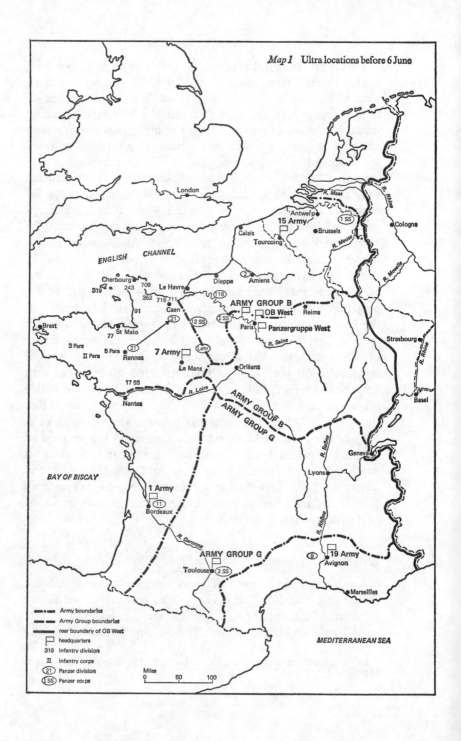

Map 1 Ultra locations before 6 June

the Spanish frontier, the figures are seven and five, and on the French Riviera seven and four. By D-Day, therefore, Ultra had identified (and in a good many cases located) well over half the garrison-type divisions which would be the first line of resistance to the landings. In addition, all the army and corps commands along the coast had been identified at least once, many of them together with evidence showing what units or formations each controlled. This probably did not provide more than a hard core to other information about the tactical disposition of German troops manning the coastal defences, and it no doubt fell a good deal short of what was desirable. Thus 352 Division, a field division of good quality which moved into the Côtentin in March and right up to Omaha beach a few days before the landings, received only a single mention in Ultra before the fighting began: this was on 22 January in an OKH order which provided the first evidence that this division existed but did nothing to locate it beyond showing that it was under OB West's command. In view of the initial difficulties of the Omaha landing, much has been made of the failure of Allied intelligence to locate 352 Division and some accounts appear to contain the veiled implication that Ultra might have been expected to give a hint of its position. The reason why Ultra could not be relied on to know anything about troops with satisfactory land communications has already been sufficiently explained, but it is also worth pointing out that this was not an isolated or exceptional case. For just the same reason, Ultra was even less well informed about 352 Division's right-hand neighbours in the British landing area, 716 and 711 Divisions: there was no mention at all of 716 Division in Ultra signals before D-Day and only the bare record of a fusilier battalion reaching 711 Division on 23 May.

There were two exceptions to the general rule that Ultra knew only a little about the infantry divisions which guarded the beach obstacles and which were to provide the hard shell of the defence under the scheme Rommel had devised and Hitler accepted: there were fuller reports on 77 Division (St Malo) and 91 Division (in the Côtentin) than on any others. The arrival of the newly formed 77 Division in OB West's area on 3 and 4 May was known four days later, and so was the fact that it was 8000 men strong and fit for a defensive role only. OKW declared 91 Air-Landing Division part of its central reserve for all theatres (i.e. regarded it as of high fighting quality) on 29 March and ordered it to remain in Strasbourg, but it was beginning to move into OB West's area on 4 May along with 77 Division, was allotted to 7 Army next day and directed on 10 May to a 'new area' which proved to be the base of the Cherbourg peninsula. It had in fact only been ordered there at the beginning of the month, when Jodl reminded Rundstedt that Hitler attached particular importance to Normandy, so that Ultra got the news of the move very promptly indeed and also quickly disclosed the new dispositions Rundstedt accordingly made after a tour of inspection by Rommel: LXXXIV Corps was to have under command 709 Division (Cherbourg), 243 Division (Cherbourg–Port Bail–Canville),[1] 91 Division (Carentan–Montebourg–La Haye du Puits) and 6 Parachute Regiment (Périers–Lessay).[2] Thus fuller information was available about the first line of defence near and just within the right boundary of the US sector than for any other part of the line.

With the exception of 91 and 352 Divisions and 6 Parachute Regiment, all these were static, second-quality troops. It was far more important to know the whereabouts of the armour and whether there were any other paratroops in the vicinity. Both were of superior battle capability, and the location of the armour on D-Day would determine the speed with which a counter-attack on the bridgehead could be mounted and would indicate which roads and railways should be bombed in order to delay it. In point of fact Ultra revealed far more about the paratroops which had been drafted in to strengthen the defence after Rommel's strictures[3] and about the armoured striking force than it did about the almost immobile divisions which

1. Rundstedt added a self-contradictory postscript to the effect that 243 Division was to hold back a strong mobile reserve—on bicycles.
2. Only a month earlier, 6 Parachute Regiment had been the sole OKW reserve for Reich defence.
3. To which particular attention has lately been drawn by Irving 287–99.

guarded the coast. It showed the consequences of the awkward and unsatisfactory compromise Hitler imposed on Rommel's and Rundstedt's disagreements; there was much to be said either for defending the beaches so strongly that the invasion would be repelled on them or for launching a heavy armoured counter-attack as soon as the main landing point had been identified, but nothing at all for a plan which tried to reconcile these contradictory views, scattered the Panzer divisions instead of concentrating them, and denied Rundstedt sole control of the armoured counter-attack force.

II Parachute Corps had an equipment staff at Châlons-sur-Marne on 7 February and was known to be interested in 3 Parachute Division in the Reims area, and its headquarters was at Melun on 6 April. Part of 1 Parachute Division was moving to Brest a month earlier, and a series of reports in May linked 2 (from the Russian front), 3 and 5 Parachute Divisions with II Parachute Corps and various locations in Brittany. II Parachute Corps was listed as 7 Army reserve on 30 May.

The Panzer divisions in the west were even better documented. 2 Pz was heard of in a western context in late March and firmly located at Amiens on 20 April; 9 Pz (upgraded from 155 Reserve Division) was at Nîmes in the spring and was frequently noted in the same area thereafter; on 2 May 9 Pz and two other new armoured divisions, 11 Pz and 116 Pz, were to be equipped with motor transport during the late summer months; 21 Pz was moving to a new location in March, which was known early in April to be Brittany and precisely located as Rennes a month later, and its composition figured in two later signals; 116 Pz (formerly 179 Reserve Division) was taking over 21 Pz's old positions on 22 March and was near Paris on 2 April, but its distribution along the lower Seine was not apparent from the decodes which formed the basis of several later signals; Pz Lehr (formed from several high-quality training units, it was a formidable fighting force until the disaster which overtook it at the end of July[1]) had shared in the occupation of Hungary in mid-March[2] but was also taking over a

1. See pp. 102–3 below.
2. The abundant Ultra evidence about the occupation was summarized in VL 9625 of 28 March.

workshop in Versailles, and it had thereafter appeared in OB West contexts several times before it was seen moving up to the Côtentin on 15 May.

Towards the end of April, Pz Lehr figured alongside 1, 12 and 17 SS Divisions (the first two armoured, the third lorried infantry) in one of Ultra's best hauls in the west so far. On 26 April Hitler ordered that I SS Panzer Corps, consisting of these four divisions, was to constitute the OKW reserve in the west and was not to be moved without his prior permission. Jodl's signal announcing this and the reserves for all other theatres of war except the Russian was in the hands of Allied commanders just three days later. I SS Pz Corps had been steadily located by Ultra in Brussels since the middle of December 1943 before it moved to the west of Paris later in May, and all its four component divisions were regularly reported.

A real plum, had it only been available a little earlier, was a long OB West return of 19 May which gave full details of 1 SS Pz Division's strength (over 20,000 men) and some information about its equipment; the section covering its tanks was missing, but the same return showed that 2 SS Pz, then still at Toulouse, had fifty-five Mark IVs and thirty-seven Mark Vs (Panthers), with forty-six and sixty-two respectively still to be delivered. The division had been regularly reported at Turn-hout in Belgium in late April and early May. 12 SS Pz, also in Belgium in February, could be followed to south Normandy in April and was still firmly located in the Evreux area right up to D-Day, while 17 SS Panzergrenadier[1] Division remained consistently at Tours and westwards throughout the spring and early summer. Farther south, 2 SS Pz was regularly reported between Bordeaux and Toulouse from February to May and the allocation of 11 Pz (not 10 Pz, as first intended) to the same area in early May for rest and refit was duly noted.

If to all this it be added that the transfer of II SS Pz Corps (9 and 10 SS Pz Divisions) from Normandy (to which it had come from Italy in December 1943) to the Russian front in March and April, in accordance with Hitler's decision of 26 March to accept a temporary weakening of the west in spite of

1. Lorried infantry. Abbreviated to PzGr.

his previous ruling to the contrary, could be clearly followed, then Ultra will be found to have kept a close watch on the movements of all the main armoured forces in the western theatre of the war. A sentence in the OKW War Diary lends extra sharpness to this point: the Allies were believed not to have realized that II SS Corps had left France, but OKW nevertheless ordered in mid-April that the three new Panzer divisions just mentioned (9, 11 and 116) be created by upgrading reserves in order to make good the resultant defensive weakness. In point of fact, Allied commanders knew about all this shortly after it happened and in ample time to take full account of it when making their plans for the invasion.[1]

Valuable confirmation that Ultra had correctly identified and located all the armour in the west was provided by an announcement by the Inspector General of Panzer Troops, Guderian, of his itinerary for a western tour on 20 April; this gave a splendid insight into the distribution of the armour a month before the landings. He was first to spend three days with various SS tank units at Mailly-le-Camp near Reims before calling on Rundstedt and Rommel in Paris on the 26th. After this he would inspect 2 Pz at Amiens and 12 SS Pz at Dreux, and take in a visit to Dollmann (commanding 7 Army) on the way westwards to 21 Pz at Rennes[2] and 17 SS PzGr at Thouars. Moving south, he would next see Blaskowitz (just about to take over the new Army Group G) and inspect 10 Pz at Bordeaux, 2 SS Pz at Montauban and 9 Pz at Nîmes, returning to Paris to call on 116 Pz on 8 May. Mailly-le-Camp was a well-known SS tank training area (it was reported in this connection from March to May) and it was heavily raided, with 400 casualties, while Guderian was on his way to Paris, possibly as a result of Ultra information.

1. In order not to overburden the text, nothing has been said above about units below the size of a division, several of which were reported by Ultra and later played an important part in the fighting.
2. The move, shortly after this inspection, of 21 Pz from Rennes to Caen (whence it attacked the beach-head on the afternoon of D-Day) seems to have escaped explicit mention in Ultra; it could with some probability be inferred, however, from the absence of 21 Pz from a long list of military locations in the towns (including Rennes) of Brittany and western Normandy dated 15 May. The move was evidently known from other sources.

The evidence quoted so far has been almost entirely concerned with the location of corps and divisions, so far as this could be discovered. From the middle of April onwards information about strength began to accumulate too, and this gave a different but equally valuable indication of the resistance a landing would encounter. OB West reported on the strength and state of training of two of his armoured divisions on 20 April. 2 SS Pz Division had 412 officers, 2536 NCOs and 14,-077 men; its basic training had not progressed beyond the sixth week, and only one battle-group was ready for offensive operations; there were deficiencies in NCOs, men, motor transport and signals equipment, and fuel was short. 12 SS Pz's strength was 484 officers, 2004 NCOs and 19,920 men, it was still under basic training and was short of fuel. On the same day the Denmark command reported that 363 Division (which was to be moved to France in July) was still being set up, was short of young officers, and had almost no motor transport but 8000 sick horses. A fortnight later, and again in May, 17, 84 and 85 Divisions, newly formed and belonging to the twenty-fifth conscription class, were reported pretty well up to their recently reduced establishment-strength at around 8000 men each. Just before the landings 17 SS PzGr Division was in its twenty-second week of training, short of officers, NCOs and transport, but well provided with guns.

A useful index to OB West's capacity to counter-attack a landing would have been given by two tank returns he rendered in May (decoded 6 and 7 June), had they been fully intelligible at the time. They were of a type not yet encountered in the west although familiar in Italy, and were rendered according to a pro-forma, the paragraph headings of which were not yet understood. The meanings were only penetrated when more examples of this and similar pro-formas accumulated in later months. Between them they covered 9 Pz, 21 Pz, 1 SS Pz, 12 SS Pz Divisions and some other less heavily equipped units.

Most of the statements made in a handful of wide-ranging situation reports from Rundstedt and Rommel have already been recorded, but a few additional points may be mentioned here.

Rundstedt said on 21 March that much work had lately been done on beach defences and that he considered it three-quarters complete in 7 Army area, two-thirds in 1 Army; he was improving the defensive grouping behind 7 Army by bringing 21 Pz Division up to Brittany. His report of 8 May already quoted again recorded good progress on beach defence (progress was slowed down three weeks later by a serious fuel shortage, however) and noted that 2 Parachute Division and 7 Werfer Brigade (mortars and rockets) were now strengthening the most endangered part of the front. This suggests that it was the Breton–Norman frontier area which the western command thought the most likely landing place. On the other hand, throughout the late spring the fighter command in Brittany was constantly reporting no air activity in his area, and at the opposite end of the front it was the number and intensity of the RAF's and USAAF's raids on the Pas de Calais which helped the Germans to deduce (as they were intended to do) that the landings would take place there.

Signs of a serious German manpower shortage were soon evident. At the beginning of March, Kesselring wanted to withdraw the Italian front to a shorter line because of his lack of trained troops and was still complaining in May. Keitel gave Rundstedt a solemn warning on 19 April when he said that OKW was well aware of the weakness of 1 Army in south-west France and was constantly trying to remedy it, but that the general situation forbade any reinforcement at present, so that if Rundstedt wished to strengthen 1 Army he would have to do so by transferring troops from some other part of his command. What was very likely part of Rundstedt's rejoinder was signalled on 16 May. It expressed disquiet on the same subject and talked about a duty to comb out rear echelons in order to maintain the combat strength of fighting units. These were the strongest indications yet received of the scarcity of German reserves; some other examples will be given in a moment. The formation of Army Group G to control 1 Army in south-west France and 19 Army in south-east France a week later may have been the most effective response to this warning which Rundstedt could devise, for he had long been conscious that there was a serious weakness at the junction between his and

Kesselring's commands on the Franco–Italian frontier: he had
told Kesselring and OKW as long ago as 6 January that in his
opinion it would not be possible to mount a counter-attack
against a landing on this coast (OKH thought at the end of
March that a secondary landing might be made here, timed to
coincide with the main cross-channel attack).

If considerably less can be said from Ultra about the location
and strength of GAF units in France, this is not so much because of any scarcity of information as because of the difficulty
of attaching exact significance to it. Tanks and infantry had to
be in position ready to meet the invaders, but aircraft could be
used for the defence of the Reich until the landings and then
flown to France at a moment's notice. Reports of airfield occupation in France, which were regular and frequent, were therefore valuable mainly because they showed where the bases
would be in the event of an invasion; on their own, they could
scarcely indicate the scale of the opposition to be expected. A
strength return by Fliegerkorps X (anti-shipping) for 16 May
was available ten days before the landings, and so were returns
from Fliegerkorps IX (bombers) and two fighter Gruppen, but
their value was limited by the reflection that reinforcements
would be flown in directly the emergency arose. That a plan to
do this existed was apparent in mid-March when it was announced that with the approval of Luftflotte Reich (the air
defence of Germany) General Buelowius, commanding the
close-support aircraft of Fliegerkorps II in France, would
shortly inspect 'the units which are to be transferred in case of
emergency'. There was further reference to the transfer plan
just before the middle of May.

All through the spring there was also a steady flow of information about the strength and location of GAF units in Germany, but no attempt has been made to record and analyse it
here. Maximum value could only be extracted from this sort of
evidence, from whatever theatre of war, by a statistical analysis
of the detail collected from day to day; this was undertaken at
the time by Hut 3's Air Section and by its research departments.

A GAF code was Hut 3's most regular source, and it provided material of this kind in great profusion. Only a relatively small proportion of it was signalled at once; the rest was not urgent enough in the form in which it arrived. But everything went down in the index, from which the signals were annotated, and everything went to the Air Ministry, which compiled intelligence summaries from it. Neither card-index nor intelligence summaries are now available. Without them, it has not been easy to avoid giving the quite false impression that Ultra gave a clearer picture of the German army than of the Luftwaffe. If anything, the contrary is true. But the army evidence almost speaks for itself; the significance of a division moving from one place to another can hardly be missed, and until the landings such moves were usually made with deliberation and seldom cancelled in a hurry. With an air force, the case is different. To move fighters or bombers over considerable distances is comparatively simple, and the operation can be reversed more quickly than that of a comparable number of tanks, for instance. Moreover, since GAF moves were frequent, often concerning several quite small units with different types of aircraft in the course of a single day, the broad significance of the mass of detail can only be effectively grasped when it is compiled into a statistical table and set out on a map—which, of course, every headquarters concerned did at the time. A good example of what could be done by collecting scattered evidence in this way is provided by KV 8819, which gave a complete list of GAF fighter units and their bases in mid-June; but because it was seldom necessary for Hut 3 to signal summaries of that kind, it is a comparative rarity amid the surviving evidence. This is very far from implying a paucity of information about the GAF, however, as would at once become plain if it were possible to consult the many other such compilations made at the time but not signalled. On the contrary, as D-Day approached, the locations, preparedness and strength of all the GAF units likely to be engaged came under ever closer scrutiny.

Problems of the defence

The most striking emphasis in GAF messages during the late
spring was on shortages of all kinds. Bomber units were required on 16 March to submit the names of volunteers for day
and night fighting, and since this scheme was 'over and above
that ordered by the Air Officer for Bombers' it was evidently a
second appeal. It was presumably the same scheme which was
mentioned a few days later by the Balkan air command and a
transport Gruppe, both of which referred to the strained manpower situation for the air defence of the Reich and to the need
for volunteers. Attention was drawn to another aspect of the
manpower shortage by a Berlin order of 4 May halting the
recruitment of paratroops among GAF flying and technical personnel in order to maintain operational readiness; other similar
recruiting had already been stopped. Finally, on 9 May OKL
(Supreme Command of the Air Force) refused Fliegerkorps IX
an increased establishment of bomber crews because of the
growing demands of the fighter programme and the general
tense aircrew replacement position. In view of the imminent assault, fighters were urgently needed, of course, but the competition for manpower[1] here shown was further reflected by the unsatisfactory scale of effort by all branches of the GAF from
June onwards; cries for help and complaints of the lack of it by
the army were rife, and refusals by the GAF command nearly
as frequent.[2] It was possibly manpower shortage, too, which explained why the first mention of defensive sea-mining in the
Channel for many months came as late as 27 May.

Equipment was as much in demand as men. The Balkan air
command announced a ruthless comb-out of spare parts for Me
109,[3] Me 110 and Fw 190 aircraft on 27 March in order to
maximize the production of new fighters for home defence; results were to be achieved within a fortnight, and units would

---

1. Because of the shortage of labour, even the privileged fighter pilots were
ordered to spend twelve off-duty hours a week helping to prepare new disper-
sal areas to protect aircraft from the mounting Allied air attacks.
2. See, for instance, pp. 98, 107, and 115 below.
3. Wings for the Me 109s were in particularly short supply at the beginning
of June.

have to live from hand to mouth in future. There was no reason to suppose that the comb-out was restricted to the Balkans, but rather that we had chanced to intercept the Balkan copy of a widely distributed order. The wide application of the order was taken for granted in a comment to KV 3530 of 12 May, which authorized the establishment of teleprinter links between the fighter staff of the German Air Ministry and certain factories with effect from 3 May, evidently to speed up production, and when similar links were set up between the fighter staff and front repair workshops. A connection may be surmised between all this and an OKL instruction of 28 April: in view of a recent severe decline in the serviceability of transport Gruppen, a temporary Gruppe of forty-eight Ju 52s was to be set up, and all Luftflotten were invited to contribute aircraft to it. A number of signals during the next ten or fourteen days bears out the seriousness of the transport problem, caused by Allied air attacks on roads and railways.

There were just two mentions of new types of aircraft. The names of highly qualified pilots were to be submitted by 15 March for retraining on Arado 234s, Dornier 335s and Messerschmitt 262s. The novelty and value of this information is sufficiently indicated by an Air Ministry comment appended to VL 7389 to the effect that the Me 262 was known to be jet-propelled but that the other two types were unknown. (In July the Me 262 was in fact the first jet aircraft in the world to enter operational service with any air force.) Just a month later the Director-General of GAF Equipment announced that the Me 163 would be operational sooner than anticipated but that the continual difficulties with the power-unit made it necessary for all servicing personnel to be trained by the manufacturers, Walter of Kiel. The Air Ministry comment to KV 1417, which conveyed this information, was that the Me 163 was a rocket-propelled aircraft of short endurance.

More valuable than any of this, in all probability, was the high-level confirmation received in the last pre-invasion weeks that the petrol and oil situation was becoming really serious for the enemy. Naval Gruppe West, one of its subordinates said on 19 May, had just ordered a substantial reduction in fuel consumption because of Allied raids on Rumanian oil-fields and

German hydrogenation plants, and it expected the June allocation to be considerably below previous quotas. That this was
no mere alarmist report was evident from an OKL order issued
while the assault forces were at sea and signalled to commands
just after the first troops landed on 6 June. Even essential training and production requirements could scarcely be covered with
the reduced fuel stocks consequent upon Allied action, it
stated, and the only quota-classes which could be considered
for aircraft fuel allocations in June were bombers, fighters,
ground attack and supply formations. It had been necessary to
break into the OKW strategic reserve in order to ensure the
defence of the Reich and prevent collapse in Russia. Present
stocks would have to last until the beginning of July; only very
small adjustments could be made, and then only 'provided the
Allied situation remains unchanged'. The strictest economy was
essential, and duty journeys were to be made by rail if at all
possible.

Thus during the months before the landings Ultra confirmed
that the Allied offensive against the fighter arm of the GAF and
against the oil industry was having effect; the quality of the evidence was high, because much of it came from Berlin or senior
commands, though its quantity was not very great.[1] Much the
same can be said about another aspect of the air offensive, the
effort to disrupt communications and slow down the rate at
which reinforcements and supplies could reach the armies facing the invader. As early as 1 April, only a few days after the
disagreements between the Allied commanders had been settled
and the transport interdiction plan given high priority, Keitel
complained to Rundstedt and others that OKW's directions for
the repair of air-raid damage to railways were not being carried
out with sufficient energy, and ordered maximum effort to
speed up repairs. Locomotives were so short because of air attacks in his command area by 10 May that Rundstedt asked
whether he might employ prisoners on repair work; Kesselring
had made a similar request in Italy a little earlier. In an appre-

---

1. In addition, there was a considerable number of reports of air-raid damage to towns and factories in Germany. For an appreciation of some tactics
used on these raids by the USAAF see VL 7822 of 6 March and VL 9205 of 23
March.

ciation of Allied air-raids on the night of 26–7 May, Luftflotte 3 concluded that there was a deliberate plan to prevent reinforcements reaching the front and that this plan had largely succeeded, adding that attacks on the Seine bridges pointed to a landing at or near Dieppe and thus again confirming the success of the Fortitude deception plan. Two signals in June showed that Allied raids were rendering daylight traffic between the Seine and the Atlantic coast too hazardous to be risked.

There is a similar story to tell about damage to airfields and the interruption of telephone lines. One example of the former may serve to represent the very considerable number received; 75 tons of aircraft fuel were delivered to Argentan on 6 June, but nearly half of it had been destroyed from the air less than two days later. Bomb-damage reports, whether positive or negative, enabled the serviceability of a given airfield for the next few days to be forecast with some confidence, even when a specific report on this did not (as it often did) come in later. The best proof of the success of the Allies in interrupting German army and air force telephone and teleprinter communications was the tremendous upsurge in Enigma traffic which began from the moment of the landings; it was of course in part due to the change from static to mobile conditions, but this was by no means always the reason. Rundstedt's senior signals officer reported a number of problems over repairing damaged land-lines on 17 May. An air-raid on 31 May cut the GAF's Paris–Rouen cable so badly that it was expected to be out of action for three days, interrupting Paris–Rennes and Paris–Caen contact for that period. By 8 June the navy was in even worse plight: Captain U-Boats West at Angers reported that all lines to Berlin, Nice, Wilhelmshaven, Paris, Brest and La Rochelle were down because of enemy action and that he had only one teleprinter line to Paris, which was working intermittently.

Until the heavy raids of May and June began to put land-lines out of action, comparatively little news was received about the location and equipment of the radar installations used to detect the bombers' approach: KV 2536 of 30 April, which gave the location of a Wuerzburg Giant array, was an exception, but after the landings information of this kind could often be passed on to air commands for their guidance.

Finally, as D-Day approached and the success of the operation might depend on weather conditions, the weather reports and forecasts which had for years been one of the least interesting features of Enigma traffic suddenly acquired a greater potential importance. One was sent as KV 6169 to commands with very high priority in the late evening of 2 June, for instance; it may conceivably have contributed a little to the pool of information at Eisenhower's headquarters and to the agonizing 'To go or not to go' debates of the next two or three days. Since they were very often received and decoded well before the period covered by the forecasts, and since they were often associated with intended raids by the GAF, it was often worthwhile to give them high priority during the next few weeks and to provide information on Continental conditions which were difficult for Allied weather bureaux to ascertain.

From the moment the British army left the Continent at Dunkirk in June 1940, the Germans' need for radio communications diminished sharply. Garrison conditions prevailed as soon as the invasion of England was called off in September, and the few troops left on guard were well provided with land-lines. Ultra in France and the Low Countries sank to a trickle, and the lively Enigma traffic in the Balkans and North Africa in 1941–2 and in Italy in 1943 did not spill over into the west. There, only the GAF—and principally squadrons moving from airfield to airfield, not major commands—had much occasion to use wireless telegraphy.

This situation still prevailed when the SLU was set up at Eisenhower's headquarters in January 1944. One moderately useful bit of intelligence was soon passed over this link—Hitler's proclamation of 28 January, already quoted[1]—but this arose out of Italian conditions and must have been intercepted on its way to Kesselring's troops. After this, there was almost nothing with a bearing on Overlord until the end of the first week in February, and less than one signal of any significance was passed each day until the end of that month. A higher level was

1. On p. 38 above.

reached early in March and maintained in April, although March was the more productive of the two. There were still odd gaps of a day or two even later, but May was the best month yet from the Ultra point of view, and probably saw more signals passed to commands in the west than the previous three put together. If Ultra had not told the Overlord commanders a great deal by 6 June, therefore, this was because there was not much traffic to intercept; it had in any case probably produced rather more than could have been forecast with any confidence when the service to SHAEF opened in January, and the volume of intelligence derived from this source during the first five months of 1944 was nothing in comparison with what was to come.

The number of Enigma intercepts, and hence of Ultra signals, increased with dramatic suddenness even on D-Day itself and rose still further during the following weeks, and the high traffic levels of June 1944 were maintained with remarkable consistency until the last few days of the war. There were occasional fluctuations, but never a really serious decline. A lull in the fighting might reduce signals traffic for a day or two, just as the helter-skelter out of France in the second half of August naturally increased it. New cryptographic refinements introduced at the New Year caused delays with some keys in the spring of 1945, but were countered by improved bombes. As the area within which Enigma was used grew smaller and smaller when the western and eastern fronts closed to within a few miles of each other in March and April, the total volume of traffic dropped away; but the value of what remained was increased by a much higher proportion than formerly of messages originating with Hitler, Keitel or Jodl—presumably because they could no longer rely on undamaged telephone lines. There were gradual changes like this in the type and provenance of Ultra information during the eleven months of the campaign, but astonishingly little diminution in either volume or intelligence value.

3
The first month: Cherbourg and Caen

British and American troops waded ashore in Normandy at dawn on 6 June, parachute and glider landings having been made at each end of the fifty-mile front since the previous midnight. The British did not manage to seize Caen in the first rush, as they had intended, and one of the American beaches was in acute danger for a few hours, but there was a continuous front by 12 June and both the artificial harbours were in operation by then. The inflow of men and supplies proceeded without serious interruption until the gale which began on 19 June stopped it for three days and delayed the next stage of the joint advance. The enemy did not seize this opportunity to strike a decisive counter-blow.

The Americans soon pushed northwards up the peninsula towards Cherbourg, seized the port on 26 June and immediately began to plan the break-out from the still narrow Allied perimeter which they were to achieve towards the end of July.

There was no second defence line to protect Paris once the cordon Rommel and Rundstedt had hastily thrown round the invaders should snap, and the Allied deception plan had deepened the Germans' conviction that another and greater landing would shortly be made in the Calais area. Thus although they would not denude 15 Army, the Germans began to concentrate tanks round Caen opposite the British sector to ward off the suspected threat to Paris. However, the British gained little ground and were being criticized for the slowness of their advance before they had been ashore for a fortnight. It is not entirely clear just when it became Montgomery's sole object to attract the German armour to the British front in order to reduce the opposition the Americans would have to face farther west, but a series of limited attacks near Caen (notably Epsom, 25–30 June) drew almost all the Panzer divisions to the British sector and continued to hold them there long after the city fell on 10 July. Shattered by the ill-success of his armies—for which his own meddling was in large measure responsible—Hitler looked for scapegoats, sacking the unfortunate commander of his armoured striking force and replacing Rundstedt as OB West by von Kluge.

The first days

D-Day in Hut 3 was tense with excitement, but even more with anxiety and hope. Would Ultra in the west now quickly attain the levels long familiar elsewhere, or would better land communications still restrict the enemy's use of radio, thus keeping us in the same frustrated condition of half-blindness which had been so hard to bear during the last few weeks? How soon should we begin to intercept signals from the battlefield which could show what the Germans were thinking and how they planned to tackle the invaders? How long had we to wait before being once more in a position to help Allied commanders by sending them first-class intelligence of immediate operational value?

To begin with, nothing of much importance came to hand. There were several accounts of small-scale fighting in the beach-head, but situation-reports were almost bound to be so far behind the swiftly moving events they described that they could tell Allied generals nothing they did not know already. Gradually, however, the volume of traffic and the value of its content began to rise reassuringly and within two or three days we were giving western commands the same service we had been accustomed to provide to headquarters in Africa and Italy for the past three years, supplying a continuous stream of high-grade information and an occasional item of absolutely priceless significance.

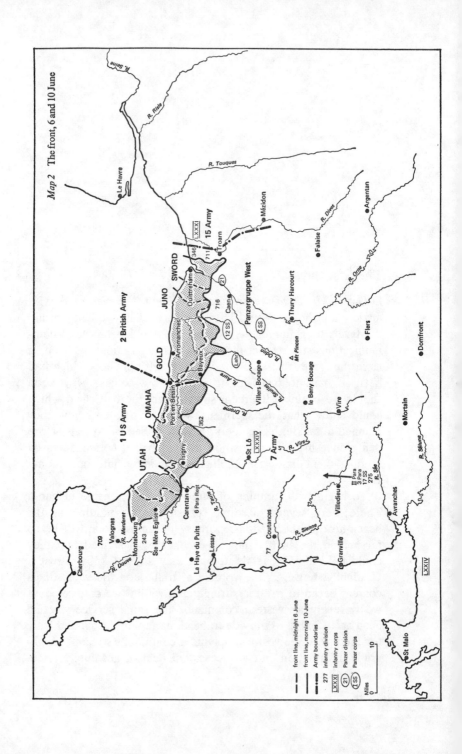

Map 2 The front, 6 and 10 June

Le Havre

R. Seine

R. Risle

R. Touques

Mézidon

15 Army

LXXXI

711

346

Troarn

R. Dives

Falaise

Argentan

SWORD

Ouistreham

R. Orne

JUNO

21

716

Caen

Panzergruppe West

Flers

Domfront

2 British Army

12 SS

1 SS

Thury Harcourt

GOLD

Arromanches

Bayeux

Lehr

Mt Pincon

△

R. Odon

OMAHA

Port-en-Bessin

R. Aure

R. Seulles

Villers Bocage

le Beny Bocage

Vire

Mortain

1 US Army

352

Isigny

R. Drôme

St Lô

LXXXIV

R. Vire

7 Army

R. Sée

UTAH

Carentan

6 Para Regt

R. Taute

Villedieu

II Para
3 Para
17 SS
275

Valognes

243

709

R. Merderet

Montebourg

Ste Mère Eglise

91

La Haye du Puits

Coutances

Avranches

Cherbourg

R. Douve

Lessay

77

R. Sienne

Granville

St Malo

LXXIV

front line, midnight 6 June

front line, morning 10 June

Army boundaries

277   infantry division

LXXXI   infantry corps

21   Panzer division

1 SS   Panzer corps

Miles
0   10

There were three principal things to look out for at once. Had surprise been achieved? How quickly would the armoured counter-attack force be assembled for a strike, and how soon would the French airfields be filled with fighters and bombers?

The complete tactical surprise of the landings is now so well known that it seems hardly necessary to add Ultra's confirmation. Such Ultra evidence as there had been during the last few days supported Rundstedt's conclusion on the evening of 5 June that there was nothing to suggest an invasion in the immediate future, and this was borne out by the first messages received that night. There were several reports about the unserviceability of coastal radar stations (they had been systematically bombed to ensure surprise), one of which was received in time to be signalled just as the landing-craft were making for the beaches,[1] and the German navy seemed reassured by the discovery that 'some of the parachutists reported were straw dummies'. (A fortnight later, the official inquiry demanded by Hitler concluded that it had been impossible to detect the invasion by radar before the moment at which these same 'parachutists' were dropped—a comforting conclusion which overlooked the fact that it was the six or seven hours *after* this which had mattered most.)

0221/6
KV 6573
0530/6
2355/5
KV 6546
0601/6

It was early afternoon before there was any sign that the scale of the landings had been properly appreciated. By then, the naval authorities[2] in Normandy had decided that they were facing a major invasion although the possibility of another in Norway could not be ruled out, and there were soon plenty of indications that Cherbourg, Brest and the whole Breton coast were believed threatened. This was enough to show that the enemy had been thoroughly confused by the deception plan and was uncertain about Allied intentions, but the only early hint of German views about the Pas de Calais, the most important 'red herring' of all, was an order for extra Flak protection for the

1500/6
KV 6635
1850/6

1. The typographical conventions which will henceforth be used to show the speed with which urgent Ultra signals were transmitted is explained in Preface, p. xiv.
2. Several of the first D-Day messages were in naval Enigma, which long continued to be a small-scale but useful source of military news; it was used to report conditions in Cherbourg, Brest and other 'fortresses' when they were under siege, for instance.

Quilleboeuf ferry over the Seine—which suggested that the threat of FUSAG to this area, on which so much effort had been spent, might not prove enough to deter Rundstedt from reinforcing the over-stretched 7 Army by drawing on the resources of 15 Army farther up the coast. Twenty-four hours later it had been made very difficult for him to do this: all the Seine crossings from Conflans to Rouen had been bombed, and north–south road traffic was only possible by going as far upstream as Paris.

Ultra knew nothing of the war-game at Rennes which kept 7 Army's divisional generals away from their posts on invasion night (save that 319 Division in the Channel Islands was temporarily under the command of a deputy when it was put on the alert at 2321 hours on 5 June), nor of Rommel's absence on leave in Germany, and it was late with news of the first armoured counter-stroke although it got the essentials: the failure of 21 Pz's hasty attack and the preparation of another by I SS Pz Corps. The most immediately useful item during the first hours was probably the news that already by midday on 6 June the British drive towards Caen was alarming the GAF enough to make them contemplate evacuating Carpiquet airfield west of the city, but it evidently proved impossible to take advantage of their panic. Conditions were not yet favourable enough for Ultra to get into its stride as a provider of battlefield intelligence; the first signs that it might very soon do so were the realization as early as 7 June that Hut 3 was handling as many Enigma messages originating in the western as in the Italian theatre of war, and a complaint two days later from Fliegerkorps II (close support) that because almost every land-line was down it had the greatest difficulty in passing its orders to the squadrons under its command and in carrying out its planned operations.

1400/6
KV 6605
2110/6

The air story was in fact very encouraging right from D-Day onwards. Warning of three raids on the beaches and on ships lying just off-shore was given before the attacks took place, one with nearly four hours to spare. A comprehensive list of moves of aircraft to the west became available early on the morning of 7 June; several single items had preceded it and more followed. Together they showed that at least seven Gruppen of fighters, one of ground-attack aircraft and one of bombers, were coming from as far away as Austria and Hungary: in many cases routes and destinations were given, making interception possible. If all these Gruppen were up to their proper strength, this means that within thirty-six hours of the landings Ultra had accounted for nearly 300 of the 400–450 aircraft with which the Germans are now known to have reinforced their western front by 10 June.

An order that bombing attacks on ships off the beaches were to be pressed home determinedly ('No possibility is to be left untried') gave a hint of anxiety about the rate of Allied reinforcement as early as the morning of 7 June. Hitler had already lost his one fleeting chance of catching the invaders before they were ready by at first refusing to grant Rundstedt's immediate request for two armoured divisions (12 SS Pz and Pz Lehr) from OKW reserve north of Orléans; too late, he now released these two and three more (2 Pz from Amiens, 1 SS Pz and 2 SS Pz from the Antwerp and Toulouse areas respectively), together with 17 SS PzGr from south of the Loire, and 3 Para and 77 Infantry from central and northern Brittany. Ultra had discovered all this by midday on 8 June, save that faulty interception obscured the number of what was evidently 2 SS Pz, adding for good measure a Panzer brigade known to be equipped with Panther and Tiger tanks, and some particulars about a planned counter-attack out of the Cherbourg peninsula on the American right wing.

It was reasonable to wonder whether 1 SS Pz would really leave 15 Army after it was learned that Allied reinforcements were being interpreted as preparation for a thrust into Belgium, where a landing was expected during the night of 8–9 June, and in fact the division stayed where it was for another week.[1] The now well-known story of the prolonged miseries of 2 SS Pz's journey from the south drove home the lesson that Hitler had missed his opportunity by delaying so long before ordering more armour up to the invasion area. Badly as it was needed in Normandy, 2 SS Pz was so harried by the *maquis* on the ground and by the RAF and USAAF from the air that it could not get there for a week. Ultra was able to follow its uncom-

1. See p. 78 below.

fortable progress closely enough for action to be taken to add
to its difficulties. Before it set off on 9 June, the division made
arrangements for emergency communications in case it had to
keep wireless silence (presumably to avoid betraying its position to the Resistance). Moving through Périgueux and Limoges en route to Poitiers two days later, it was warned to
keep open order (to reduce damage from air attack) after
crossing the Loire. Army Group B was anxious to get it to the
front as quickly as possible, but had first to collect enough
motor transport; this would take time, it said, and warned the
division that meanwhile 'some operations against guerrillas con-
not be avoided'. Shortage of petrol held the division up on the
road from Poitiers to Tours, and an attempt was made to get
some from 1 Army, whose command it had just left. By the
time it reached its destination, XLVII Corps near the centre of
the front, on 15 and 16 June, there was greater need for it else-   0800/18
where, and it was switched to St Lô early on 18 June to help in   KV 8707
blocking the American advance.   2129/18

    When 17 SS PzGr was put under Panzergruppe West (after
an hour and a half directly under 7 Army), this mobile strike
command emerged briefly but disastrously from the shadows in
which, so far as Ultra was concerned, it had lurked hitherto.
Geyr von Schweppenburg, its commander, did not reach Pan-   p.m./8
zergruppe West's battle headquarters until 8 June; just as he   KV 7171
did so, and received his orders, Ultra twice reported the posi- 2044/9
tion of the headquarters, the second time with a pin-point loca- p.m./9
                                                               KV 7225*
tion. A bombing attack—clearly the result of these signals—   0439/10
completely destroyed this headquarters on the 10th, and so
many of Geyr's staff were killed that Panzergruppe West was
not operational again for more than a fortnight.[1] The counter-
stroke planned for the day of the raid was halted in its tracks
(it was first put off for twenty-four hours and handed over to I
SS Pz Corps to direct, but then cancelled before it started), and
the OKW War Diary speaks of a 'crisis'. 'We should have been
better off without wireless,' commented Rommel's chief of intelligence later, but he suspected nothing at the time because a
British aircraft had been observed reconnoitring the target be-

----

1. cf. p. 82 below.

fore the raid. It was at about this moment that the initiative passed decisively to the Allies, and Ultra may justly claim a share of the credit for bringing the change about. By making it possible to wipe out Panzergruppe West's headquarters staff, Ultra helped to paralyse the nerve-centre of the armoured striking force and to frustrate Rommel's plan for a concentrated blow to split the bridgehead in two and drive the invaders back into the sea. The consequence was to compound the mistake the German command had already made—that of frittering away its tanks in 'penny-packet' attacks—and to compel them to go on making the same mistake for lack of a workable alternative. Above all, it convinced both Rommel and Rundstedt that their situation was very serious indeed.

Other bombing targets, of less individual importance but still eminently worthwhile, were offered about this time by the first of what were to become familiar reports giving the exact location of petrol or ammunition dumps. Thus KV 6860 showed where a trainload of Flak ammunition had been halted only a few hours previously, and KV 7267 located an ammunition depot 10 km south-east of Falaise on the Argentan road the day after it was opened to supply the shells for the deadly 88-mm guns with their dual anti-aircraft and anti-tank role (airfields all over Normandy and Brittany had been running out of these shells the day before). Similarly, Luftflotte 3 grumbled on 8 June that fuel economy was necessary because 7 and 15 Armies controlled all the stocks in the area but had no barrels to deliver it in; on the other hand, the chief supply officer at OB West had no fuel at all at his disposal next day, nor had some unspecified army units near Caen. Information of this sort enabled the Allied air forces to make the shortages still more acute by bombing targets which were often very precisely indicated.

Morale was in equally short supply in some quarters. Gunners belonging to the garrison of the Îles de Marcouf off Utah beach 'were soft, and had to be forced into action' and heavy bombing in the Flers–Condé–Argentan area for two successive nights meant that some soldiers were 'showing signs of nervous exhaustion' as early as 8 June—small wonder, when

Rundstedt himself admitted that raids by thousands of bombers were stifling every attack his tanks attempted. By this time, too, a personal reconnaissance of his front by General Marcks, commander of LXXXIV Corps, had discovered that 716 Division, which had held the beaches at the western end of the British sector, had lost two-thirds of its men and equipment. When OKL in Berlin said that Allied anti-aircraft fire was already heavy enough by the second night to force the bombers to fly so high that they could not find their targets, it did not seem likely that the GAF was in much better heart.

The American sector

Even before the gap between Utah and Omaha beaches was completely closed, and while the key towns of Isigny and Carentan were still in German hands, there was plenty of evidence that the American landings were already regarded as a serious threat to Cherbourg, the western shore of the Côtentin, and places still more distant. Preparations to demolish the harbours of Granville and even Brest were being made by 8 June. Just after midnight on 9–10 June, 7 Army told Luftflotte 3 that a breakthrough to Cherbourg could only be prevented if help was immediately forthcoming; a few hours earlier the troops in this area had been 'hard pressed' and in urgent need of the air support thus asked for, and before midnight on the 10th we knew that Rundstedt (evidently unable to believe that tired men and scanty aircraft could save the town) had given orders for the destruction of Cherbourg harbour to begin at once and had refused to rescind them in spite of local protests about the bad effect they would have on morale. So much for the 'hard shell' policy and the coastal defence of *Festung Europa!*

Frantic efforts were made to plug an ugly gap that was developing at the base of the peninsula. There was an urgent call for lorries to bring up II Para Corps to 'the exposed coast' early on the morning of 9 June and 3 Para and 17 SS PzGr Divisions were rushed into the breach; a comprehensive account of these movements and the positions to be taken up in the St Lô area became available two days late. Another message of 9

0100/9
KV 7244
0709/10

1031/10
KV 7389
2319/10

0800/9
KV 7105
1329/9

June, to the effect that 77 Division was being sent to Valognes[1] because a fresh division was essential to deny the Allies possession of the 'decisive' port of Cherbourg (German planners had long ago decided that an invasion could not succeed unless Cherbourg were speedily captured, and the artificial harbours had not yet opened their eyes), was also delayed by decoding difficulties, but was considered so revealing that it was signalled with high priority nevertheless.

To secure the base of the Cherbourg peninsula and prevent an Anglo–American link-up across the marshes at the mouth of the river Vire, Pz Lehr was ordered on the 9th to hold Isigny at all costs (a little later its battle headquarters was pin-pointed some miles farther east at Hottot, but the target seems not to have been accepted). Next day Rundstedt listed all his dispositions between here and the coast at Avranches, revealing too that parts of 2 Pz and 9 Pz had reached the invasion area but that 19 Pz (very ill-equipped), 1 SS Pz and 116 Pz were still being held aloof from it in north-east France and Belgium.

A period of some twelve hours from the late evening of 11 June to the middle of the following day was Hut 3's busiest since D-Day and in all probability also its most profitable. In quick succession several pieces of evidence came in about a counter-attack on Carentan, which the US VII Corps had just captured. No doubt they reflected Rommel's wish—of which Ultra had no direct knowledge—to transfer his main attention westwards and ensure the safety of Cherbourg before dealing with the British sector, and if so they neatly illustrate how a major tactical decision could be inferred from an accumulation of inter-linked details and how directly useful Ultra signals could be.

Amid a flurry of orders for air-raids in support of attacks in the neighbourhood of Caen, one message concerning the American front stood out that evening: it gave the positions of 352 Division and 3 Para Division, instructed them to join up on both sides of the St Lô–Bayeux road as far west as possible, and added that 17 SS PzGr Division was assembling in the same general area. Before long, it became clear that 17 SS in-

a.m./9
KV 7480
1534/11

1600/9
KV 7451
1042/10

1300/11
KV 7591
0008/12

early a.m./12
KV 7662
1101/12

---

1. South of Cherbourg, in the middle of the peninsula.

tended a counter-attack on Carentan in the morning. The operation must have been postponed during the night, since at midday we had an urgent request for GAF raids from 1300 hours
to soften up the enemy before 17 SS went in, probably at 1500;
this information was signalled to 1 US Army with nearly two
hours to spare. A great deal of supporting local detail followed:
17 SS's assembly area was described as south-west of Carentan
and west of St Lô, and the object which the counter-attack was
intended to frustrate emerged from an intelligence appreciation
to the effect that the Allies were trying to cut off the Côtentin
peninsula (Naval Group West spoke of 'the fateful importance
to Greater Germany' of the forthcoming battle and urged everyone to fight to the last). The intended ground operation was
again called off before it started and was postponed until the
following morning, but it was too late to stop the GAF—
Fliegerkorps II had evidently not cured the trouble which was
hindering its operation on the 9th, for 'the signals situation'
now prevented it from redirecting the aircraft which were to
support the troops. 17 SS PzGr duly attacked early on the
morning of 13 June, but Bradley had been forewarned and had
brought his tanks up to deal with the SS lorried infantry. Bradley's guarded account (published in 1951) specifically attrib-
utes the warning to his Chief Intelligence Officer, who was of
course the Ultra recipient at 1 US Army, and thereby makes it
all but certain that the victory was due to Hut 3's series of signals.

    With the pressure on their flank and rear thus relieved, the
Americans could advance more freely to north and west against
diminishing opposition. II Para Corps put in its 'remaining reserves' against them on 14 June and was supported next day by
LXXXIV Corps, but operations and even movement were so
seriously hampered by shortages of motor transport, petrol,
ammunition and guns that the Corps appealed to Goering. That
the whole of 7 Army was in the same predicament appeared
from an inquiry whether the navy could ship 60,000 tons of
supplies a day from Bordeaux to Breton ports to meet its needs,
and the reason was no doubt the 'total Allied air superiority',
preventing all daylight movement, complained of by LXXXIV
Corps, which had already lost its commander in an air-raid. As

0745/12
KV 7671
1316/12
1000/12
KV 7678
1419/12

1 US Army drove on, it was kept constantly informed of the confusion into which its advance was throwing the enemy. 243 and 709 Divisions lost contact with Cherbourg on 16 June (243 had no reserves forty-eight hours later), 352 Division had such 'slight fighting strength' that it doubted its ability to hold on and was soon running out of ammunition, 3 Para suffered 'heavy losses', and 77 Division's withdrawal left the west coast open to the Americans on 17 June. General Schlieben, commanding one of the two battle-groups into which LXXXIV Corps was split by the American thrust, had no sooner begun to lead his men back towards Cherbourg, along with the navy and the GAF, than he had an altercation with the Fortress Commander about the way in which Hitler's latest 'no withdrawal' order should be interpreted. Their dispute was summarily resolved in Schlieben's favour next day, when Hitler appointed him Fortress Commander under 7 Army, with orders to defend the town to the last and the east coast for as long as possible. OKW warned him to look out for surprise Allied landings on the coast, and detailed instructions for a slow fighting withdrawal on the port were added by Rommel and Fahrmbacher, Marcks's temporary successor as Commander of LXXXIV Corps.[1] Every day counted for the outcome of the war as a whole, they both urged, but a less rhetorical reason for their insistence had already been revealed—it would take a week to demolish Cherbourg harbour.

Schlieben's correspondence with his superiors lent an air of comedy and bombast to the last days of Cherbourg, and it probably held more entertainment than intelligence value. Hitler demanded to know what elements of 243, 77 and 91 Divisions were in Cherbourg. Impossible, replied Schlieben, they are too mixed up, and added that they were also too old and too exhausted for their task. To Rommel he complained that his men were not only old but 'pill-box minded' garrison-troops who would never stand up to the strains about to be imposed upon them, and demanded reinforcements if Hitler's order were to be carried out. Rommel sent him a parachute regiment by air and a grenadier regiment by sea just before the harbour was

2230/17
KV 8618
0950/18

---

1. Von Choltitz took over the Corps on 20 June.

closed. On the eve of the final assault on the 22nd, Hitler signalled 'Defend as Gneisenau did at Kolberg,[1] defend to the last
pillbox. The eyes of the German people and of the whole world
are upon you' and received the solemn reply 'I will do my
duty'. By the following evening, with all his reserves committed,
Schlieben was back to his earlier mood, complaining that his
troops were useless because the best had already been weeded
out for the eastern front, and incoherently signalling that he
was completely out of 'anti-tank resources' without specifying
whether he meant guns or ammunition. Rundstedt bade him
farewell with a 'historic importance . . . last man, last round'
message, and as the Americans broke in Schlieben comforted
himself with the thought that they had wanted Cherbourg ten
days earlier. By the morning of 25 June he was asking Rommel
whether it was necessary to sacrifice his remaining troops by refusing to surrender. Stretched beyond capacity by competing
demands, on the previous evening Jagdkorps II had refused a
request for fighter support by Pz Lehr on the central front in
order to help Schlieben in his extremity, but now quickly
switched to the Caen sector as the Epsom battle began.

With the fall of Cherbourg on 26 June, silence fell not only
on the garrulous Schlieben but almost as completely over the
whole western sector of the Allied front until the first days of
July. While 1 US Army prepared for the break-out which was
eventually delayed for another month, the Germans took such
steps as they could to prevent anything of the kind: the diver-
sion of 2 SS Pz Division to St Lô and Périers as soon as its long
journey from the south was over,[2] the positioning of 77 Division at La Haye du Puits and the bringing up of Werfer Brigade
8's rockets and mortars to II Para Corps were signs of a determination to block any future American attempt to turn west
into Brittany or south to the Loire. It was useful to know that
nevertheless the coast at Coutances was still thought vulnerable

---

1. August Graf von Gneisenau (1760–1831), Prussian general, stubbornly
defended Kolberg against Napoleon's besieging armies in 1807 until hostilities
were ended by the Peace of Tilsit. He played a leading part in the subsequent
clandestine military reforms, was Blücher's chief of staff at Waterloo and (with
Scharnhorst and Clausewitz) is regarded as one of the founders of the nine-
teenth-century Prussian army.
2. See p. 67 above.

to a thrust from St Lô on 23 June, just after 2 SS Pz had been withdrawn into Army Group reserve to cover that area, even though no advantage could be yet taken of it. For the moment, the limelight was focused on the British sector.

The British sector

The attempt by 2 Army to over-run Caen directly after the landings having failed, on 9 June Montgomery ordered Dempsey to capture the city. Progress was impeded by the persistent attacks which Hitler demanded when he rejected Rommel's request to concentrate on the American front—for instance, that of LXXXI Corps near the mouth of the Orne on 12 June, of which Ultra gave ample notice—but Rundstedt was still holding much of his armour (1 SS Pz, 2 Pz and 116 Pz) well away from the beach-head because of an invasion alarm in Belgium and Holland.

2100/11
KVs 7605,
7615
0313/12

Although this comprehensive statement by Rundstedt was dated 10 June, it was not available for signalling until 14 June. It did not therefore bring the news of 2 Pz's arrival, which was apparently the chief influence in deciding Montgomery to concentrate henceforth on pulling the German armour on to the British front round Caen so that the Americans could break out farther west, but it was somewhat disingenuous of him to claim that 2 Pz 'suddenly appeared' on the 14th, for Ultra had revealed its march to an assembly area only thirty-five miles away on 12 June—that is, well before its infantry was first identified in action. Its arrival filled the awkward gap in the German front which had made possible the attempt to outflank Caen by way of Caumont, forced 7 Armoured Division's withdrawal from Villers Bocage, and led to a temporary slowing down of the British advance which denied the RAF the airfields they had expected to occupy by now, and caused Tedder's unjustifiable remarks about a 'crisis'.

0730/12
KV 7707
1701/12

The activities of I SS Pz Corps and its component divisions (Pz Lehr, 12 SS Pz, 21 Pz, 716 Divisions and Werfer Bde 7, according to an order of 11 June) round Caen were kept under regular review at this time, and so were the movements of 116 Pz farther east. The main German effort, however, was spent in

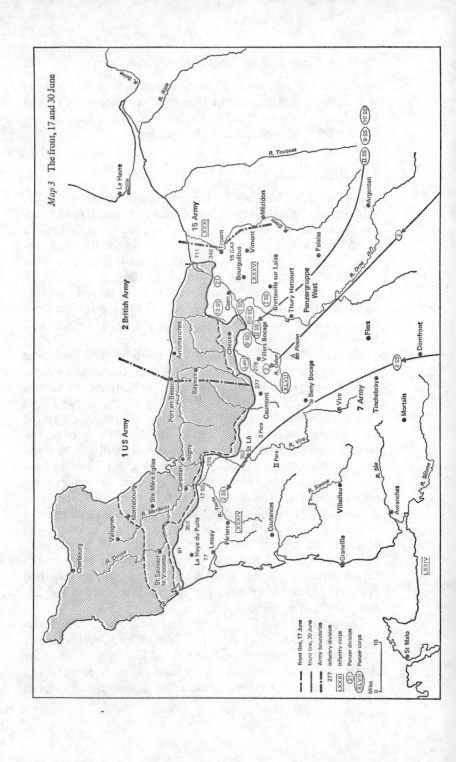

Map 3 The front, 17 and 30 June

counter-attacks on the Orne bridgehead between the sea and Troarn (due east of Caen), one of which was signalled with high priority between five and six hours before it was due to take place, and they brought up LXXXVI Corps from the south to a position between LXXXI on the coast and I SS Pz in order to pack the ring round Caen still more tightly. A major event at this point was the receipt of the first large-scale tank return since D-Day. It was dated 15 June and covered I SS Pz Corps (the divisions just listed, and Heavy Pz Abteilung 101—i.e. all the armour yet in action, except 2 Pz and 2 SS Pz in the centre and west) but, as was sometimes the case with material of this kind, it was difficult to decode and was consequently five days old before it could be signalled. Summarized, it shows the corps to have had 129 Mark IV tanks and forty-six Mark Vs (Panthers) immediately serviceable, together with some seventy heavy anti-tank guns; twenty-one Mark IVs, eighteen Vs and thirty VIs (Tigers) were under short repair, two IVs and eight VIs under long repair (12 SS Pz Division had gained a few serviceable tanks during the four days since it made an earlier return). A few days later, a complement to this operational report turned up in the shape of three successive supply returns (for 19, 20 and 21 June) by the same corps; they disclosed a shortage of heavy infantry guns, anti-tank guns and mines, and reported a decline in the serviceability rate of motor transport.

Naturally enough, there was not a whisper in Ultra of the conference between Hitler, Rundstedt and Rommel at Margival near Soissons on 17 June (in an atmosphere 'somewhere between confusion and chaos', according to Speidel), and useful current news for the next few days was confined to the imminent arrival of 1 SS Pz Division (with about 100 tanks, half of them Panthers) from Belgium to replace 716 Division[1] in I SS Pz Corps, the location of the boundary between I SS Pz Corps and 2 Pz Division of XLVII Pz Corps (the division shifted a little eastwards to conform), the forecast of an attack on I SS Pz

1. 716 Division was sent south to 1 Army; some elements were ordered to proceed on foot to the entraining station at Le Mans, and by side roads to avoid large movements in the opposite direction on the main routes (presumably 1 SS Pz).

Corps, a statement of the casualties suffered and replacements required by Pz Lehr and 21 Pz—in round figures 16 per cent, or 2000 men, in each case—and repeated confirmation that 116 Pz was still staying well away from the battle.

It was particularly fortunate that 116 Pz was so well documented at this particular time. The intelligence about it was valuable on two grounds: first, that although 1 SS Pz had after a week's hesitation been moved from Belgium to supply the needs of Normandy, the only other first-class Panzer division in the north-east was being retained there—and secondly, that this was plainly in response to the continuing FUSAG threat. The shuffling movements of 116 Pz betray the anxieties of a command trying to meet dangers from two opposite directions at the same time with limited resources. The division was still firmly located on the Seine, where it had long been, on 11 June, evidently guarding the river-crossings against the possibility of Montgomery breaking out of the Orne bridgehead and making for Paris or the Pas de Calais.[1] Two days later it was said to be moving to the south bank of the Somme (that is, fifty miles farther away from Normandy and nearer FUSAG and Calais), but its battle headquarters had actually crossed the river to a village just outside Abbeville on the north bank. By 15 June it had already begun retracing its steps, however, being variously reported as having 'just arrived' near Le Tréport (some twenty-five miles nearer the Seine than Abbeville) and as having its battle headquarters farther inland and nearer Dieppe. Since this location was confirmed next day, it was no doubt here that Rommel paid a visit to its commander, Graf von Schwerin, on 19 June, and it was clearly still thereabouts when it complained on the 23rd that no one was even bothering to send it situation reports on the Normandy fighting, for its headquarters had only moved a few more miles back towards the Seine by 25 June. By now it mattered little that news then dried up for a fortnight; 116 Pz was not heard of again until 9 July, when the imposition of wireless silence seemed to herald a major move which did not in fact take place for another three weeks.[2]

1. cf. p. 90 below.
2. cf. pp. 103–4. Irving 349 now connects 116 Pz's inactivity with the plot against Hitler.

On the eve of the battle for the crossings of the river Odon south-west of Caen (Epsom), which began on 25 June, there came to hand the first of a long series of late decodes in an obstinately difficult army key. They were timely in spite of being a week old, for they located heavy reinforcements just outside the battle area and gave away Hitler's decision (taken on 11 June in response to gloomy reports by Rundstedt and Rommel on the first few days' fighting) to shift II SS Pz Corps (9 and 10 SS Pz Divisions) back again to the west from the Russian front and to move more infantry (including some from 15 Army, the Fortitude area) towards Normandy as well. The first news was

18 June
KV 9364
0605/24

that on 18 June twenty-seven trainloads of II SS Pz Corps had arrived in the area of OB West, twenty-one of them at Nancy. Four hours after this had been signalled with high priority, we could report much more in the same vein, but this time with only three days' delay instead of six. By 21 June seventy-eight trains of 9 SS Pz had been unloaded within Rundstedt's command, sixty-two in Nancy and the rest in the general area Alençon–Laigle–Dreux–Nogent-le-Rotrou, west of Paris;[1] fifteen trains of 10 SS Pz were unloading in the same area, forty-seven between Nancy and Saarbrücken. In addition to all this armour, 353 Division was approaching St Lô from western Brittany, 276 Division (from Bayonne) assembling between Domfront and Flers, 266 (also from Brittany) moving to south-east of Avranches and 16 GAF Field Division on the way from Holland to locations west of Paris. After this, the remainder of the same message seemed tame by contrast although it yielded several valuable additional details. A highly profitable twenty-four hours ended about dawn on 25 June when

18 June
KV 9473
0409/25

Werfer Bde 9 (destined for LXXXIV Corps) was also found west of Paris and forty-six trains of 363 Division and 6 Para Division were detected at Lille.

Since similar information about these and some other reinforcements being hastily brought up to seal off the invasion area continued to come in for several more days, it will be best to summarize it all now even at the price of operating a double

---

1. On 24 June OKW, Luftflotte 3 and 5 Jagd Division were very concerned to give fighter protection to troop movements in this area, in spite of Allied air superiority.

system of chronology for a moment. Movement reports dated 23, 25 and 30 June were decoded between 1 and 5 July and signalled as xLs 393, 488, 644, 655, 661 and 786. By the last of these dates it was possible to conclude (among much else) as follows:

(i) The staff and corps troops of II SS Pz Corps and the whole of 9 SS Pz Division had reached the western theatre by 23 June; most of 10 SS Pz had arrived too, but some of it was still in the neighbourhood of Saarbrücken on the German border, not in Normandy.

(ii) By the same date a good deal of 1 SS Pz had reached the battle area; its Panther tanks were at Rouen.

(iii) 16 GAF Field Division had cleared the Dutch frontier by 25 June and some of it was assembling just behind the Orne front at Mézidon on the 30th.

(iv) SS Panzer Abteilung 102 (Tiger tanks) was on the way from north Germany to Normandy by 23 June but its movement was still incomplete two days later.

(v) 276 Division was moving ahead of 277 Division from the south of France; it had passed Angers on route for Flers on 23 June, but part of 277 was stuck south of the Loire.

It is not easy to determine how much of all this will have come as a surprise to Hut 3's customers in spite of the decoding delays, and how much they probably knew or suspected already from non-Ultra sources. For instance, 21 Army Group is said to have 'learned on 20 June that 1 SS Pz Div had begun moving from Belgium three days before'. Since kv 8881 was signalled on 20 June, it could on that ground have been 21 Army Group's authority—but its content was dated 19 (not 17) June; 21 Army Group may therefore have had other sources which Ultra confirmed and expanded. The situation is much the same over II SS Pz Corps. According to the official history, unspecified 'evidence' of its arrival from Russia was in 21 Army Group's possession on 24 June, the day when kv 9364 was signalled and apparently four or five days before its component divisions were identified in combat. This makes the decisive importance sometimes accorded to the 'suddenness' of its appearance difficult to understand, but at the same time underlines the tremendous value of the Ultra warning that heavy reinforcements were certainly approaching the battle area. The essentials of this warning were in Montgomery's hands just before Epsom began on 25 June, and the course of the battle showed what good use he made of it.

So far as the other formations mentioned above are concerned, Ultra seems clearly to have been first in the field with news of 16 GAF Division and SS Pz Abt 102; they were signalled on 24 June and 1 July respectively, and are first mentioned in operational histories on 6 and 10 July.

Ultra information was not particularly plentiful during the Epsom battle (25–30 June), but it was of high tactical quality; all the principal corps and divisions engaged were reported at least once every day, and their intentions sometimes discovered.

1115/27
KV 9826
1516/27

Pz Lehr reported 'heavy losses' on the first day, but under 'the dynamic leadership of General Bayerlein' had destroyed 170 armoured vehicles since the landings. It continued in the thick of the fighting until ordered to be relieved by 276 Division on

a.m./30
XL 230
1714/30

30 June.[1] The bulk of the intercepted traffic concerned I SS Pz Corps. We knew the tank strength it could muster in its position on the eastern flank of the British salient across the Odon at the end of the battle on 1 July: 1 SS Pz Division had fifty-four Mark IV tanks, twenty-six Mark V (Panthers) and thirty-one assault guns, 12 SS Pz Division twenty-five IVs and twenty-six Panthers, while twenty-five of the twenty-eight Tigers with which Heavy SS Pz Abt 101 had started the day were in the repair-shops by nightfall. The corps' petrol and ammunition supplies began to run dangerously low at once, and the petrol situation was becoming 'more acute every day' on the 27th. The corps or its component divisions frequently reported the point at which they would concentrate their main effort, and the corps itself remained 7 Army's spearhead until the fighting died down.

---

1. Ellis i. 319 dates this relief 5 July. See p. 84 below.

II SS Pz Corps did not enter the battle until 29 June. At dawn, 9 SS Pz Division was moving up to tackle the Allied breakthrough west of Caen, but soon postponed its effort. Next day it gave long notice of an intention to attack Cheux, a communications centre in the middle of the Allied salient, during the night 30 June to 1 July. Only a little over four hours separated the German and the British times of origin of this signal, making it among the speedier performances by Hut 6 and Hut 3, and when it was dispatched there were still several hours to go before 9 SS Pz's intended attack. It must surely have been this long notice which allowed the preparation of the tremendous artillery barrage which snuffed the attack out on the morning of 1 July and caused one of 9 SS Pz's officers to warn those approaching the locality 'Abandon hope all ye who enter here'.

0500/29
XL 70
1325/29
1200/30
XL 227
1612/30

There was considerable activity around the Allied bridgehead east of the Orne at the time of Epsom. Some well-aimed bombs on its headquarters (not Ultra-directed, so far as can be ascertained) perhaps discouraged 116 Pz from coming too close. LXXXVI Corps was expecting to be attacked by the enemy it was trying to contain on 28 or 29 June, so its Flivo demanded that the bridge over the river at Bénouville be destroyed from the air; a raid was laid on, but a signal disclosed this well in advance.

1200/28
XL 9
0029/29

A considerable reorganization of the command in this sector and of the distribution of forces round the whole lodgement area was undertaken at the end of the month. Hitler decreed that 'divisions of the 22nd wave' (i.e. conscription classes recently called up) be brought forward to create an infantry reserve and to enable exhausted divisions to be moved back for rest and refit. Thus 352 and 716 Divisions were to be relieved and sent south, while 271 and 272 Divisions, transferred from Army Group G like 276 and 277 Divisions already mentioned, were placed so as to guard the Somme and Seine against a British thrust from the direction of Caen. Panzergruppe West, restored to duty after the annihilation of its staff three weeks before and once again under 7 Army (itself now led by SS General Hausser, formerly of II SS Pz Corps), took charge of the four corps round Caen which constituted the only solid protection for Paris and the V-weapon coast—I and II SS, XLVII and LXXXVI. Thus (2 Pz having edged a little eastwards) all the Panzer divisions in northern France were concentrated against 2 British Army except 2 SS Pz which (deprived of its Panther tanks by the bombing which had blocked the railway south of Angers) was anxiously watching from St Lô for signs of the break-out by Bradley's Americans with which Rundstedt knew that the exhausted II Para Corps would be unable to cope.

The tremendous value of accurate foreknowledge of these new arrangements scarcely needs stressing. It was of absolutely prime importance to know that all the armour (except one weak division) had been successfully attracted to the British front and that Montgomery had thereby achieved his object of reducing the opposition to the break-out now being planned in the American sector. It is therefore worth pointing out that all the Ultra evidence was in the hands of Eisenhower and Montgomery between 1 and 4 July, several days earlier than the date given in the published accounts.

As the battle along the Odon approached its climax, Rundstedt and Rommel were summoned to confer with Hitler at the Berghof above Berchtesgaden. A few days before, the most powerful concentration of armour Rundstedt had yet been allowed to assemble had stood poised for a crushing blow at the invaders; Epsom had forestalled and nullified it. Rundstedt had been denied a free hand and knew that he had been forced to conduct the defence in the wrong way. Now the consequence was that the massed British tanks might suddenly burst out of their constricting perimeter at almost any time and create havoc in open country where there was no way of stopping them. As Geyr was to urge directly Rundstedt got back from Bavaria, a planned withdrawal followed by elastic defence would at least ensure that the Germans sometimes held the initiative, whereas obstinately to maintain the present lines of containment round Caen was to surrender it permanently to the enemy by permitting him to attack when and where he pleased. But Hitler would have none of such realism. A few hours after returning to his headquarters, Rundstedt nevertheless actually authorized Rommel to disengage Army Group B, but a countermanding 'no retreat' order came from Hitler and OKW as soon as they heard what he had done. Enraged by the defiance, Hitler now dismissed both Rundstedt and Geyr. In their places he appointed von Kluge (who had agreed with the Führer at the Berghof conference but was already implicated in the secret opposition to him) and the Panzer General Eberbach. All this can be claimed as the result of Epsom and in justification of Montgomery's policy of attracting all the German armour to the eastern corner of his front.

As if stunned by these momentous events, Ultra became rather uncommunicative at the beginning of July. The 'Red' was still broken regularly, but it carried little news of the first importance; the intermittently difficult army keys, which had yielded most of the news about II SS Corps, grew obstinate again, so we had no hint of the Berghof discussions or their aftermath. With one side licking its wounds and the other busy preparing for its next move, the front was quiet by contrast with the immediately preceding weeks. Only the American sector was comparatively active, as Bradley made an abortive effort to secure a suitable start-line for his forthcoming offensive; but since this properly belongs to the story of the breakout it will be deferred until the next chapter.

Apart from a routine confirmation that the Allied build-up south and east of Bayeux had been seen from the air, the first serious news from the British sector since Epsom ended was confirmation that 276 Division had relieved Pz Lehr,[1] together with the additional information that Lehr was going into Corps reserve behind 276 and 2 Pz; there was also a report on the front line of XLVII Corps, which controlled all three divisions. That Lehr was 'ready' next day in the expected position aroused no particular speculation until the sudden discovery that it was moving to the area west of St Lô during the night 7–8 July. Its staff had got halfway there by the next afternoon, and the division had reached its distination and was preparing to attack under LXXXIV Corps by the 10th. This was

1200/5
XL 858
1746/5

2300/7
XL 1196
0654/8

0215/10
XL 1492
1403/10

---

1. The relief was first reported on 30 June. See p. 81 above.

the first move of a Panzer division from the British to the American front.

By 6 July the location of the armour round Caen was being regularly reported again, and it was discovered that 12 SS's tank state on the 7th was forty-four Mark Vs serviceable plus nine undergoing long repair, thirty-six Mark IVs serviceable plus seven on long repair, a considerable improvement over its last return. The order of 9 July that 116 Pz was to keep wireless silence suggested that at long last this division might be about to take the final step which would precipitate it into the fighting. The capture of Caen next day was marked not by any reference to the cratering the British bombing had caused nor to the piles of rubble which impeded the advancing troops, but instead by several standard reports of the location and intentions of Panzer divisions (only one of which was received in time to be of much operational value) and by another exchange of infantry for armour: 277 Division was relieving 9 SS Pz on 10 July and completed the job next day.

General

Several other aspects of Ultra intelligence cannot easily be assigned to one sector of the front more than another, notably air operations. Yet warnings of bombing raids or fighter sweeps, plans to lay sea-mines off the beaches or to reconnoitre the approaches to them, were signalled in advance of the action on most days in June and quite often three or four times in a single day. Whether forewarning could be given, and if so how much, depended partly on when 'Red' broke and partly on when the German orders were issued; but since as a rule the new key was 'out' within a few hours of the midnight change, and since Luftflotte 3 usually issued its night-operation orders during the afternoon and its day orders about dawn, the feat was accomplished more often than not with an hour or two to spare. Then, a few days after the event, the formation carrying out the raid would file a return stating the number of sorties, of aircraft lost or damaged, of pilots ready and machines now serviceable. Battle order and action report combined enabled a continuous running record of air activity to be maintained, the enemy's loss-rate and the difference between intention and performance to be accurately measured, and the current strength and readiness state of every GAF unit to be known at any moment. From June onwards, the whole of the GAF's operational life on the western front was under constant surveillance; KV 8819, for instance, listed the Geschwader base airfields of every GAF fighter unit in France on 18 June, and XL 1505 gave several days' notice that the first Me 262s (the new jet fighters) were expected to operate from Orléans and Châteaudun about 14 July. The location of new airfields and their serviceability after the constant Allied bombing raids were regularly reported, together with fuel and ammunition stock returns by authorities at all levels from individual airfield up to Luftgau, and the distribution and equipment state of all the Flak in France. Flakkorps III was particularly assiduous in daily returns which detailed the whereabouts of every battery and recorded the serviceability of guns of all calibres, often indicating whether they were currently being employed in an anti-aircraft or an anti-tank role. In view of the continuing menace to tanks of the 88-mm AA gun, these returns were probably as useful to the Allied armies (because they showed where the gun-line was, and how dangerous its weapons) as to the RAF and USAAF, and the value of the dual-purpose 88-mm was driven home by the frequent GAF complaints of its abuse through employment in ground fighting.

Serious shortages of various kinds, but particularly of fuel and transport, began to show up within a week of the landings, and soon every day brought a new complaint. II Para Corps was short of transport and was compelled to have its petrol brought from Paris only at night (to escape the attentions of marauding aircraft) as early as 13 June, and 21 Pz lost half its current stocks in a bombing raid a week later. No fewer than five supply returns from I SS Pz Corps were noted between 20 and 27 June. The first two reported no exceptional difficulties (save that anti-tank weapons were running short and that the accident-rate among transport vehicles was mounting alarmingly because of the constant night journeys), but by 23 June fuel and ammunition expenditure were out-stripping supply; heavy fighting on the first day of Epsom made this situation still worse, because no fuel allocation had been received for some time, and it was 'daily becoming more difficult' according to the last of these five returns, dated 27 June. Bombs destroyed 600 tons of fuel at the army depot north of Poitiers on 16 June, the quartermaster's department of 7 Army had no stocks at all on 5 July and was forced to tell units to fetch what they could from OB West's dumps, probably not realizing that several of these were empty. Comparison of several successive stock reports from Luftgau Belgium–North France had already shown that GAF fuel supplies were also steadily diminishing because of the heavy consumption induced by battle. Realization of the stringency penetrated to the highest levels before the end of June. An OKW circular of the 24th, said to be based on experience gained by OB West, tried to make the best of a bad job by pretending that energy and initiative on the part of transport column leaders and the skilful use of bad weather periods would get supplies through in spite of the Allies' superiority in the air, but Keitel knew that this was not enough. Only twenty-four hours after his staff issued this circular he turned down a request of Rundstedt's for more motor transport on the ground that he (Rundstedt) already possessed full powers to commandeer what he needed; the GAF and the navy could easily spare the small quantities required,[1] as the overall fuel situation would not in any case permit an extra allocation for additional vehicles. Finally, he reminded Rundstedt of an earlier OKW order for the maximum possible use of producer gas in place of petrol.[2] Because of the 'extremely strained motor transport fuel situation' Sperrle (Commander, Luftflotte 3) prohibited all operationally inessential travel on 7 July.

Two reports from OB South-West (Kesselring), dated 11 and 30 June, showed that shortages like these were also prevalent in Italy; the second of them gave chapter and verse for the losses the German forces were suffering through their lack of

1. This was not the navy's view. Naval headquarters in Normandy had complained on 12 June that it was already feeling the pinch because it had surrendered so many vehicles to the army and the GAF.
2. The GAF was soon under orders to use producer gas or horse-drawn transport for supply journeys.

mobility and the shortage of spare parts. That things were no better in districts remote from either battle-front appeared from scraps of information about three Panzer divisions which had for some time been located in the west, formally as reserves but actually in an incomplete state of establishment: 9 Pz on the Rhône, 11 Pz outside Bordeaux and 19 Pz in Holland. The last would, of course, come into action as soon as the expected landing along the Channel–North Sea coast took place, yet on 9 June it lacked all heavy weapons (they were being applied for by XLVII Corps and may have arrived a fortnight later) and was regarded by OB Netherlands as 'inadequate even for defence against an air-landing'. An incomplete report on the stage reached in setting up all three divisions, dated 25 June, showed shortage of equipment having its effect. 9 Pz had only four Mark IV tanks and no Panthers, some of its infantry was still on foot for lack of lorries, and it was short of NCOs. One of the Panzergrenadier regiments of 11 Pz was mobile only in buses or on bicycles, but it was nearly up to strength although it was insufficiently trained, its motor transport was only a mixed bag and 'shortage of lorries hampers its employment as a Panzer division'. (It was clearly prudent of Hitler to decide on the 29th 'not to employ it as a Panzer division at the battle-front'!) As for 19 Pz, it was short of petrol and still only fit for local defence and a static role.

Evidence like this was particularly welcome because it could reassure Allied commands that the strain of war was beginning to tell on the German supply organization at the same moment as they were suffering from a serious—though temporary—logistical setback themselves. The great gale of 19–22 June totally destroyed the American and badly damaged the British Mulberry harbour, and almost halted the inflow of men and supplies for three days. By the time it ended, Dempsey's 2 Army was three divisions below its planned strength, and American operations were soon restricted by an ammunition shortage. The gale undoubtedly gave Rundstedt time to strengthen his defences with troops and artillery, but no sign is detectable in Ultra that he or anyone else realized the extent of the opportunity presented by the temporary imbalance of the Allies or sought to take advantage of it. In so far as a stepping-up of air attacks was one means of doing this, the explanation is no doubt the shortage of properly trained pilots which became acute about this time. At a fighter conference about 20 June, the Gruppenkommandeure of III JG 54 and III JG 26 gave it as their opinion that severe losses over the bridgehead could only be avoided by flying in large formations, because newly arrived pilots were poorly trained and there were few experienced leaders. The Air Officer for Bombers in Berlin explained on 24 June how a small fuel allocation could best be used to train just enough pilots to make good the losses being suffered, and both reports gave other evidence that the bottom of the barrel was being scraped for pilots and aircraft. Confirmation was given to all this at the highest level in a Goering order of 5 July. Because of the recent intolerable losses and in order to preserve the lives of indispensable leaders, flying by commanders of fighter, bomber and ground-attack units was to be limited to the following scale, according to the number of aircraft engaged: Staffelkapitaene—six, Gruppenkommandeure—fifteen, Geschwaderkommodore—twenty-seven (but forty-five for day fighters).

Whereas the Allies could still make good all their losses at once, it was therefore plain that the Germans could not. OB West reported total casualties of 47,070 (including six generals and 897 officers) between 6 and 25 June, and this suggests much the same loss-rate as that of the Allies for the same period, but he did not say how many of them had been replaced.[1]

More than a dozen appreciations of the Allies' probable next move, drawn up by a variety of authorities, provided clear evidence that the Fortitude threat to north-east France and the Low Countries remained effective throughout June and early July; over half of them consisted of little more than the predic-

---

1. xl 356. Compare xl 786 for 6–23 June, xl 1792 for details of some divisional casualties at an unspecified date, and Ellis i. 307–8. A footnote to Ellis i. 308 quotes an Army Group B document as authority for a figure of 80,783 German casualties by 7 July and points out that the Cherbourg figures were not known until the end of June, i.e. after the above OB West report. According to Irving 374, Army Group B had only received 6000 replacements by 12 July.

tion of an early landing somewhere in this area (the navy, always more jumpy than the other services, twice committed itself to forecasting a landing 'tonight', on the second occasion because radar jamming like that before D-Day had been noticed). The south coast of France was intermittently favoured by OB West, areas as widely separated as Denmark and the Aegean were mentioned as possibilities, and on one occasion the broadcasting of *messages personnels,* as on D-Day, was held to augur a landing 'anywhere'. The diversity of landing places canvassed was proof enough that the Germans were as much in the dark as ever about future developments.

Four of the dozen or more appreciations (two of them directly from Foreign Armies West, two clearly derivative from it) carried greater weight than the rest because they were more closely reasoned by a higher authority and because they agreed in many of their main conclusions. According to a Foreign Armies West Intelligence Summary of 22 June, 'Army Group Montgomery' had between twenty-two and twenty-four formations already ashore and another ten or twelve in reserve, whilst FUSAG, in a strength of twenty-eight large formations plus three or four airborne divisions, stood ready and waiting in southern England and might be used in a *coup de main* against Brest. From an ambiguous reference to 'Army Group Patton' it was not clear whether or not FUSAG was regarded as identical with it. Ten days earlier, OKH had seen these same airborne divisions' most likely employment as a new landing between Seine and Somme so that 'the two Army Groups' could operate together towards Paris before the end of July, and in so doing OKH had anticipated some of the points made in an OB West appreciation of the events of the week 19–26 June. This asserted that the Allies were twice as strong in the British as in the American sector although on a much shorter front, and drew the conclusion that in early or mid-July 2 Army would capture Caen and drive towards Paris on the Caen–Lisieux–Evreux axis, while FUSAG would land between Seine and Somme and encircle Le Havre before forming the other arm of a pincer movement on Paris which the mobile forces behind 15 Army were insufficient to repel. The Americans in the Côtentin would resume their attacks round Carentan at the beginning of July and would push on towards Coutances to cut off the Germans in the peninsula. 19 Army in the Rhône valley was in no better case than 15 Army on the Channel coast, for only 9 Pz Division ('not yet fully mobile'—as, indeed, has already been noted) and 341 Assault Gun Brigade could seriously confront a force landed from the sea. On 30 June Foreign Armies West agreed that the Caen and Carentan operations were both imminent but believed that 'Army Group Patton' would not be employed until Cherbourg could be fully utilized in late July.

These intelligence appreciations, particularly that over the signature of Rundstedt, the man responsible for conducting the battle, are illuminating in several ways. They show in the first place how completely the threat posed by FUSAG and by the absence from the field of a man with General Patton's fearsome reputation was mesmerizing the enemy. Not only has he been made to hesitate before reluctantly moving a few divisions from north-east France to Normandy—which was the primary purpose of the Fortitude deception plan—but he has been deluded into misunderstanding why the British sector was more thickly packed with men, guns and tanks than the American. The deception plan was designed to distract his attention from the western end of the front and blind him to the enormous scope of the break-out which Bradley was even then engaged in planning; these appreciations show not only that this has been successfully accomplished (the American objective is seen as simply Coutances on the west coast, the attack on which was in fact only the preliminary to a gigantic sweep round to the east), but also that Rundstedt has been fooled by Montgomery's concentrations outside Caen into a gross misconception of the whole Allied strategy. There was indeed to be an envelopment, but the leverage provided by the second arm of the pincers was to come from south and west, not north and east—nor was Paris the sole objective!

But this is not all. Rundstedt's wrong conclusions perfectly illustrate the difference between the conditions under which the opposed intelligence services were now operating. Deprived of their agents (who had either been locked up or 'turned' to feed false information back to Berlin via the Abwehr headquarters in Hamburg), denied all but the rarest reconnaissance flight over England[1] by the overwhelming air superiority of the Allies, unable to break any but the lowest-grade Allied codes and so easily lured into misinterpreting the results of their own Y-Service—with these handicaps Rundstedt's intelligence staff would have needed second sight to reach the right conclusion. On the other side of the lines, Bradley and Montgomery now knew—thanks to Ultra—how incorrect was Rundstedt's assessment of their plans and how weak his hand. He had been allowed to bring some armour up from the south, some from Germany, some even from the Russian front, and he had diluted the forces guarding the Straits of Dover and the Belgian coast—with what result, in his own eyes? That both his north-eastern and his southern flanks were too weak to resist determined assault—and this at a moment when his centre was about to give way as the British forced the crossings of the Odon and stormed Caen against the best of his armour. Ultra did not hear Rundstedt's 'Make peace, you fools' on the telephone to Keitel, but on almost exactly the same day it exposed the reasoning behind his despairing words.

Where might fails, courage or self-deception may supply the lack. The conclusions reached in an interview between Hitler and Kesselring were being widely circulated about 9 July, no doubt for propaganda purposes. 'Keynote of the fighting is to gain time. A few months may be decisive and bring equilibrium of forces. . . . Fighter production satisfactory; heavy tanks, assault guns, flying bombs, long-range rockets and new types of U-boat afford hope and will soon make themselves felt. The prerequisite for saving the nation is to fortify the troops psychologically.' Instead, they were to receive in quick succession the shocks of the American break-out, defeat at Mortain and encirclement at Falaise.

1. A contemporary German report, quoted in Ellis i. 307, said that no photo reconnaissance even of the effects of the V1 attacks on London was possible, and Jones 422 states that there was no photo reconnaissance of London between 10 January and 10 September. Irving 363 has Hitler passing round air photos of V1 damage in London at the Berghof conference on 30 June, however.

4

The break-out and the Falaise pocket

Further operations were already being planned as Caen fell: Goodwood across the Orne south-eastwards, and Cobra, the American break-out in the far west. They were to start on 17 and 18 July respectively. Was Goodwood intended simply to hold the German armour on the British front still longer, thus facilitating the American drive, or was it designed as a breakthrough in its own right? Montgomery seems to have changed his mind while it was in progress.

Just before Goodwood, Rommel tried to give Hitler a last warning that victory in Normandy was impossible, but on 17 July he was severely injured when his car was shot up from the air. Feldmarschall von Kluge, already OB West since 3 July, at once took over Army Group B as well, and combined the two functions until he was dismissed in mid-August. On 20 July the plotters tried to kill Hitler at his headquarters in East Prussia.

Goodwood seriously eroded German strength, but it was checked after a few hours and called off after two days—partly because of the bad weather which also caused the postponement of Cobra until 25 July. Cobra was an instant success, and the Germans' discomfiture was increased when the British joined in at Caumont in the centre of the front. The fall of Avranches on 30 July opened a corridor down the coast through which the Americans could advance south and east. To exploit the opportunity, an American Army Group was called into being under Bradley[1] (it was numbered 12 instead of 1 so that FUSAG could retain its notional existence a little longer). Bradley promptly gave Patton his head with 3

1. See Figure 4 for the new Allied command set-up.

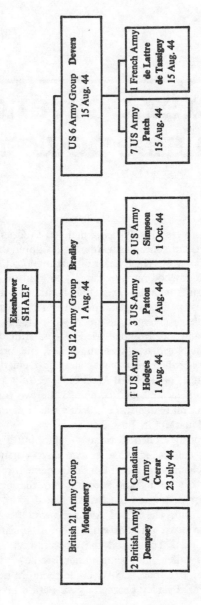

Figure 4 The Allied land command as finally developed

Notes: Dates are those on which each formation became operational. 6 U S Army Group came under Eisenhower's command on 15 September 1944. Montgomery continued to direct all land operations during August 1944. Eisenhower took active personal command on 1 September. During the Ardennes offensive 1 and 9 U S Armies were placed under 21 Army Group from 20 December; 1 Army reverted to 12 Army Group on 18 January and 9 Army on 4 April.

Army, loosing him towards the Loire and Orléans through country where there were no prepared defences; within five days he had turned the German southern flank by reaching Mayenne and Laval. Meanwhile the British had taken Mt Pinçon, the key feature in the centre of the old front, and were pressing hard on the northern flank of what was now rapidly becoming a deep German salient.

Hitler tried to counter the American offensive by attacking from east to west, but the 'madness of Mortain' completely failed to cut the slender supply-line through Avranches upon which the American advance depended and did not check Bradley's planned encirclement for a moment. By persisting with the attack for four days (7–11 August), however, Hitler preserved the salient long enough to turn it into a deadly pocket, a killing-ground from which two German armies were already finding it difficult to escape by 12 August. For by then 1 Canadian Army (in action since 3 July) was pressing close to Falaise from the north, while Patton was only a few miles away to the south when Bradley halted his northward thrust at Argentan on 14 August and turned his face towards the Seine. The jaws never quite closed on the fleeing Germans, but huge numbers of men and vast quantities of material were trapped. Patton and 3 Army were near Paris by now, aiming to cross the river a little to the north of the city.

At this moment, another American army landed on the French Riviera, and Hitler called 15 August 'the worst day of my life'. Dismissed as the scapegoat for another's mistakes, von Kluge committed suicide two days later.

The material

The last few days of June and the first three weeks of July turned out to be one of the few relatively lean periods for Ultra in the west. The volume of traffic dropped when the front became temporarily stabilized soon after the fall of Cherbourg, and was slow to pick up again until Cobra brought about a resumption of mobile warfare a month later and raised traffic-levels to unprecedented heights. But if Ultra information was for a time rather scarcer than it had been lately, some of the decodes were obtained in quicker time than usual and the news they contained was even more up to the minute than hitherto. Almost all of them came from GAF sources, however. While this by no means denied us knowledge of the ground fighting—the Flivos used GAF links to report the movements of army units, and so did the parachute divisions, which belonged to the Luftwaffe—a transient difficulty with army keys deprived us until towards the end of July of the tank-returns and supply pro-formas which had been invaluable during the first few weeks.

From the intelligence point of view, fate dealt the cards kindly. If there had to be a period of relative famine, it was probably easier to endure it in these three weeks than at any other time during the whole summer. The fullest possible information was needed in the precarious early days of the lodgement, and again during the break-out and pursuit in August; mid-July, on the other hand, was a time of limited operations in

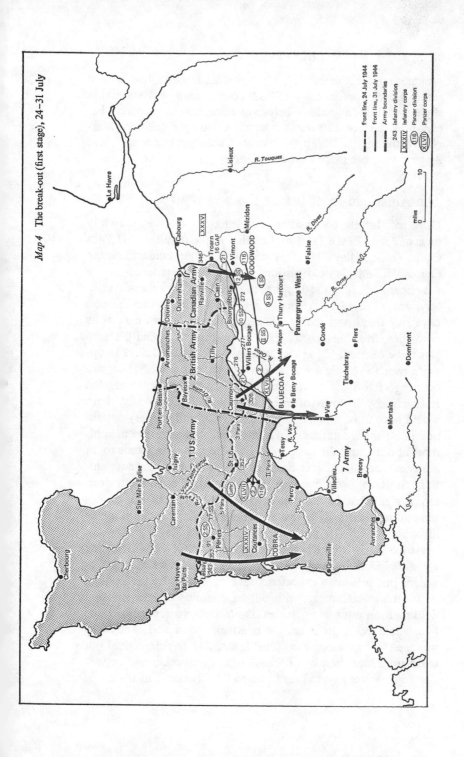

Map 4   The break-out (first stage), 24–31 July

front line, 24 July 1944
front line, 31 July 1944
Army boundaries
243   Infantry division
XXXVI   Infantry corps
116   Panzer division
XLVII   Panzer corps

miles
0   10

Le Havre

R. Touques
Lisieux

Cabourg
Ouistreham
Ranville
Troarn
16 GAF
Vimont
Mézidon
XXXVI
21
116
GOODWOOD
12 SS
Caen
272
1 SS
346
R. Dives
Falaise
Bourguébus
Douvres
Arromanches
Tilly
Bayeux
Port en Bessin
10 SS
277
Villers Bocage
9 SS
11 SS
Thury Harcourt
R. Orne
Condé
Flers
Panzergruppe West
1 Canadian Army
2 British Army
R. Odon
276
2
R. Vire
A Mt Pinçon
R. Aure
Caumont
XLVII
21
326
BLUECOAT
le Beny Bocage
Vire
Tinchebray
Domfront
Tilly
3 Para
St Lô
352
II Para
1 US Army
Tessy
R. Vire
R. Vire-Taute Canal
Isigny
Lessay
Périers
XLVII
2
116
7 Army
Bréecy
Percy
Villedieu
St Mère Eglise
Carentan
St Père
R. Taute
Lessay
243
91
353
2 SS
17 SS
LXXXIV
Coutances
COBRA
Granville
Avranches
Mortain
Cherbourg
La Haye du Puits

preparation for the coming offensive, and rather less was at stake. Be this as it may, Ultra's contribution was somewhat slighter in July than either before or after, and the account that can now be reconstructed is correspondingly thinner. Mercifully, the famine began to abate as Cobra got under way, and August was once more a time of plenty.

The American front before the break-out

Ultra was largely confined to the American front in the early days of July. On the 1st it told us that in the opinion of II Para Corps (on Bradley's left) the day would soon come when the German infantry would no longer be able to stand up to the Americans because the latter was supported by superior artillery, well directed from the air; 3 Para Division in fact claimed on 5 July that it was losing 100 men a day, or 97 per cent of its casualties, from this cause. If even the present Allied pressure was to be resisted, II Para went on, the GAF would have to operate over the battle area 'at least for short periods' (how did Goering relish this contemptuous disparagement of the Luftwaffe by its own offspring, the parachutists?) and there would have to be a better supply of mortar and artillery ammunition. Neither requirement was met, for both were repeated almost at once, and the news must have been very welcome to an American command just beginning to suffer from an ammunition shortage itself because of the effects of the previous month's gale but on the point of going all out at St Lô, Carentan and westwards to secure a proper start-line for future operations.

At the base of the Cherbourg peninsula LXXXIV Corps was equally gloomy. It reported the battle headquarters of all its divisions just before an expected attack on 3 July. By the evening its front was collapsing, with only a battalion of 353 Division holding firm; after heavy losses like today's, its report said, the line would be in great danger if attacks continued. The story was the same all along the corps' front: 243 Division could not clean up a local break-in because it was too weak, and casualties (details were given) had caused 77 Division and the corps itself to use up all reserves, although both claimed defensive successes.

0936/6
XL 1027
2255/6

2000/9
XL 1468
0757/10

2 SS Pz was now momentarily called out of Army reserve and put under LXXXIV Corps to meet another expected attack; its fuel, artillery and ammunition state was reported, and then it was suddenly struck off the corps' strength again and ordered to assemble at Périers, once more as Army reserve. Before LXXXIV Corps could in consequence repeat its old complaint that it had nothing left to counter a thrust down the coast to La Haye, von Kluge took the unprecedented step of moving armour from the British to the American front, sending Pz Lehr to help LXXXIV Corps west of St Lô. Ultra gave more than

2300/7
XL 1196
0654/8
1800/9
XL 1447
0022/10
1840/9
XL 1456
0426/10
0215/10
XL 1492
1403/10

thirty-six hours notice of the move,[1] which was not complete until the early evening of 9 July, but did not manage to send Allied commanders a copy of LXXXIV Corps' order to its new subordinate for an attack across the Vire–Taute canal until a little while after the planned zero hour 'early on 10 July'.

The immediate threat to the German line was averted by battle-groups of 2 SS Pz, which on 10 July prevented a breakthrough on LXXXIV Corps' front at just the point where the corps had expected it and then settled down astride the Carentan–Périers road, but in most other respects the news was bad from the German point of view everywhere between St Lô and the sea. There were more reports of heavy losses and 'last reserves' on 11 July, and strenuous efforts to hold the Allies at bay left 2 SS Pz in need of petrol and most types of ammunition for several days and cost it twenty-two tanks, seven guns and seven lorries. A little to the east, II Para Corps was so weakened that it did not expect to hold out if attacks were

2130/11
XL 1713
1244/12

renewed on the same scale, and it urgently needed small arms to make good losses in 3 Para Division, which was down to only 35 per cent of its proper strength. Only Pz Lehr, which had fought side by side with 2 SS Pz in the Vire–Taute canal action, refrained from complaints of this kind.

However, to judge from a sudden spate of casualty-returns and operational reports about the strength of units which occurred in mid-July, the loss-rate in men as well as in material

---

1. cf. p. 84 above.

was causing considerable alarm about this time. A return of 10
July, covering the five divisions of LXXXIV Corps and presumably referring to a single day's fighting, gave a total of 578
killed, wounded and missing. Pz Lehr only suffered twenty-six
casualties that day, but it reported 'heavy losses' from its battle
headquarters south-west of St Lô on the 13th. Twenty-four
hours later, LXXXIV Corps was so weakened by heavy casualties, particularly among officers, that it could no longer hold its
ground in face of the battering meted out to it by gunfire and
bombs. On the same day II Para Corps reported nearly 6000
casualties in the period 6 June–14 July.

It was presumably these figures which led on 15 July to an
even more emphatic repetition of the previous day's statement
that heavy losses had so reduced the corps' fighting strength
that 'even the bravest troops' would not be able to prevent a
breakthrough to St Lô when the expected new attack came.
These statistics were of course only a fraction of the whole—total German casualties in the western front between 6 June and
16 July were later known to have numbered approximately
100,000, including 2360 officers—but they were enough to
show that the manpower resources of both the corps holding
the line opposite the 1 US Army were becoming so stretched
that, however stubborn the resistance which was to keep the
Americans out of St Lô for another three days, even the senior
local German commanders expected the breaking-point to
come at any moment. These commanders do not seem to have
foreseen the magnitude of the disaster which was soon to over-
whelm them—for the capture of St Lô was only a preliminary to
the blow which smashed open the gap through which Patton's 3
Army was to drive, rolling up the whole German front in the
process—but by reporting their apprehensions in Enigma they
let Bradley and Montgomery know, as they planned Cobra,
that the opposition would not be difficult to crack.

The arrival of reinforcements did not lighten the Germans'
gloom in the week before the blow fell. On 19 July 5 Para Division suddenly appeared under LXXXIV Corps, to be followed by 275 Division two days later. A message which gave
the precise location of both these divisions was decoded in time
to be signalled several hours before the American advance

19 July
XL 2823
1647/20

early/21
XL 3284
0657/24

began, and later on the same day it was confirmed that 5 Para was sandwiched between 17 SS PzGr and Pz Lehr in the St Lô–river Taute sector. The new arrivals strengthened the defence near the coast, where the Americans struck most violently, but at the same time 17 SS PzGr detected 3 US Army on its front, and II Para Corps around St Lô pointed out that 352 and 3 Para Divisions were so exhausted by weeks of continuous combat that they were simply unable to close gaps which might be driven into their lines.

An exchange between the commander of II Para Corps, Meindl, and General Student, the hero of the 1941 air-landing on Crete and now commander of the Parachute Army, was even more revealing. Meindl complained on 20 July that the fighting power of his paratroops was dwindling steadily and that two requests for new drafts had gone unanswered; the critical situation of the last few days had forced him to put in the few replacements he had received as soon as they arrived—with the result that 90 per cent of them became casualties in a very short time, because they were young, untrained men, most of whom had never thrown a hand-grenade, fired more than a few rounds of live ammunition, or learned much about machine-guns, entrenching-tools and camouflage. Even after allowance is made for the pardonable exaggerations of a general anxious to persuade his superiors of his plight in order to get their help, this message had a twofold value: it confirmed that the divisions on what would in a few days' time become the left flank of the American thrust were incapable of mounting an immediate or effective counter-attack, and it also betrayed the likelihood of a gradual decline in the quality of the handful of parachute divisions which now constituted the élite of the German infantry. Student's answer did little to alter this impression: 2500 volunteers were on the point of being sent off, he said, but Meindl must remember that the chief reason for the present difficulties was the constant demand for paratroops on all fronts; he had drawn OKL's attention to this many times and was sure they would not allow standards to fall. During the short interval that elapsed between question and answer, Meindl forecast an American thrust either south-eastwards or south-westwards from St Lô which the depleted German divisions would be unable to block, and on 22 July asked Student to divide the 2500 volunteers into two parties: 1000 men to a training depot at home, and 1500 to 3 Para Division to restore part of its fighting strength.

Coming on top both of the anxieties of 20 July, with its contradictory reports of the success and failure of the plot against Hitler in which he was himself implicated, and of the strain of trying to decide whether Caen (where Goodwood had just ended) or St Lô would be the springboard for the next Allied offensive, these repeated warnings that neither of the two corps he had set to guard the base of the Côtentin peninsula was capable of fulfilling its task may have been the final straw which broke von Kluge's nerve.

The break-out

1400/24
XL 3338
1909/24

The effectiveness of the carpet-bombing of Pz Lehr and 5 Para with which Cobra began on the morning of 24 July was reported so quickly that it may have done something to lighten the gloom spread by the accidental dropping of some of the bombs in the Americans' own lines. When there was no immediate follow-up, LXXXIV Corps thought it had smashed the ground attack by massed artillery fire (in fact, the attack was postponed for twenty-four hours because of the weather), but also gave away its conviction that it could only go on using up ammunition at this rate if it received more regular supplies. Its evening report delivered the corps' complete order of battle into Allied hands before the assault was renewed next morning.

1800/24
XL 3399
0448/25

1000/25
XL 3527
0447/26

In view of the immediate and sweeping success of Cobra, there are surprisingly few dramatic highlights in the Ultra signals, which give an essentially straightforward account of operations moving too swiftly for intelligence to keep up with them, but an occasional item underlines the chaos into which the German command had been thrown. Thus 2 SS Pz (and indeed the whole of LXXXIV Corps) were soon both desperately short of 88-mm shells to use against the American tanks, and the corps reported heavy casualties and a deteriorating situation before dawn on 26 July and vainly brought up a battalion of 275 Division to block the penetration south-west of St Lô.

A curious feature of this engagement is the discrepancy between the austere terms in which Pz Lehr reported its appreciation that the enemy was trying to punch a hole in its front and what later became known of its sufferings at the moment when this report was being drawn up. A sentence from the account given later by the divisional commander, General Bayerlein, of the raid by 1600 Flying Fortresses which almost wiped out Pz Lehr on the morning of 25 July has become famous: 'By midday the entire area resembled a moon landscape, with bomb craters touching rim to rim.' Cut off from his men by the subsequent American advance, Bayerlein eventually came across a stray vehicle, which carried him back to 'the rearward elements of my otherwise annihilated formation'. Nothing about Pz Lehr beyond routine movements came to light through Ultra for several days, and it was not reported unfit for battle until 28 July nor pulled out of the line until the 31st (even then, a battle-group remained near Villedieu as late as 2 August). Only on 5 and 6 August were reports more in keeping with Bayerlein's account intercepted on their passage through official channels, and they were not decoded until several days later still. On 5 August the divisional operations officer said that his men were 'badly battered and no longer fit for operations': only 150 Panzergrenadiers from a single regiment were capable of fighting and they had no more than thirteen tanks and half-a-dozen guns; sufficient cadres were left for the division to be made battle-worthy if it were brought up to strength again, but it would need a month's rest first. Next day II Para Corps made the division's tally of tanks only nine and rated its fighting value 'hardly even IV' (the lowest category, fit only for static defence).

To return to the opening day of Cobra: there were useful indications in Fliegerkorps IX's orders at 1300 hours on 26 July that the Germans were being surprisingly slow to appreciate that the main Allied effort was now being made on the west coast rather than at Caen—its fighters were to operate over St Lô and its heavy bombers in the Caen area. Not until twenty-four hours later was the priority reversed, but the corps then told the bomber formations that only by their most strenuous efforts could the gap in the front be closed and a strategic success by the Allies be prevented. Several vain attempts were made to halt the American advance and II Para Corps (already down to a rifle strength of only 3400 men) was rendered still less capable of effective resistance when told by von Kluge's Chief Quartermaster that he could not send it any more howitzer ammunition because there was none available.

With his enemies already in Coutances, von Kluge tried on 28 July to block their farther advance with armour, drawing 2 Pz and 116 Pz from the central and eastern sectors, with XLVII Corps to co-ordinate them. Within twenty-four hours of his decision, Ultra had pieced together the essence of it. The first sign was a report of II Para Corps' front line which placed XLVII Corps on the 'wrong' side of it, and occasioned the cautious comment 'no other evidence for transfer of XLVII Corps from right to left of II Para'. Very soon afterwards it was discovered that 2 Pz had moved westwards from its previous position due south of Caen the previous evening, but its combination with 116 Pz and the latter's exact location had to wait until the next day.

0630/29
XL 3934
1254/29

1930/28
XL 3943
1404/29
1000/30
XL 4067
1629/30
1200/30
XL 4085
1840/30

The most striking thing about all this was the discovery that 116 Pz had at last left 15 Army and the Somme.[1] Under pressure from von Kluge, Hitler had released it ten days earlier, and it had at first gone to Falaise, but all this had passed unremarked by Ultra. Its departure from the Pas de Calais has been seen as the end of Fortitude: 'Thus the spectre of Patton's Army Group had finally been laid,' writes Irving. Masterman on the other hand claims that Fortitude survived until 25 October, and an appreciation drawn up by Foreign Armies West just as 116 Pz was beginning to move confirms that FUSAG was still very much alive at that time. There had been 'extensive regrouping in FUSAG (the Patton formation)' Foreign Armies West began, but it still contained between thirty-two and thirty-five British and American divisions; its employment against Norway was no longer probable, because a decision would be sought in France and Belgium, but 'it still may be brought to bear elsewhere'.

It was soon evident that there was little chance of stopping

1. See p. 78.

the Americans, in spite of the arrival of these reinforcements. Ordering all its heavy bombers out at midday on the 29th, Fliegerkorps IX exhorted the crews to 'extreme effort' to close the gap at Avranches and deny the Allics a strategic success. XLVII Corps and 116 Pz were short of ammunition and fuel and the latter suffered such heavy losses that it was forced to postpone its counter-attack. There was no coherent front for twenty miles inland from the west coast (where 243 Division was surrounded and reduced to a strength of only 200 men) on the morning of 30 July, so that in Luftflotte 3's opinion the 'break-through crisis' was not yet over. This was the 'terrible mess' which von Kluge tried to clean up by taking command of 7 Army himself and Ultra had reported its seriousness by the night of 30–31st. By midday, 7 Army's flank was wide open, and its orders were arriving too late for LXXXIV Corps to carry them out. Fuel was so short that tanks were running dry on the battlefield and irreplaceable transport being abandoned, blocked roads were delaying supplies and causing corps and divisions to get mixed up; even far away on the right 3 Para Division was 'worn out' and down to a strength of 1500 men, and maximum air effort was being called for to prevent a further American advance south and south-east of Avranches.

As his 12 Army Group came into operation on 1 August, Bradley's first orders were to exploit his advantage in just this way—he directed 1 Army on Mortain and Vire, 3 Army on Rennes and Fougères with the subsequent duty of clearing Brittany—but within two days the situation had developed so promisingly that he told Patton to face east with the bulk of 3 Army, leaving only one corps to clean up Brittany with the help of the Resistance. Having telephoned his fears to Hitler, von Kluge was allowed to denude Brittany by moving 2 Para Division to Normandy but was denied permission to withdraw 319 Division from its non-combatant role in the Channel Islands. Nearly two months after the landings, the war of movement was about to start. Its scale and duration were in large measure determined by the extraordinary order Hitler gave von Kluge on 2 August—to prepare a counter-thrust by four Panzer divisions through Mortain to Avranches and the sea. Before examining this, however, events on the British front since the fall of Caen must be recorded.

The British front before the break-out

The week between the capture of Caen and the short-lived Goodwood offensive, the same week which was to be Rommel's last as a field commander, saw frustratingly few Ultra signals, as has already been remarked. We were able to give no warning of the multiple defence lines south-east of Caen—unsuspected, it seems, by 2 Army Intelligence—which brought Goodwood to a halt so quickly, but we did manage to keep track of the movements of most of the Panzer divisions and to show that the Germans were in a continual fret about new attacks from almost every quarter. Thus 21 Pz, out towards Troarn due east of Caen, was already expecting to be attacked again while the British were still sorting themselves out amid the heaps of rubble on the right bank of the Orne; just a week later, one of the Goodwood bomb carpets was laid across the road the division was holding. General Buelowius, commanding the fighters of Jagdkorps II, was less accurate when he read tank concentrations west and south-west of Caen as indications of a new attack there on 15 July, and ordered every possible aircraft into the air to break them up. His superior, Sperrle of Luftflotte 3, was better informed. Just after midnight on 15–16 July he correctly forecast a large-scale attack (which would be 'decisive for the course of the war') to take place south-eastwards from Caen 'about the night of 17–18th'. By midday—that is, thirty-six hours before Goodwood was launched—this forecast was in the hands of those who were at that moment putting the finishing touches to the plan of attack, and it was soon followed by the operational orders to bomber squadrons which Sperrle based upon it.

0001/16
XL 2287
1030/16

Several intended movements were discernible among the divisions packing the ring round Caen which Goodwood was designed to break, but fear of imminent attack prevented most from being carried out. 9 SS Pz, which had been holding the south-west sector alongside 10 SS Pz, with 276 Division in its rear, was to be withdrawn on 15 July but was still fighting near

Gavrus next day. Early on the 16th 272 Division took over 1
SS Pz's front, but 1 SS Pz did not move far. More noteworthy
was the behaviour of 12 SS Pz. It too was coming out of the
line on 11 July, but maintained a battle headquarters in the
south-eastern outskirts of Caen nevertheless. Lost to sight for a
few days it reappeared early on the 17th, demanding air cover
early/17   for a move from the same general area to a position northwards
XL 2383   from Lisieux, twenty miles back, whence it would be able to
0306/17   pounce on the spearheads of that drive from Caen towards the
Seine which had so long been the Germans' nightmare, condi-
1600/18   tioning them to fall in with Montgomery's plan and put their
XL 2604   armour where he wanted. One of the division's headquarters
1901/18   was later located en route to Lisieux. These two signals are another good illustration of the high tactical value Ultra could
sometimes have: the first will have been received by all the Allied headquarters which could make use of it five or six hours
before 12 SS Pz began to move, and both were among our
quickest jobs—just three hours from German to British time of
origin.

Allied artillery-spotter aircraft had lately been the subject of
frequent complaint: on 12 July, for instance, XLVII Corps and
2 Pz Division (on the central front about Caumont) grumbled
that they were 'overhead the whole time'—only to be silenced
by Jagdkorps II's rejoinder that it could only operate at the
most vital spots and that Army Group B had ordered it to concentrate its main effort on another part of the front. This was
evidently east of the Orne, for soon Panzergruppe West,
LXXXVI Corps and 21 Pz Division all combined to proclaim
themselves 'thrilled and grateful' for support recently received.
Bouquets like this had not often come the GAF's way since the
landings, but there were two more in the same week. Air patrols were said to have reduced the army's losses of motor
transport, and at nightfall on 17 July 10 SS Pz Division reported 'great joy' in its ranks at that day's raid by Fliegerkorps
IX, which had kept the enemy's artillery quiet for twenty min-
utes(!).

Soon after Goodwood opened on 18 July, 1 SS Pz captured a
map from a British aircraft which force-landed just south of

Caen, but there was no indication that it gave away anything vital. Possibly the most useful piece of information from Ultra during the forty-eight hours' severe fighting was the news that due west of the city 16 GAF Field Division had been so badly smashed by 19 July that what was left of it had been taken over by 21 Pz, which had itself had to give ground the previous evening after at first making some progress with a counter-attack.

Goodwood was called off on the 20th. For the next ten days, however, we were frequently able to report that divisions in all parts of the front expected it to be renewed shortly but disagreed about the point at which the blow was likely to fall. The GAF estimated that between 800 and 1000 tanks were massed south-east of Caen, and 1 SS Pz (right in the front line) predicted a thrust from here towards Falaise. Both were no doubt taken by the German command as confirmation of the belief— already manifest through Ultra for several weeks, and now known to have been firmly held at this moment by Speidel and Eberbach—that a break-out on this general line towards Paris was imminent. We were able to give this sector continuous coverage during the last days of July, and a large number of divisional locations or short-range moves—most of them decoded very quickly—made it abundantly clear that a very strong defensive screen was still being maintained at the eastern end of the Allied bridgehead. At the same time Ultra provided regular evidence that the presupposition behind these arrangements continued to dominate German thinking. Jagdkorps II and Fliegerkorps IX orders for the 26th and 27th still put the main air effort outside Caen, and did not shift it to St Lô until the night of 27–28th (that is, some thirty-six hours after Cobra began); we gave five or six hours' warning of the change.[1] Caumont was not mentioned as a target until after the start of 2 Army's new offensive there, and again notice that it was to be bombed was given in time.

1345/27
XL 3702
1630/27

1300/30
XL 4088
1930/30

Between the framing of Montgomery's orders for the Caumont attack (Bluecoat) on 27 July and their execution three days later, the situation upon which they were based had undergone a considerable change. As already explained, two Panzer

1. cf. p. 103.

divisions (2 Pz and 116 Pz under XLVII Corps) had been moved westwards to protect the rear of 7 Army from too close an American encirclement. This shifted them from the eastern to the western flank of the new British attack, and was known before Bluecoat started.[1] On the same day, 28 July, as this move was first detected, Ultra also revealed that more armour (only fifty-three tanks in fact, but we did not know this for several days) was moving from the Caen front to the eastern edge of the Bluecoat area—21 Pz was reported to be leaving LXXXVI Corps on the Orne later that evening, after being relieved by 272 Division. Not only was this news delivered in just two and a quarter hours, but it also presents something of an intelligence curiosity, in that it almost seems to show Ultra reading von Kluge's mind in advance. No hint of 21 Pz's destination was given in the Enigma message which underlay XL 3877, but in the circumstances (the success of Cobra) 21 Army Group and 2 Army are more likely to have interpreted the news as indicating that it was moving westwards than that it would replace 116 Pz as 'longstop' between Caen and Paris. Yet the British Official History quotes the Panzergruppe West War Diary as authority for the statement that von Kluge only decided to move 21 Pz after news of Bluecoat reached him on the 30th. It was not until this stage that Ultra found out where 21 Pz was going—Cahagnes, just outside Caumont and directly in the path of the assault 2 Army was shortly to make on Mt Pinçon.

2000/28
XL 3877
2214/28

0630/31
XLs 4179,
4187
1423/31

The plot against Hitler

Ultra gave no preliminary warning of the 20 July plot, for naturally the conspirators could not entrust their secrets to the Wehrmacht communications network until they controlled it. Events moved too swiftly after their bomb exploded at Hitler's East Prussian headquarters about midday for Ultra to give any news before Hitler's broadcast in the early hours of the next morning proved to the world that he was still alive whatever might have happened to him during the day. Such information

---

1. See p. 104 above.

as the source did provide was meagre at best, and it was presumably a perhaps excessive concern for security which prevented any of it from being signalled for several days. The first indications came when Keitel and Doenitz informed the services that Fromm, Hoepner and von Witzleben (respectively Commander of the Home Army, an out-of-favour Panzer general and a former OB West) were the leaders of the plot, and that Hitler had appointed Himmler in place of Fromm. The most dramatic item had originated a few minutes earlier but was not decoded until it was already out of date. It was timed 2010 hours 20 July, had the special Führer-Blitz priority, announced itself as from 'von Witzleben, Commander-in-Chief of the Armed Forces', and ran: 'The Führer is dead. I have been appointed Commander-in-Chief of the Armed Forces, and also . . .'. The text broke off at this point, and the interruption fixes the moment at which the plot failed in Berlin.

0100/21
XLs 3329,
3472
1834/24

Other messages were of less general significance. Just after Doenitz and Keitel made their announcements, a GAF Signals School directed its subordinates to honour requests for the provision of aircraft by the SS immediately but by no one else except Hitler, OKL or the commanders of Luftflotte Reich and its own immediate superior. During the following day an air reconnaissance unit sent a sycophantic message to its political commissar to assure him that its morale was high and that it deplored the 'murderous attack', and the communications squadron of Army Group B announced that flights outside his area by the Army Group commander or his Chief of Staff required the permission of Goering or Himmler. Two messages at the end of the month gave glimpses of the way the plotters were being hunted down. The first, dated 29 July, was cryptic: 'Search for minister over. Search for Oberbürgermeister[1] continues'; the second showed the police on the trail of a fugitive, General Lindemann, who was suspected of being somewhere in the Aegean on his way to a neutral country.

---

1. Carl Goerdeler, formerly mayor of Leipzig.

Mortain and Falaise

Some time on 2 August Hitler telephoned to von Kluge an order to replace armour by infantry in the line and to assemble at least four Panzer divisions for a heavy blow westwards to the coast at Avranches. A confirmatory signal was timed 2315 hours and passed on to Army Group B just after midnight. It was a sudden snap decision, for it had not been mentioned the previous evening when Warlimont (deputy head of the Operations Staff of the OKW) was sent off on a special mission to the western front, and Warlimont only heard of it at Army Group B's headquarters on the 3rd.

As an abstract conception, the idea had something to recommend it. The coastal road had only been in American hands for three days, and all 3 Army's supplies had to pass along it; if it were cut, the spearheads of the incipient American enveloping movement would wither and die (this point was specifically made by XLVII Corps when it attacked). But the practical obstacles were insuperable. The process of disengaging and assembling so much armour was bound to be long and difficult (even Rommel had not managed it under the more favourable conditions of early June), and the weight of Dempsey's and Bradley's blows from opposite directions was already threatening to hammer the life out of 7 Army before so far-reaching a plan to rescue it could be put into operation. Moreover, the shortage of motor transport, upon which the effective use of armour directly depended, had just been highlighted by a circular issued by the Inspector-General of Panzer Troops after consultation with Keitel at OKW. Addressed to all SS and police authorities, it said bluntly: 'Men and tanks are standing ready, but I lack lorries, tractors, passenger cars (particularly Volkswagen), carbines, field kitchens and war equipment of every kind', and appealed for them to be surrendered to the army immediately. Lastly, Hitler's order overlooked the probability that a new drive to the west would increase the likelihood (great enough already on 2 August) of 7 Army being surrounded and crushed to death. This possibility was converted into the disaster which soon overtook the whole of Army Group B by one

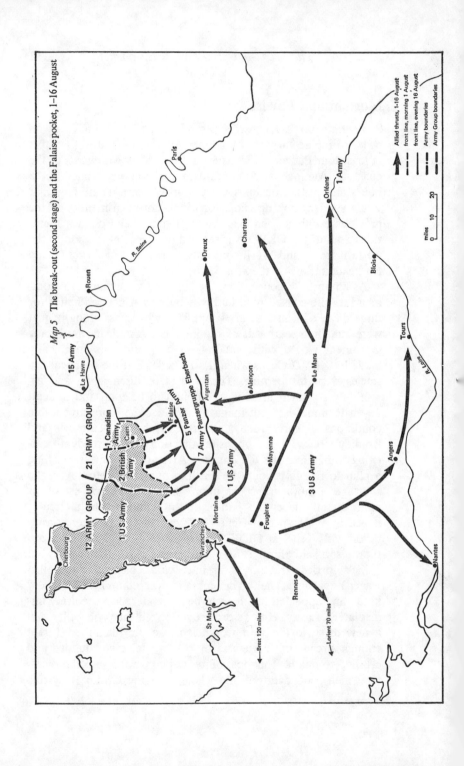

Map 5 The break-out (second stage) and the Falaise pocket, 1–16 August

15 Army

Le Havre

R. Seine

Rouen

Paris

21 ARMY GROUP

12 ARMY GROUP

Cherbourg

1 Canadian Army

2 British Army

Caen

Falaise

5 Panzer Army

Argentan

7 Army Panzergruppe Eberbach

Dreux

Chartres

1 US Army

Alençon

1 U S Army

Mayenne

Le Mans

1 Army

Orléans

Avranches

Mortain

Fougères

3 US Army

Angers

Tours

Blois

R. Loire

St Malo

Rennes

Brest 120 miles

Lorient 70 miles

Nantes

miles
0   10   20

Allied thrusts, 1–16 August
front line, morning 1 August
front line, evening 16 August
Army boundaries
Army Group boundaries

thing above all: Hitler's intention was known to the incredulous Allied commanders in time for them to take steps to counter it and to make Hitler's order the agent of his own army's destruction.

Foreknowledge at this juncture and on this scale made Ultra security more vital than ever. The Allied command had always planned to begin the eastward advance to the Seine from about the line it had now reached; here was Hitler proposing, by a large-scale attack in the opposite direction, to double its effect and to run his head into a noose of his own devising. Hotter news there could hardly be, yet no unwise use of the information was made, and the secret was safely kept. 'How does the enemy learn our thoughts from us?' Hitler had asked a few hours before he issued his order; but, still trembling from the shocks of 20 July, he had ascribed it to the plotters' treason.

Montgomery did not know what Hitler intended when, pursuant to the plan drawn up before D-Day, he issued new instructions on 4 August, directing the Americans to aim for Paris and 1 Canadian Army (which had just become operational) to strike down towards Falaise, but there could not have been a bolder counter-move. If both new drives were successful, 7 Army and Panzergruppe West (renamed 5 Panzer Army on 6 August) would be surrounded unless they extricated themselves by retreating speedily eastwards instead of attacking westwards. Montgomery's directive did not explicitly mention the possibility of an encirclement—indeed, he pointed 12 Army Group in too easterly a direction for it, and did not make a junction with the Canadians its main objective—and he seems only to have done so on 8 August, after the German attack had begun. It is more surprising that the fear of being encircled does not seem to have occurred to von Kluge until the previous day, 7 August, just before Hitler ordered him to push on regardless of risks and thereby 'bring about the collapse [!] of the Normandy front'; we intercepted his operations report for the week, which set out his fear of being caught in a trap, and it did not perhaps much matter that we could not decode it until 13 August, when encirclement was already an accomplished fact.

Whatever misgivings he may have had about the wisdom of Hitler's original astonishing order, von Kluge made new dispositions in accordance with it on 3 August, arranging for an attack on both sides of Sourdeval (a few miles north of Mortain) by XLVII and LXXXI Corps with 2 Pz, 9 Pz and 116 Pz and elements of 2 SS Pz and 17 SS PzGr. There was no evidence of this in Ultra, but there were signs of the withdrawal of the front by which he hoped to free the armour and of the impediment to his plans caused by the British attack, which forced him to rush II SS Pz Corps in to plug a dangerous gap at almost the same moment as Hitler was having his 'inspiration' and to hold 21 Pz, 9 SS and 10 SS Pz Divisions in that sector for several days. The formations listed by von Kluge were a shade less well reported, but 2 SS Pz, 2 Pz and 116 Pz were clearly located in the Sourdeval area until 116 Pz was relieved by 84 Division on the night of 5–6 August, while 9 Pz and LXXXI Corps were coming from the south and the Channel coast respectively but had not yet arrived.

0700/2
XL 4437
1408/2

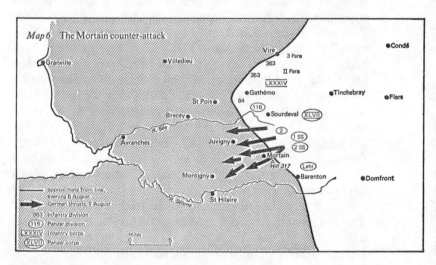

Map 6   The Mortain counter-attack

News of the German attack came in several signals during the evening of 6 August. The first asked for night-fighter protection for 2 SS Pz in an attack through Mortain (which the Americans had just captured) south-westwards to St Hilaire, another a few moments later said that XLVII Corps would attack with 116 Pz, 2 Pz, 1 SS Pz (which had been assem-

1400/6
XL 4991
1912/6

1300/6
XL 4997
1948/6

1700/6
XL 5027*
0011/7

bling far away at Falaise the previous night) and 2 SS Pz. The most explicit of them timed the attack for 1830 hours (only ninety minutes after the German signal was sent; ours went out at midnight), gave its start-line as Sourdeval–Mortain and its first objective as the north–south road from Brécey to Montigny ten miles ahead, and said that it would be conducted by 'strong forces of five Panzer divisions'. The attack did not in fact begin until after midnight–this, like the discrepancy between four and five divisions, no doubt reflects the confusion which prevailed in the German command that day–so that at any rate the first two of our signals had time to arrive before the event.

The Germans did not even reach their first objectives. Plentiful information about the fighting came in throughout the next few days, and a great deal of it could be signalled five or six hours after the German original (sometimes sooner–several of our fastest deliveries belong to early August); it made cheerful reading in Hut 3, deprived as always of news from Allied sources, but probably told Montgomery and Bradley little they had not already learned from their own battle reports. Some elements of 116 Pz were already in retreat at dawn on 7 August, for instance, and at midday 1 SS Pz complained that it had been brought to a standstill by fighter-bombers, while hostile aircraft had prevented the GAF from coming to its rescue, with the result that it decided to withdraw for the night. The sustained, violent and (thanks to Ultra) well-prepared attacks by 83 Group RAF and IX US Air Force were in fact one of the turning points of the battle. Another was the heroic resistance of the American 30 Division, isolated and surrounded on Hill 317 just east of Mortain, but there seems to have been no Ultra information about it beyond the statement that 2 SS Pz, which had recaptured Mortain at dawn, was still trying to take St Hilaire, one of its first objectives, in mid-afternoon. Of more lasting value was confirmation during the evening that, notwithstanding the small advance so far made, the attack would be continued next day: Hausser of 7 Army ordered XLVII Corps to keep at it and to drive on to Avranches, but a return (unfortunately not available for another three days) of its available guns and small arms casts doubt on its capacity to do so: nei-

ther 116 Pz nor 2 SS Pz had any 88-mm anti-aircraft/anti-tank
guns at all, for example, and although 2 Pz was somewhat better off with eight, it had fewer light and medium howitzers.

With 3 US Army ranging almost at will up the Loire valley
next day (8 August), Ultra was able to show how the German
command was losing grip of the situation on what was now its
southern flank but had so recently been its undefended rear. All
road movement was impossible because of enemy fighter-
bombers, complained both LXXXIV Corps and 2 SS Pz during
the morning, and a regimental commander on II Para's left
boundary completely lost control of his men, who were running
away under the slightest Allied pressure. By evening, American
tanks were in Le Mans and Tours, making the situation as far
east as Blois 'obscure', and attempts were already under way to
cobble together elements of Pz Lehr and 9 Pz to block them, as   1030/8
well as to form a new defence line behind Mortain. The situa-   XLs 5282,
                                                                        5292
tion here was the more acute because of the swift success in the   2208/8
afternoon and evening of 6 August of the British XXX Corps'
assault on Mt Pinçon, which might otherwise have anchored the
German defence; there was very little news of this, save about
some of 10 SS Pz's difficulties, but after it 12 SS Pz, which had
been brought across from Caen to strengthen the defence, had
only thirty-four serviceable Mark IV tanks out of a total
strength of fifty, and only twenty Panthers out of thirty-four.

Measures were already being taken to bring some order out
of the chaos which threatened Occupied France and to antici-
pate and halt a general advance by the Allied armies by constructing a defence-line east of Paris. Ultra quickly got wind of
them, but at first only in fragments and often out of time-
sequence. The first became known when the Military Commander of north-eastern France reissued an OKW order on 5
August, but the decode was five days late. It provided for the
'immediate development of a rearward position' from Reims to
Châlons and the Marne–Saône canal by a special staff empow-
ered to use 'the severest measures' to conscript French civilians
between the ages of sixteen and sixty and to commandeer en-
trenching tools and excavating equipment. Before this could be
signalled, we had passed on the news that 1 Army headquarters
was moving from Bordeaux to the neighbourhood of Poitiers,

closer to the flank of 7 Army, and that on 7 August it had appointed officers to take charge of local operations in Nantes,
Angers and Tours. An even woollier Hitler order than usual of
the same date for the defence of 'fortresses' (Brest and St Malo
were already cut off, and when 1 Army moved out the U-boat
bases on the Atlantic coast were soon to suffer the same fate)
completed the outline of a pattern that held broadly true for
several weeks: speedy evacuation of all France except the
north-east, which was to be held as a forward defence of the
Reich frontier. The urgent business of controlling Army Group
B's operations kept von Kluge near the front, and he left Blumentritt, his Chief of Staff, in charge at OB West. From there
Blumentritt sent him a wide-ranging set of proposals on 8 August. These could not be decoded until the 14th, but even then
it was still useful to know of his suggestion that 1 Army should
be transferred from Army Group G to Army Group B, that
LXIV Corps should fill the gap which was beginning to open
on the upper Loire at the junction with 19 Army, that 6 Para
Division was moving to Chartres and a static division being
brought from Germany to Paris, and that Blumentritt considered the situation urgent enough to warrant 15 Army surren-
dering two divisions from Belgium and Holland without waiting
for replacements.

The daylight hours of 9 August saw us continuing to provide
news of more emergency measures by the other side. Among a
large number of routine Flivo reports of divisional locations,
the most striking items were that a new formation, LVIII
Corps, was taking over command of 2 SS Pz (and presumably
other divisions too), that 9 Pz and 708 Divisions would cover
the exposed southern flank around Domfront (708 Division
was coming from the south-west, and even 1 Army was not
sure how many train-loads of it had started out that morning),
and that Army Group B had ordered up 11 Pz from the south
to Blois and Chartres.[1] All this had been passed to SHAEF, the
two Army Groups and all others concerned by the late evening.

Excitement at the significance of the intelligence we were
providing at a moment which might be decisive for the whole

---

1. Hitler subsequently countermanded von Kluge's order for 11 Pz's move;
see p. 158 below.

campaign was already intense in Hut 3 at midnight, but it soon rose still higher. Good fortune sent me on duty then, and I can still vividly recall the exhilaration of the next few hours; in recollection they surpass even D-Day for the volume and importance of the information Ultra produced. The size of the net which was being drawn round Army Group B, and the number of divisions which would be caught in it, clearly depended on whether Hitler persisted with his foolhardy attack or whether he ordered a general retreat before the Americans had got far enough east to prevent an escape. 'We checked him hourly at Mortain', wrote Bradley later, adding that he needed forty-eight hours from 8 August to complete the envelopment. Aerial reconnaissance—to which he was of course referring—could show what the Germans were doing at a given moment, but not what they intended to do an hour or two later. Only Ultra could give warning of their plans in advance, and in the early hours of 10 August it did so superbly.

We intercepted orders issued by von Kluge the previous evening which called for a renewal of the attack 'probably on the 11th' although there might be a postponement. We were able to signal the crucial first part during the night; the second part (listing the troops to be employed) came in later and went out early the next afternoon. This resolved the issue conclusively. Whatever his misgivings, von Kluge had allowed himself to be over-ruled by Hitler. For the next twenty-four hours at least there would be no retreat; Bradley would have almost as much time as he needed, and the Allies could proceed in the confident expectation that if they acted quickly they would be able to surround most of the German troops in northern France.

1800/9
XL 5461*
0349/10
1800/9
XL 5516
1436/10

The orders were issued by von Kluge in his capacity as commander of Army Group B (he had doubled this with OB West since Rommel was wounded). They called for an attack on the southern wing of 7 Army to be led by General Eberbach (for whom a new staff would be provided under von Kluge's own son) 'after regrouping and the bringing up of decisive offensive arms'. Eberbach's objective was to be 'the sea at Avranches, to which a bold and unhesitating thrust through is to be made'. The assembly area and start-line would be communicated verbally, but Mortain–Domfront was envisaged; the attack was intended to go in on the 11th, but there might be a postponement of twelve or twenty-four hours. Troops engaged would be XLVII Panzer Corps, LVIII Reserve Panzer Corps, 2 Pz and 116 Pz Divisions, 1 SS, 2 SS and 10 SS Panzer Divisions, the main body of 9 Panzer, two rocket brigades and some army artillery (we had already known about the last four for several hours). To ensure the success of the 'decisive thrust', 5 Panzer Army (where Sepp Dietrich was to take over in place of Eberbach) and 7 Army were to hold their lines to the last man and the last round.

1530/9
XL 5470
0530/10

Twice in three days Ultra had given information of unsurpassable quality; first, sufficient advance warning of the Mortain attack to nullify it completely and to assist in inaugurating a riposte which was to turn Cobra from victory into triumph and to make an orderly German withdrawal to new defence lines impossible, and now (with at least twenty-four hours in hand) the certainty that the attack would be persisted in long enough to ensure the almost total dissolution of von Kluge's forces.[1] It might be thought that only anti-climax could follow. The truth was far otherwise. These were some of Ultra's most prolific days of the whole war; unprecedented amounts of Enigma traffic were being intercepted, and most of it was decoded with such rapidity that signal after signal could be prepared so close to the German time of origin that each seemed more urgent than the last and the mind could scarcely hold on to a myriad details long enough to comprehend the relation of one to another. Unexpected quantity brought no decline in quality, but was so great that for the period of the Falaise pocket a mere selection from the bewildering riches poured out by the source must serve to show how Ultra depicted the confu-

1. Group Captain Winterbotham gives a rather different account of the first ten days of August in *The Ultra Secret* 147–54 (Lewin, *Ultra* 337–9 derives from it.) There appears to be no Ultra warrant for a number of his statements, in spite of the circumstantial detail with which he surrounds some of them. Several can, however, be approximately reconciled with the signals by a change in dating. There were three stages in the Mortain attack: (1) Hitler's order of 2 August, of which Ultra knew nothing, (2) the attack order of 6 August and (3) von Kluge's renewal order of 9 August, both of which Ultra reported in time. It seems possible that Group Captain Winterbotham's memory confused stages (2) and (3) with (1).

sion as a swift and terrible fate overtook Hitler's armies in Normandy.

Von Kluge's orders were not the last important item on 9 August. The move back of a number of fighter Gruppen to Germany for rest and refit, and their replacement by others, gave away the whole relief plan and—remarkably enough— showed that a revised version of it put into force that day actually reduced the number of fighter Gruppen serving in France from seventeen to thirteen. Two divisions previously reported (6 Para and 49 Divisions) were still on the way to reinforce 7 Army, and by midnight next day we had signalled the positions occupied that morning or afternoon by most of the divisions and corps in the thick of the fighting (in three cases adding that they were short of petrol, ammunition or transport), located Eberbach's headquarters, and discovered that 1 Army was to hand over to LXIV Corps in Bordeaux and move to Fontainbleau by rail (its exact time of departure, 0600 hours 12 August, came through a little later).

By way of contrast, the most important 11 August items were not available until late that night or the following morning: the assembly area of 116 Pz Division (which was coming out of the line), the battle headquarters of Army Group B, a list of new army boundaries to come into force as soon as 1 Army arrived, and news of so serious a petrol shortage in XLVII Corps that several Panzer divisions could barely move (thirty of Pz Lehr's tanks were completely immobilized next day). Our first intimation that von Kluge realized he might be surrounded came into this category; he had feared it already,[1] but his repetition of it now, though delayed, was decoded before the earlier message.

The new destination—Alençon—of 116 Pz became apparent the next day as part of a major shift of emphasis to the southern flank whereby LVIII Corps took over from XLVII and the GAF concentrated its efforts in the Le Mans area at the army's request. All this was signalled during daylight. Two useful bits of information were subject to delay: reinforcements for 1 Army to help it fill the open spaces south-west of Paris, and a

1. See p. 113.

reasoned case by Hausser of 7 Army for giving up the westernmost tip of the pocket in order to strengthen the front round Falaise, Flers and Domfront. Something like the second part of this argument was already being put into practice by 13 August, when it was described in a GAF situation report which was signalled currently. A recognition that the Canadian drive towards Falaise was threatening to strangle Army Group B by closing its only escape route was apparent from an extraordinary Army Group B order that every tank and assault gun arriving from Germany, no matter for whom intended, was to be delivered to 5 Panzer Army. A similar air of emergency breathed through instructions to units in Paris to be on the alert for expected landings by the British 8 Airborne Division and against believing exaggerated rumours of Allied successes put about by French civilians.

This was the moment when Bradley halted Patton's northward thrust at Argentan (lest the violent closing of the trap be-

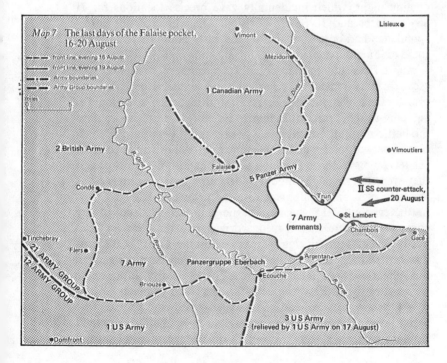

Map 7   The last days of the Falaise pocket, 16-20 August

tween there and Falaise cause the collision of Allies as well as the capture of enemies), directing him forward to the Seine instead, and when Eisenhower broadcast to the troops to 'go flat out'. Ultra, too, moved rapidly. Among a dozen or more divisional and other locations signalled currently on 14 and 15 August, an appreciation by I SS Pz Corps which was forwarded in just over two hours and a series of messages about a withdrawal stand out. At 1100 hours on 14 August Eberbach aligned himself with the view Hausser had expressed on the 12th, admitted that Hitler's orders could not be carried out by saying that it was impossible to clear up the situation by attack, and offered to protect the withdrawal of 7 Army and 5 Pz Army to the Falaise–Argentan line provided the fuel and ammunition situation permitted; three hours later he needed 400 cubic metres of fuel for the purpose and could not get it by air supply. Discussion between him and von Kluge appears to have ended in an order for the withdrawal of 7 Army during the coming night, which incidentally gave precise locations for II SS Pz Corps and 10 SS Pz Division. The whole of this correspondence had been signalled by the early hours of 15 August, some of it a great deal sooner.

1900/14
XL 6234
2114/14

1700/14
XL 6322
0854/15

Apart from holding Argentan (the southern bastion of the escape-route) which he regarded as essential, Eberbach was also looking over his shoulder at the threatening situation developing round Trun, to the north. For three or four more days the battle round the contracting pocket raged with particular violence between Trun and Argentan as the Allies strove to close the ten-mile gap through which the German armies must pass if they were to escape. Morale was declining in this bottleneck as losses in men and equipment rose, according to XLVII Corps on the evening of 15 August, but the only tactical detail of any consequence concerned a wedge driven into the German lines north-west of Trun by eighty tanks late on the 17th. II SS Corps was ordered to counter-attack and clear it up, and a signal to this effect was dispatched with highest priority just twelve hours after the order was given—too late to be of much use, no doubt, at a time when the best targets were being provided by aerial reconnaissance and no other source of intelligence could keep up with the speed of events. With the exception of several

2100/17
XL 6896
0916/18

signals locating II SS Corps in the mouth of the pocket, ordering it to cover Vimoutiers, and showing that it controlled 2 SS, 116 Pz and Pz Lehr Divisions (which were even more valuable in retrospect because of the counter-attack II SS Corps was shortly to deliver from outside the pocket), most of the fifty or sixty pieces of tactical information derived from Ultra during these hectic days were probably out of date by the time they reached Allied headquarters in France, although they were often only a few hours old when dispatched with high priority. It will have been of more lasting value to know in the early hours of 16 August that in the course of the previous evening Flakkorps III had notified OB West that it had put five more heavy batteries at the army's disposal for use in an anti-tank role, since the Falaise situation was very serious and the troops there not far from collapse. Stray hints of the carnage and destruction being wrought in the pocket were given by the news that 708 Division's battle strength was only sixty men and 3 Para Division's 1920, and by a report from 116 Pz which showed that it had only thirty-eight tanks and eleven guns left.

early/16
XLs 6605,
6648
2047/16,
0211/17

Early on 16 August von Kluge conferred with Hausser and Eberbach (who had lost so many of his staff officers that he could no longer control his strike force), and it was evidently their joint recommendation to Hitler which von Kluge submitted and we intercepted. They had insufficient tanks and petrol to clear up the situation on the south side of the pocket, von Kluge said, and would have to move back into a switch position (he sketched its location) while 2 SS Pz tried to halt the Allied advance on Trun by counter-attacking. 'To a certain degree' orderly retreat through the bottleneck was still possible, but the least hesitation would bring serious consequences, and the situation demanded that the pocket be evacuated with all speed. He ended with the words, 'I request corresponding order.' We did not get Hitler's reply, but we could soon infer that he had admitted defeat and given it, for during the afternoon Army Group B ordered a withdrawal to the line of the river Orne, starting at once.[1] These two crucial signals, marking the end of

1600/16
XL 6607
2048/16

1. In point of fact, von Kluge for once acted independently when he issued the Army Group B order. Hitler's formal consent was not given until after the withdrawal had begun.

the battle of Normandy, were sent out within a minute of each other; the information in the second was not yet five hours old. Less than twenty-four hours later, an OKW order completed the picture of German collapse. All troops of Army Group G west of Orléans, Clermont-Ferrand and Montpellier, except those of 19 Army actually engaged in the Rhône valley against the new landings in the south, were by Hitler's order to retire at once behind the water-line Seine–Yonne–Canal de Bourgogne.

0940/17
XL 6753
1408/17

Instructions were promptly issued for some of the Orne bridges to be used for east–west supply traffic and others for the retreat, and the publication of a list of Seine ferries in working order already suggested that there would be no halting at least until the river stood in the way of pursuit. By the next afternoon retreat *to* the Orne had officially become retreat *beyond* it: von Kluge telegraphed 'Situation both sides Falaise necessitates quickest possible withdrawal across the Orne' and 5 Panzer Army (struggling to hold the northern wall of the corridor) urged 7 Army to make haste to get out that night. At the same time, OKW made von Kluge responsible for ensuring that all V-weapon installations were so thoroughly destroyed that the victors could draw no conclusions about the method of operation.

1630/17
XL 6905
1124/18

Ultra did not know that von Kluge had been 'lost' in the pocket while taking cover from air-raids on 15 August—his conference with Hausser and Eberbach was one of his first actions on returning to duty next morning—nor that he was dismissed and committed suicide on the 17th. As so often, however, it gave a glimpse of the essentials almost at once. As soon as Feldmarschall Model took over as OB West on the evening of 17 August he ordered Hausser and Eberbach to meet him at 5 Panzer Army headquarters at 0630 next morning: a signal conveying this information was dispatched only nine hours after they met.

p.m./17
XL 6929
1534/18

Signs of a manpower shortage

If most of the complaints about heavy casualties already recorded must be discounted as the natural consequence of weeks of bitter fighting, temporary in impact because soon to be made

good, there also came to light during July and August a number
of unmistakable signs of an underlying manpower shortage
which was much more serious because quite irreversible.

Two of the most striking indications of it were also among
the earliest to come to our notice. In a remarkable statement on
13 July, SS Operations Headquarters coupled the sending of a
thousand reinforcements to I SS Pz Corps with the reservation
that it was impossible to foresee when future losses in 1 and 12
SS Pz Divisions could be made good. If the SS, whose head
(Himmler) had the ear of Hitler, could not undertake to maintain the strength of the élite armoured divisions which had been
specially set up the previous autumn, it seemed natural to
doubt whether anyone could do better, and to infer a serious
manpower problem in the Greater German Reich. Less than a
week after this, OB West made the casualty return for the period 6 June–16 July which is now regularly quoted: approximately 100,000, including 2760 officers. Its most striking features were the bald comment that the replacements received
covered only 12 per cent of wastage, and the reflection that
while the Allies could make good their losses at once he was
unable to do so; in spite of the disbanding of 165 Reserve Division and the cannibalizing of others to provide replacement
drafts, the situation remained serious (because losses were increasing daily) and enforced a search for further emergency
measures. Confirmation that the Germans were running short of
men was to be found in the conscription of sixty-year-olds, the
oldest class yet called up, and in OKH's announcement that it
considered 709 Division (which had manned Utah beach on
D-Day) and several smaller units already disbanded. (It has to
be remembered, of course, that by now the British Army had
reached its maximum size and that 59 Division was about to be
broken up; but since American numbers were still on the increase this altered the balance of the alliance without diminishing its strength.) Home Army units in the Ruhr were ordered to
train drafts as fast as possible and send them up to the front,
the crews of U-boats in Brest, Lorient and St Nazaire which
could not be made ready for sea by the first week in September
were to take over army duties so as to release soldiers for the
'fortresses', and at the height of the battle in the Falaise pocket

Jagdkorps II ordered fighter squadrons to complete the training of new crews within twenty-four hours. Lastly, an extremely involved communication about aircrew training from Berlin to Luftflotte 3 on 15 August appeared to conclude that petrol[1] rather than manpower was the factor limiting the output of pilots, but at the same time it clearly revealed how hard the air-training schools had been hit, and how fuel and aircrew difficulties were combining to undermine the future of the Luftwaffe by restricting the supply of trained pilots coming forward and so threatening to nullify the recent increase in the output of fighter aircraft from the factories and the technical advance which was putting jet planes into service.

A second casualty return, covering the two months 6 June to 6 August instead of the six weeks of the previous figures, confirmed the impression already gained: 3219 officers (including fourteen generals) were reported killed, wounded or missing, and 141,046 NCOs and men; 19,914 replacements had arrived, and 16,477 more were on the way. At about a 25 per cent replacement rate, this represented an improvement over the previous month, but still meant that the Wehrmacht was wasting away fast. There is no doubt that this was the case. But coming on top of the crushing victory of Falaise, news like this was heady stuff, particularly if interpreted as heralding an imminent German collapse. Allied progress in the first weeks after the landings had been slower than expected, and the advance had begun in late July instead of late June. Once started, however, it had accelerated well beyond expectation. It had been hoped to reach the Seine about the beginning of September and to capture Paris in October, but now both had been successfully accomplished within a week between 19 and 25 August. In consequence, a mood of optimism—ill-founded, as it proved —soon permeated Allied thinking: 'The August battles have done it, and the enemy in the West has had it' was the view of a SHAEF Intelligence Summary towards the end of the month,

1. That the petrol situation was really acute by now was evident from many references to shortage of supplies, and most notably in extremely stringent regulations issued by Luftflotte Reich on 4 August, under which no aircraft whatsoever were to be refuelled without a Luftflotte Reich fuel voucher except aircraft being ferried to their operational stations and communications flights for Hitler, Goering, OKW, OKH, OKL and OKM.

and on the 28th Brooke, the British Chief of the General Staff, thought that 'The Germans cannot last much longer.' A Joint Intelligence Committee appreciation of 29 August was even more categorical: 'Germany's acute shortage of battle-fit manpower is now taking direct toll of her fighting capacity in the field.' It is an uncomfortable speculation that Ultra's incontrovertible evidence may have inadvertently fostered this impression by diverting attention from the fanatical resistance to be expected from the depleted armies, and that by so doing it may have promoted the over-optimistic outlook which was soon to prevent some of its own warnings from being heeded.

5

Pursuit to the Rhine and West Wall

American troops crossed the Seine on 19 August, the day that Paris rose and the pocket was finally closed between Trun and Chambois. The pursuit—'a foaming torrent which nothing could stem'—began in earnest on 25 August, when the Americans liberated Paris and the British XXX Corps crossed the river farther downstream. It went on at a rate of forty or fifty miles a day until, 'strangled by its own success', it stopped abruptly in the north with the capture of Antwerp on 4 September and more gradually farther south as the American 1 and 3 Armies met stiff opposition in the West Wall[1] at Aachen and in front of it along the Moselle by the middle of the month. Men were exhausted from lack of sleep, and supplies could not reach them in sufficient bulk to nourish any further immediate advance. (Here probably was the only success of Hitler's 'fortress' policy: SHAEF had expected to be using other French ports besides Cherbourg by the time the front had moved so far east, but supplies of all kinds still had to come in over the Normandy beaches. Le Havre did not fall until 12 September nor Brest for another week, and both ports had been thoroughly demolished.)

When Montgomery briefed General Horrocks for XXX Corps' advance, he told him, 'The Germans are very good soldiers and will recover quickly if allowed to do so. All risks are justified—I intend to get a bridgehead over the Rhine before they have time to recover.' This was all he needed to say then about the grandiose plan he had put forward a week earlier—a paralysing stroke at the industries of the Ruhr by a thrust with forty divisions across the flat

---

1. The Germans never used the term 'Siegfried Line' which was invented during the 'phoney war' of 1939–40.

north German plain. Some purely military considerations favoured the proposal, and so did the suddenly prevalent notion that a total German collapse was in any case imminent. Model did in fact panic, presenting Hitler with an impossible demand for twenty-five infantry and five Panzer divisions to prevent his front from giving way altogether, and many German writers have argued subsequently that it was the right policy for the Allies to pursue because it offered a fleeting opportunity (before some sort of coherent defence was hastily re-established during the first week of September) for them to end the war in 1944. The long and vulnerable southern flank which such a thrust would have exposed argued against it and in favour of Eisenhower's 'broad front' strategy, but the decisive factor was the likelihood that the friendly Anglo–American partnership would be fatally weakened on the political plane if American public opinion resented (as it probably would) the glory of victory being reserved for the British. Eisenhower allowed Montgomery to monopolize enough transport to reach Antwerp, but he had practically decided against the 'forty-division thrust' by the day the advance from the Seine began, and he started to put the 'broad front' policy into effect as soon as he took direct control of the armies on 1 September and Montgomery ceased to be Land Force Commander. By coincidence, Rundstedt returned as OB West on the same day, Model remaining in command of Army Group B (see Figure 5).

While the generals were locked in argument, the forward troops were making unexpectedly rapid progress, and new American forces landed under General Devers on the Riviera coast closed up so quickly that they were put under Eisenhower's command on 15 September and a single front established from the North Sea to the Swiss border. Thus the next moves had of necessity to be made at a moment when the situation was changing faster than at any time since D-Day, and before the main lines of future strategy had been decided—indeed the operation (Market Garden) which has come to be known simply as 'Arnhem' seems to have been planned while one strategic concept reigned but executed when another had replaced it. The mistakes had been compounded in advance by the failure—inexplicable in retrospect, but perceived at the time by only a very few (Hitler was one of them)—to clear the approaches to Antwerp directly the docks were captured intact on 4 September. So long as the Germans held both shores at the mouth of the Scheldt, they could prevent the port from being used to supply the forward troops by denying access to it from the sea. The first convoy did not enter Antwerp until 28 November, eighty-five days after the capture.

The Allies had lost momentum before Market Garden was launched on 17 September. Airborne troops were dropped to capture and hold three river-bridges until relieved by land forces driving up a narrow corridor towards them. The first two-thirds of the operation were successful, though slower than intended. When the attempt to hold Arnhem bridge ended in failure on 25 September, all hope of a quick victory disappeared.

Figure 5 Later re-arrangements of the German land command in the west

1 September–9 November 1944

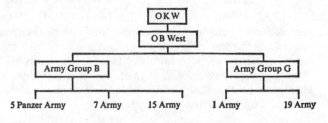

10 November 1944–6 April 1945

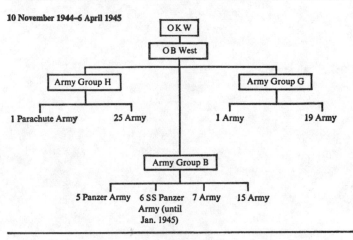

7 April–7 May 1945

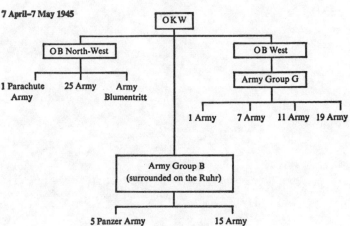

The intelligence: volume and distribution

The prodigious volume of traffic intercepted and decoded during the first half of August was maintained or even exceeded throughout the period of the pursuit. It was not until about 10 September that a serious diminution could be sensed, and even this was soon temporarily blurred by the consequences of the Arnhem operation.

General Westphal later wrote that when he became Chief of Staff to Rundstedt on the latter's reappointment as OB West at the beginning of September, he found the military telephone system completely inadequate to the demands that had to be made upon it, and complained that it sometimes took as long as twenty-four hours for a message from OB West to reach Rundstedt's immediate subordinates in Army Groups B and G. After the worst of the pursuit was over, Guderian made swingeing criticisms of the state of army signals which effectively bear out both Westphal's points. 'After line communications had broken down', Ultra revealed him saying,[1] the higher command had ceased to have a clear picture of what was happening and consequently made its decisions either late or unrealistically, and he singled out certain officers for blame. Between them, Westphal and Guderian explain why Ultra flourished so tremen-

---

1. Guderian's message was dated 12 September, Hut 3's signal 20 October. This is therefore one of the more extreme examples of a late decode retaining intelligence value in spite of the passage of time. Rundstedt evidently followed up the complaints by demanding improvements, but the result remained unknown.

dously in August and September,[1] and how it was that the extremely important but sometimes controversial information to be discussed in this chapter came into the possession of Allied intelligence at all. For at only one other stage in the course of the campaign in the west—the Ardennes battles at Christmas 1944[2]—is it likely that the release of Ultra material will compel as radical a revision of accepted views as in the case of the failure to exploit the capture of Antwerp properly and to discern in time the likelihood that stiff opposition from two of the best German Panzer divisions would be met by the airborne troops dropped to capture the bridge at Arnhem.

From about 10 September, there was some decline in the volume of Ultra traffic in the northern sector of the front (if allowance is made for the transient emergency of Arnhem) which must have been due to the restoration of the land-line network to a more satisfactory condition, but in the south—where presumably old lines had not been repaired nor new ones laid—the level remained very much the same as it had recently been. By mid-September we were therefore usually better informed about Army Group G and 19 Army in Alsace and about what had lately been the dangerous hinge between the two Army Groups which 1 Army had been hastily brought up from Bordeaux to control—that is to say, about the sectors of 3 and 7 US Armies —than about the rest of the front.

How far back will they go?

Defeat turned into flight so precipitately that OB West's plans to halt on successive defence-lines were constantly overtaken by events. Confident of their own momentum because they met so little serious opposition for the first few days, the Allied generals were also assisted by a regular service of information from Ultra about the enemy's hope that he could turn and stand in a

---

1. Lewin badly antedates a later truth when he speaks of the Germans returning to 'safe telephone and teleprinter links' soon after Falaise, and is mistaken when he writes that 'for Ultra, the law of diminishing returns took over in September 1944'. With only short-lived fluctuations, Hut 3 continued to be extremely busy with both western and Italian traffic until the end of the war. (See pp. 246–7).
2. See below, chapter 7.

series of positions which were always called 'lines' even though it was plain that most of them were not prepared defences but only lines on a map.

Thus on 13 August General Kitzinger was given additional powers to develop the Somme–Marne–Saône–Jura line on which work had already been started:[1] 'All possible means' were to be used, OB West allotted weapons to the Somme –Marne section, LXVII Corps was assigned to protect this area, Luftflotte 3 was considering on the 18th whether to release 6000 men for construction work, and by the end of the month one part of it was said to be ready although another was still being worked on. In conformity with Hitler's order to evacuate southern France, OKW instructed Army Group G to retreat at once to the southern part of this line (Seine–Yonne–Canal de Bourgogne) on 17 August, and on the 20th Hitler repeated this, extending the line to Dijon, Dôle and the Swiss frontier. This was a comprehensive order by Hitler which revealed the whole plan of withdrawal as then envisaged, and added that 7 Army and 5 Pz Army were to fight in and around Paris without regard to the destruction of the city; decoded only after a four-day delay, it was nevertheless dispatched before the Allies had crossed the Seine and while the fate of Paris still hung in the balance. (Hitler's later order for the use of severe measures like the execution of ringleaders and the blowing up of houses to deter revolt, which ended 'Never, or at any rate only as a heap of rubble, must Paris fall into Allied hands', was intercepted when Army Group B passed it on, but by the time it could be signalled the peaceful surrender of the city was already being negotiated.) Model even hoped to improve on Hitler's plan in the northern sector; ten days later a highest priority signal showed him intending to defend a line farther to the west (Dieppe–Senlis–Soissons–Marne and the Marne canal), gave all his dispositions, and listed Army and Army Group head-quarters. His hopes proved vain, and before long Admiral Channel Coast was ordering the demolition of Dieppe harbour as the Canadians approached and 2 Army crossed the Somme.

By now it was clear that there could be no stopping before

1. See p. 116 above.

the West Wall, where OKW was expecting Allied tanks to arrive at any time when on 2 September it hastily confirmed previous orders to begin putting the wall into a defensible condition after four years of neglect (since 1940 some of its guns had been removed for use elsewhere). The West Wall consequently figured regularly in Ultra signals during September. The German commanders knew so little about it that on the 3rd Westphal wanted details of its course and particularly of the extent to which it blocked the frontier around Trier, for an Allied thrust there could tear the whole position open before it was made defensible.[1] The GAF command arrangements for protecting the Wall were announced and instructions issued for raising emergency garrisons; according to Doenitz, 150,000 men were employed on 500 kilometres of fortifications by 12 September. Even more striking than the scale of effort (which did not manage to hide how much needed doing, for by the 17th Hitler was 'constantly receiving reports' that the position was not ready) was Rundstedt's repeated insistence that the Wall must not be breached, because 'there is no second position'. By the date of this last signal (19 September) Ultra had shown that resistance would greatly stiffen as the Allies approached the West Wall and confirmed that once this outer crust was penetrated there was nothing but the bravery of its soldiers to protect the Reich. A high-sounding Order of the Day from Rundstedt said the same thing more loosely for public consumption. 'The fight for German soil must increase fanaticism. Every pill-box, every village, to be defended until the Allies bleed to death. It is no longer a question of operations on a grand scale. The only task is to hold our positions or be annihilated.'

Single thrust or broad front?

Long before this, however, we were able to outline the strategy of the German withdrawal and to indicate where the enemy most feared sudden attack while still off balance and before a

1. German anxiety about a gap in the defences south of Trier is examined on pp. 137–8 below.

defence could be prepared. Several directives from Hitler and a series of operational orders by Rundstedt gave most of this invaluable information. A particular interest attaches to it, because it was provided during the weeks when the Allies were facing the same problem in reverse themselves and were painfully trying to determine their own strategy. The debate over the riskier 'single irresistible thrust' and the safer but slower 'broad front' policy was therefore conducted by men who knew how their enemy proposed to extricate himself and what he most wanted to avoid whilst doing so. The Allied generals were not balancing possibilities or speculating in a vacuum; they knew what the Germans hoped and feared, and could take this into account before they made up their own minds.

The controversy over rival strategies takes on new proportions when it is realized that while it was going on in late August and early September Ultra was telling all the main participants how anxious Hitler and Rundstedt were about two other areas as well as the Low Countries—Aachen and the Moselle valley from Metz to Trier (particularly the latter, which they regarded as their point of greatest weakness). The repeated calls to prepare the West Wall were in fact calls to protect Aachen, which was always likely to see the first invasion of the sacred soil of the Reich because it was the nearest to the enemy; and when Hodges' 1 US Army captured a newly constructed strongpoint soon after reaching the Wall on 12 September, the immediate reaction was to proclaim that every part of it was to be held 'until annihilation'. The Moselle and Saar routes into Germany invited Patton, the greatest thruster on either side, but the Germans were even more concerned for another reason—through this area ran both the escape-route for the miscellaneous force streaming back from the south-west of France and the uncertain boundary between the two Army Groups. To rescue the mixed bag of 100,000 or more Wehrmacht personnel and civilians crawling slowly from Bordeaux towards Dijon, Nancy and safety, and the even larger number coming up from the Riviera, would, at a time of growing manpower shortage, be in a sense to make good the loss by bomb, shell and capture at Falaise. But there is always a risk that the seams may not be stitched tightly enough along the boundary-lines between ground commands, and the ominous talk about a 'gap' along their route referred to the absence of forces adequate for their protection, not to an empty space between Eisenhower's and Devers' spheres through which they might escape. By revealing these anxieties to the Allied commanders, Ultra demonstrated that pressure applied in the Moselle–Saar region might create an opportunity for exploitation as rapid as anything that could be achieved in the north. It is a natural inference that Ultra seems to favour the 'broad front'.

As early as 20 August, when the Falaise battle was barely over, Hitler sent Rundstedt and Kesselring, his commanders in the west and south-west respectively, a comprehensive survey of the way they were to conduct their operations; his main object was to ensure the co-ordination of the various movements of withdrawal—arranging, for instance, that 19 Army should retreat over the Mont Cenis to join Kesselring in Italy if it could not reach Rundstedt at Dijon in time. The directive was still highly illuminating when it was decoded and signalled four days after it was composed. We had in any case been able to transmit a similar order by Rundstedt, also dated 20 August, much more rapidly; its main interest was that it showed Rundstedt as much concerned with the open southern flank of Army Group B as with the defence of Paris, for he ordered XLVII Pz Corps from 15 Army across to 1 Army, which had handed over responsibility for organizing the retreat from Bordeaux to LXIV Corps and assumed that of protecting the escape-route instead.[1] How long the route would need protection was shown by a LXIV Corps report of 21 August: the 100,000 soldiers and civilians it was trying to shepherd back could not reach Moulins (not much more than halfway between Bordeaux and Dijon) before 12 September at the earliest.

early/20
XL 7261
0033/21

Both LXIV Corps and 19 Army seemed painfully slow to their superiors, and Rundstedt and Blaskowitz in turn urged them to hurry up lest the Allies south-east of Paris cut their route before 1 Army could protect it. On 28 August Rundstedt urgently drew Blaskowitz' attention to this area, where he was to join up with 1 Army, but by the 31st American troops had

a.m./25
XL 7872
1730/25

---

1. See pp. 116–17 above.

taken advantage of a gap in the German front north-east of Troyes, outflanked XLVII Corps, and closed in on Verdun and Metz. Hasty defence measures were to include the employment of two new Panzer brigades (105 and 106) for it was becoming 'a matter of life and death' to secure Army Group G's north-western flank: 250,000 German nationals could only be got out if it held, and precautionary measures were also to be taken to hold the Vosges passes (19 Army's first direct access to Germany after its long journey from the south coast) as well as to develop the defence of Verdun. Due east of Verdun, in the Saarland, which Blaskowitz now regarded as the danger area, Rundstedt was already 'resting and refitting' three Panzer divisions.

Patton's tanks ran out of petrol at Verdun on 31 August, and were kept short for Montgomery's benefit for the next four days. These were also days of mounting German anxiety in the area Patton was threatening and still farther south. 1 Parachute Army had to be rushed north from here to meet the emergency along the Albert Canal, and the two Panzer brigades were so slow to turn up (although they moved off in such a hurry that they left some of their repair workshops behind) that Flakkorps III offered to take their place even though this would mean its own destruction.[1] On successive days at the beginning of September Rundstedt's Chief of Staff first informed Jodl that the gap from Belfort in the south almost up to Nancy could not be closed until Army Group G arrived (estimated dates of reaching Dijon were now 9 September for LXIV Corps and 12 September for 19 Army), and then saw the blocking of the German –Luxembourg frontier from Trier southwards as absolutely essential, because an Allied thrust here would tear open the West Wall before it could be prepared for defence. (As to where the Wall ran, he coolly recommended 1 Army, which was to defend this part of it, to discover its course from an officer in Kaiserslautern!) These two signals revealed more

1. Flakkorps III had taken similar action at Falaise (p. 123 above), but its offer was against standing orders. Instructions that Flak artillery was not to be used in ground fighting were repeated at intervals, as recently as 27 August by Keitel himself. The practice was said to have resulted in Flak batteries being over-run before they could come into action effectively, to a reduction in the air defence of road traffic, and to the loss of irreplaceable equipment.

than a hundred miles of weakly held territory, some of it of course still well out of Allied reach. Finally, the Hitler order of 3 September which transferred a reinforced Parachute Army to the Albert Canal ended with a refusal to move Panzer brigades north as well and announced an intention to concentrate them instead in the area of Army Group G—in order, as later became clear, to mount the counter-attack on 3 US Army of which we were able to give advance warning three days later.

0915/6,
2000/6
XLs 9310,
9332, 9333
2015/6,
0007/7,
0039/7

On the basis of Ultra intelligence alone, then, there was little to choose between the opportunities presented on the lower Rhine and on the upper Moselle and Saar, and much to be said in favour of a quick and shattering blow in the latter region. Ample information about each was provided with equal accuracy. But military action can never be determined on intelligence grounds alone, even if the source be as good as Ultra. Many other things—considerations of politics and national pride, transport, supply and the condition of the troops in the two areas among them—settled the question in favour of Arnhem. A study of contemporary Ultra does suggest, however, that the balance should have been very finely struck indeed.

Highlights of the retreat

So much Enigma traffic was forced on to the air and decoded by the bombes during the great retreat that late August was one of Hut 3's busiest periods. Our output was so great that the movements of most of the major German army and air force units at this time can still be reconstructed in considerable detail from the immense numbers of location reports received—up to a hundred in a single day—and this does not take account of the strategic or tactical significance which was distilled from many and gave them their chief value. While it would of course be tedious to reproduce more than a tiny selection here, the tremendous bulk of the whole should not be overlooked, for it enabled the enlarged staffs which were now working on Ultra at home and abroad to weave an even tighter intelligence net round the Wehrmacht than before. Nor did this apply only during the retreat across France. As the German armies neared and crossed their own frontiers, wireless telegraph stations

Map 8 The great retreat

FRISIAN ISLANDS
Cuxhaven
Emden
Bremen
ZUIDER ZEE
Amsterdam
Rheine
Osnabrück
Münster
Rotterdam *Lower Rhine* Arnhem
R. Waal Nijmegen
Flushing
WALCHEREN
Breskens
Ostend
R. Maas
Tilburg
Venlo
Albert canal
RUHR
Paderborn
Wesel
Düsseldorf
London
Portsmouth
Calais
Antwerp
Boulogne
PAS DE CALAIS
Lille
Louvain
Maastricht
Cologne
Brussels
Hasselt
Liège
Aachen
Bonn
Remagen
Koblenz
Prüm
Frankfurt
EIFEL
R. Schelde
R. Meuse
ARDENNES
Bastogne
Luxembourg
Dieppe
CHANNEL ISLANDS
Cherbourg
Bayeux
Le Havre
Amiens
R. Somme
Beauvais
Laon
R. Aisne
Verdun
Saarbrücken
Trier
R. Sauer
R. Moselle
Mainz
Mannheim
Kaiserslautern
Karlsruhe
Caen
Rouen
R. Oise
Senlis
Soissons
Reims
Metz
Brest
Evreux
Paris
Châlons-sur-Marne
Nancy
Strasbourg
St Malo
R. Marne
Chartres
R. Seine
Sens
Troyes
Epinal
VOSGES
Colmar
Mulhouse
Orléans
R. Yonne
Langres
Marne-Saône canal
Belfort
Basel
Lorient
Angers
R. Loire
Canal de Bourgogne
Dijon
Besançon
Berne
St Nazaire
Dôle
JURA
Poitiers
Moulins
Châlons-sur-Saône
La Pallice
R. Saône
Vichy
Geneva
Limoges
Lyons
Clermont-Ferrand
Grenoble
Mont Cenis pass
Turin
Bordeaux
R. Garonne
R. Rhône
Montélimar
Genoa
Orange
Avignon
Toulouse
Montpellier
Marseilles
Toulon

- - - front line, 31 July
——— front line, 30 September
▨▨▨ West Wall

miles
0   100

which had not previously been heard began to open up inside the Reich, and through them Ultra—which had hitherto been practically restricted to the GAF there—started to penetrate Germany in earnest for the first time. And just as the cryptographers' skills had by now reached levels of sophistication which enabled them to break traffic which would have baffled them formerly, so with the techniques of the intelligence staffs at Bletchley and in London: the new and unfamiliar sorts of information now discovered were grafted on to a solid trunk of experience and soon bore abundant fruit.

Fighter and bomber Geschwader began to leave their familiar airfields for new destinations even before the retreat began. Hasty transfers accounted for some of the losses which reduced Jagdkorps II's effective fighter strength to 149 aircraft by 18 August, and during the next few weeks a gradual rise in the number of its serviceable machines provided a rough index of the GAF's recovery: 203 on 24 August, 279 on the 26th, 285 on 1 and 2 September and 337 on the 7th. Sixty of these new aircraft were detected in transit to JG 27 early enough on the night of 27–8 August for their dawn landing to be signalled as a possible target. About this time Goering changed his order of early July that Staffelkapitaene, Gruppenkommandeure and Geschwaderkommodore should only fly when sufficiently escorted,[1] insisting instead that they fly once a day, once in two days and once in three days respectively; the natural inference is that there had recently been such a shortage of aircraft that the earlier rule was now amounting in effect to a total prohibition on combat flying by any of these officers. As things settled down after the initial confusion of retreat, the GAF began to circulate long lists of units' new locations for its own information. Intercepted and decoded, these lists told the Allied air forces where to find and destroy their enemies; one of them was signalled with such meticulously detailed annotations that it almost amounted to a summary of Fliegerkorps IX's recent history. Something of a curiosity in this line was a report of the

1. See p. 89 above.

street-number of the house at Heerlen near Maastricht where Jagdkorps II established its headquarters on the evening of 2 September; it was signalled next morning and was thus a potential target for precision bombing.[1] Orders on two successive days at the end of August that day and night fighters should be concentrated in Germany for home defence sharply revealed current priorities—industrial production was evidently to get better protection than the fighting troops.

The Allied air superiority was by now causing even more serious transport problems than before. Flakkorps III complained on 19 August that the roads had become twice or three times as dangerous in the last few days and that individual cyclists and pedestrians were now being picked off. A week later there was the sad tale of a jetty at Rouen completed at 1700 hours on 25 August and destroyed in a fighter-bomber attack five minutes afterwards. Scarity of transport led to fierce competition for the little that remained, and so to a quarrel between Model and Sperrle shortly before the latter—victimized for permitting an eclipse of the Luftwaffe which he was not given the means to prevent—was dismissed from the command of Luftflotte 3. Rundstedt had ordered Luftflotte 3 to surrender 5000 tons of transport space to the army; Sperrle (backed by Goering, as Commander-in-Chief of the GAF) refused, pleading his own needs, whereupon Model appealed to OKW and asked for an immediate decision. Model may have won, for Luftgau Belgium–Northern France later complained that it had given up so much transport to the army that it could not operate properly. Conflicts like this could be settled more easily within the looser but yet more unitary and more self-contained Allied system, where the Supreme Commander had authority over all three services.

Tank and gun strength-returns were much rarer than in the recent past. Three of the few received referred to I SS Pz Corps —not, unfortunately, to II SS, which was to do the damage at Arnhem. The first of them, dated 25 August, when the corps for the moment did not include a Panzer division, showed no

---

1. Oddly enough, another similar target turned up almost at once—1 Army headquarters in the golf club house 12 km east of Luxembourg on the Trier road on 4 September.

tanks except six Tigers (plus six more said to be on the way), but over a hundred guns of various calibres; during the next two days the number of guns dropped a little but that of Tiger tanks rose to ten out of forty-three serviceable, with the remainder under repair. The only tanks mentioned in an incomplete return from 7 Army on 9 September (they belonged to the newly arrived Panzer Brigade 105) were '18 (?)Panthers' (the type was queried in the German original), and an artillery return for 1 Army on 11 September was also rather inconclusive but suggested scarcity rather than plenty. The evidence was too slight to bear much weight of interpretation, but the situation seemed to have got worse rather than better since Rundstedt had been told on 29 August that the not very princely number of sixty-one Mark IV tanks and thirty-four assault guns had been allotted to the whole of his command.

Somewhat surprisingly, there were fewer indications of fuel and other shortages than had been usual ever since the spring, but three in early September were of potentially great significance. Goering imposed severe fuel restrictions on the whole Luftwaffe at the beginning of the month, and a few days later stock-returns from two fuel-issuing authorities could be used (because we had seen earlier returns from them) as the basis of a calculation which showed that GAF fuel-stocks in France had declined dramatically since D-Day: then, Luftflotte 3 had disposed of 21,000 and 10,000 tons respectively of the two standard types of fuel, but now of only 2000 and 1400 tons. On the same day, 7 September, Guderian informed the Army Groups in Russia and Norway (one of which had just reported a fuel situation 'strained to the utmost') that in future weapons could not be allocated in advance by monthly quota, and that small arms and guns up to the calibre of medium field howitzer would only be available in quite small quantities. (It was assumed that copies of the same circular had also been sent to Rundstedt's and Kesselring's commands, but that we had not intercepted them.)

At the end of the first week in September Himmler (Commander-in-Chief of the Home Army since the 20 July plot, as well as head of the security services) announced that no one was to cross the Rhine from west to east without express permission, and ordered that standing patrols of officers be set up to prevent unauthorized crossings. Further signs of the lowered morale this suggested soon came to light: theft, drunkenness and desertions among the troops retreating from the Balkans; disorderly 'every man for himself' conduct by naval personnel fleeing from the south of France, abandoning 'immense quantities' of irreplaceable rubber-covered cable in the Vosges from where it could not now be moved; and another order by Himmler of 13 September, alerting SS emergency units which had been put on standby on 20 July and used since to put down civil disturbances.

Finally, among miscellaneous items with varying degrees of interest, there may be noted the new locations of OB West and 5 Pz Army at Koblenz (7 Army having now recovered from the disaster at Falaise and taken over the latter's responsibility in the field), careful instructions for the evacuation of everyone and everything concerned with the V-weapon sites, hints that two worn-out divisions were moving to the west from Russia and an assault gun brigade from Denmark to the front at Aachen (there was of course not the slightest sign of any move in the contrary direction), an OKW order for the posting of surplus GAF officers to the army, and details of shortages of food and soap in the Channel Islands.

Antwerp

A review of the Ultra evidence throws a harsh light upon the unhappy story of Antwerp, which was useless to the Allies for nearly three months after its sudden capture on 4 September because the Germans held both banks of the Scheldt and could prevent ships from approaching it. The need for a quick decision about how to exploit the unexpected advantage the undamaged docks could give unfortunately coincided with a major command change (Eisenhower took direct control of the fighting on 1 September)[1] and with the controversy over the

1. At the beginning of September SHAEF apparently lacked a communications network adequate for the control of operations, which it had not needed while Montgomery was Land Force Commander. An important telegram about future strategy, dispatched by Eisenhower on 5 September, did not reach Montgomery for four days. It is curious that both sides were experiencing the same difficulties at the same time, although for different reasons (see p. 133 above.)

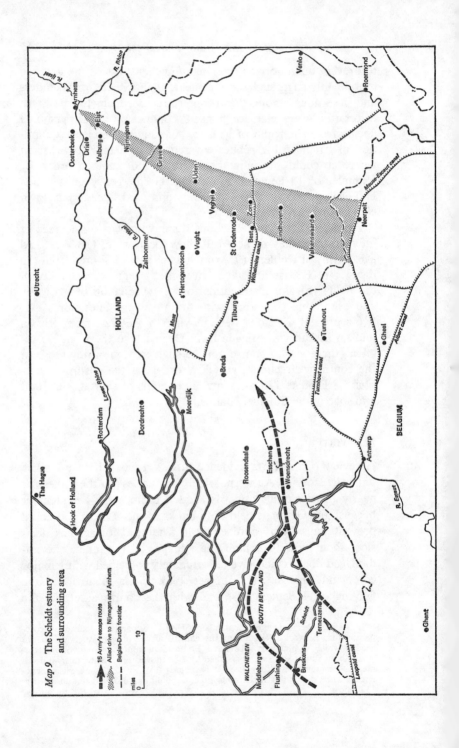

Map 9 The Scheldt estuary and surrounding area

15 Army's escape route
Allied drive to Nijmegen and Arnhem
Belgian–Dutch frontier

miles
0   10

R. IJssel
R. Rhine
Arnhem
Oosterbeek
Driel
Eist
Valburg
Nijmegen
Grave
Uden
Veghel
Zon
Best
St Oedenrode
Eindhoven
Valkenswaard
Neerpelt
Meuse-Escaut canal
Venlo
Roermond
Utrecht
HOLLAND
Zaltbommel
s'Hertogenbosch
Vught
R. Maas
Lower Rhine
R. Meuse
Wilhelmina canal
Tilburg
Breda
Turnhout
Turnhout canal
Gheel
Albert canal
BELGIUM
Antwerp
R. Escaut
Esschen
Woensdrecht
Roosendaal
Moerdijk
Dordrecht
Rotterdam
Hook of Holland
The Hague
SOUTH BEVELAND
WALCHEREN
Middelburg
Flushing
Breskens
Schelde
Terneuzen
Leopold canal
Ghent

'single thrust' and the 'broad front'; but after every allowance has been made for the distractions these caused it is still difficult to understand why it was not apparent from the start that the value of Antwerp as a supply port depended as much upon control of the seaward approaches as upon possession of the harbour itself.

Neither in the orders Eisenhower issued on 24 August, preparatory to taking over the command, nor in Montgomery's directive of the 26th is there any reference to the approaches, although both envisage the early occupation of Antwerp. Admiral Ramsay, Naval Commander-in-Chief, drew SHAEF's attention to the importance of the Scheldt estuary on the very day the advance halted at the dockside, but no effective heed was paid until the middle of the month, when it was already too late because the enemy had organized his defence. On 10 September Eisenhower specifically authorized Montgomery to defer clearing the approaches until after the Arnhem operation, and when four days later Montgomery directed 1 Canadian Army to free Antwerp he could still write 'our real objective is the Ruhr. But *on the way* we want the ports of Antwerp and Rotterdam', although he knew that Bradley's advance was already held up for lack of supplies.

The first Ultra reference to the impending loss of Antwerp was a request for the thorough demolition of the harbour on 28 August. This was only to be expected, but the central issue was put with unmistakable clarity by Hitler in an order of 3 September which made exactly the same point as Admiral Ramsay next day. In view of the threat to Antwerp, he told Army Group B that he attached 'decisive importance' for the conduct of future operations to holding Boulogne, Dunkirk and Calais, 'Walcheren island with Flushing harbour, a bridgehead round Antwerp and the Albert canal as far as Maastricht'.[1] Here was the explicit intention to hold both banks of the Scheldt, the

.m./3
KLs 9219,
248
835/5

---

1. This all-important order also laid down two other lines of strategy: the preparation of 1 Para Army to block advance into Holland (see p. 156 below), and the dangerous gap at the junction of Army Groups B and G (discussed on pp. 137–9 above).

strategy which prevented Antwerp from being used to supply
the front-line troops until the end of November and enabled the
retreating 15 Army to take Arnhem in the rear via the
Breskens–Flushing ferry and the South Beveland isthmus.
Through the medium of Ultra all the Allied authorities concerned knew of Hitler's views by the evening of 5 September,
just twenty-four hours after Antwerp fell, but they do not seem
to have adjusted their own actions accordingly.

Nor was this by any means the only evidence of the primary
importance attached to the Scheldt estuary; on the contrary,
confirmation of it built up fast during the next ten days. Army
Group B orders of 4 and 5 September were designed to carry
Hitler's directive into effect, and the local naval authorities
echoed his views next day. If news of ferryings across the estuary to Walcheren and South Beveland (which now began to
come in almost every day) and of divisional and corps locations
there or on the adjoining mainland might at first have seemed to
suggest the evacuation of at any rate the southern shore, this
interpretation was no longer possible after an order which Hitler
sent to 15 Army on the morning of 7 September; it was signalled the same afternoon. Since there were not sufficient forces
to recapture Antwerp, said Hitler, 'it must be ensured that the
Allies cannot use the harbour for a long time'; accordingly, the
mouth of the Scheldt was to be blocked by occupying and obstinately defending both Walcheren and the area round Breskens. If further proof were still required, it was provided by a
series of signals giving consequential corps and divisional locations.

a.m./7
XL 9409
1646/7

Twice in the space of four days Ultra had given unequivocal
warning that Hitler intended to render the capture of Antwerp
vain, and shown that he would succeed unless immediate steps
were taken to frustrate his intention. It is difficult to understand
why no serious effort was made to open the port by driving his
armies off the banks of the Scheldt while the momentum of
their headlong retreat still lasted, particularly since far grander
schemes for the invasion of Germany—which could not be realized unless petrol, food and ammunition to sustain them came

in through Antwerp—were being actively discussed. It was the first time that plain Ultra evidence on a matter of major importance had been disregarded; another, equally disastrous, was to follow almost at once.

Arnhem

The most likely explanation—acceptable, however, only with hesitation and bewilderment—of this astonishing oversight is to be found in the extreme optimism which the tremendous successes and swift advances of late August encouraged at all levels of the Allied command. This at least is the way most recent writers have explained otherwise inexplicable actions which certainly prolonged the war and may have thrown away the chance (if one ever existed) of ending it in 1944. But the release of the relevant Ultra signals makes it even harder than before to accept this explanation as a sufficient excuse for two costly mistakes.

Although an occasional voice was raised against facile optimism, a general euphoria had set in before the end of August. It was well established by the time the Antwerp docks were captured and it was still prevalent when the airborne troops were dropped round the Rhine bridges in Holland on 17 September. During the intervening fortnight, both sides were in fact badly overstretched. The Germans were in trouble because the haste and chaos of retreat almost cancelled out the improvisation which had extricated from the pocket men who might otherwise have been trapped and had enabled General Student to assemble enough troops to stop 21 Army Group's advance on the line of the canal which runs south-east from Antwerp—'the most terrifying thing of all was the progressive erosion of the fighting formations'. The Allies' difficulties proceeded mainly from the simple fact that they were getting farther and farther from the only harbours which could supply them while at the same time deploying more men on a wider front than ever before. So far as the truth about the Germans' troubles was known (and Ultra's part in this was considerable), it encouraged the Allied commanders to think that they could force a decision before the winter simply by pressing forward and keeping the enemy on the run. As the September days passed there was added a strong desire to find suitable employment for the airborne troops (the most highly trained of the remaining reserves, still unused except partially on D-Day) which were becoming 'like coins burning a hole in SHAEF's pocket' because so many of their intended operations were cancelled at the last minute as the speedy advance over-ran each planned objective in turn.

Prevailing trains of thought can be gauged from a Joint Intelligence Committee appreciation of 5 September which suggested that German resistance might end by 1 December or even sooner. This gave endorsement at the highest level to a view which had already been widespread for a week[1] and which remained current until the lessons of Arnhem began to sink in at the end of the month. The few dissentients included Churchill and Roosevelt, but when Churchill minuted on 8 September 'It is at least as likely that Hitler will be fighting on 1 January as that he will collapse before then', he had long lost his former power to intervene in tactics as well as to direct grand strategy and was thinking in political rather than military terms. Optimism seems to have dominated most minds throughout September.

This was the atmosphere in which the Arnhem operation was planned. It had a dulling effect on thought (plainly traceable in most of the pronouncements in the 'broad front' controversy, which so lacked verbal precision that it is often hard to see what they were intended to mean) which made it easy to dismiss the inconvenient and mutually supporting evidence of Ultra and photographic reconnaissance instead of examining it with the care its provenance deserved. Even Ultra's strong indications that two or more Panzer divisions were quartered on or near the Market Garden battlefield could not penetrate the wall, 'cemented by confidence, complacency and an uncharacteristic refusal to weigh evidence', which some of its recipients had erected to protect their presuppositions. The Ultra evidence greatly strengthens the case for 'a bridge too far' because it shows that the officers who emphasized the risks involved were

1. See pp. 126–7 above.

fully justified in doing so. The most senior of them were Generals Bedell Smith and Strong,[1] respectively Chief of Staff and Principal Intelligence Officer at SHAEF, both of whom of course saw Ultra. Their objections were waved aside by Eisenhower and Montgomery. Sir Brian Horrocks claims with some justification that 'those responsible for the higher direction of the war in the west faltered' when they halted him at Antwerp, and admits that he himself was still suffering from 'liberation euphoria' when, as commander of XXX Corps, he gave the order to advance up the road that led to Arnhem. But he makes an equally serious charge when he goes on to call the encounter with II SS Pz Corps 'our first bit of bad luck' and claims that he had not been warned of its presence, for this implies that—contrary to usual practice—the essence of an important piece of Ultra had not been passed down to corps level in disguised form. Why not? Was it because the likelihood that there were two SS divisions near Arnhem called the wisdom of the whole operation in question? Similarly, although Ultra knew on 5 September that II SS Pz Corps was in southern Holland, the possibility was not mentioned in the regular SHAEF Intelligence Summary until 16 September.

During the three or four weeks before the Arnhem operation, Ultra regularly produced intelligence about II SS Pz Corps (9 and 10 SS Pz Divisions) whose quick but allegedly unexpected counter-attacks at Arnhem denied 1 British Airborne Division the success its bravery deserved. By the first days of September this intelligence—greater in bulk than that about any other formation involved—pointed unequivocally towards the country between XXX Corps' front line and Arnhem.

As soon as it turned away after its unsuccessful attack on 20 August, II SS Pz Corps set a steady course for the Low Countries. It had already suffered heavily (it reported the loss of 120

1. However, the SHAEF Intelligence Summaries, which were issued over General Strong's signature, continued to encourage an optimistic outlook throughout September, insisting that the Germans could not possibly make good their losses or offer resistance short of the West Wall, and that 'No force can be built up in the West sufficient for a counter-offensive or even a successful defensive' (Summaries of 2, 9 and 16 September).

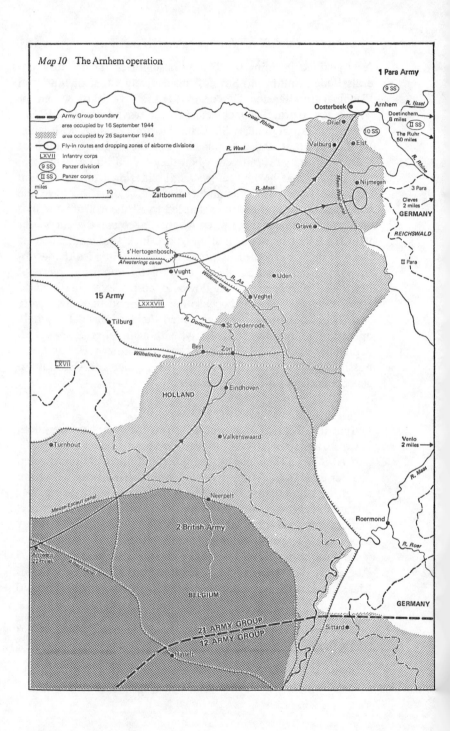

Map 10 The Arnhem operation

Army Group boundary
area occupied by 16 September 1944
area occupied by 26 September 1944
Fly-in routes and dropping zones of airborne divisions
LXVII infantry corps
9 SS Panzer division
II SS Panzer corps

miles
0   10

1 Para Army

9 SS

Oosterbeek ● ─── Arnhem   *R. Ijssel*
Driel ●   Doetinchem
                           8 miles
10 SS   II SS
Valburg ●   ● Elst   The Ruhr
                           50 miles

Lower Rhine

R. Waal

● Nijmegen   3 Para

Zaltbommel   Cleves
                           2 miles
R. Maas   **GERMANY**

Grave ●   *REICHSWALD*

s'Hertogenbosch   II Para
Afwaterings canal

● Vught   *Willems canal*   ● Uden

15 Army   *R. Aa*

LXXXVIII   ● Veghel

● Tilburg   *R. Dommel* ● St Oedenrode

Wilhelmina canal   Best ●   Zon ●

LXVII

HOLLAND   ● Eindhoven

● Turnhout   ● Valkenswaard   Venlo
                                         2 miles →

                                         R. Maas

● Neerpelt

Meuse-Escaut canal   Roermond ●

Antwerp   *R. Roer*
22 miles

2 British Army

BELGIUM   **GERMANY**

21 ARMY GROUP
12 ARMY GROUP   Sittard ●

Hasselt

tanks and an unknown number of men the previous day), and the additional casualties now incurred led to the ordering up of 600 replacements from Germany to Beauvais and to an urgent demand by its commander, General Bittrich, for 111 new Mark IV and V tanks on the 26th. It was at this moment that the retreat began in earnest, and for the next ten days the corps could be traced moving back across north-eastern France. Having rallied near Evreux, on 26 August it shifted corps headquarters nearer to Beauvais to pick up the replacements. A couple of days later it was to go to Soissons and Laon, and it continued to proceed in an easterly direction under 5 Pz Army. On 2 September several Panzer divisions, 9 and 10 SS among them, were back in Belgium with orders to rest and refit to the west of Liège. The continuing retreat forced Army Group B to change this on 4 September into an instruction that these divisions should remain active for the moment but that any elements not operating should rest and refit in the Venlo–Arnhem–s'Hertogenbosch district of south Holland—that is to say, astride 21 Army Group's intended line of advance. Next day Army Group B ordered the staff of II SS Pz Corps to Eindhoven (forty miles south of Arnhem and right in the path of Horrocks's XXX Corps) to direct the refit of 2 Pz, 116 Pz and 9 SS Pz Divisions; 10 SS Pz was farther south-east at Maastricht. Thereafter, news of II SS Pz Corps dried up for several days (this was the moment when the re-establishment of land-line communications began once more to dim our chances of eavesdropping in the northern sector), but on 9 September there was an urgent call for aerial reconnaissance to establish whether Aachen or Arnhem was the Allies' chief objective, and on the 14th Army Group B's headquarters was reported at Oosterbeek on the outskirts of Arnhem,[1] whence Model personally directed the German reaction to the airlandings three days later.

The temporary cessation of reports about II SS Pz Corps means that the Ultra evidence was neither complete nor entirely up to date when the paratroops dropped on 17 September: by

p.m./4
XL 9188
1152/5

1730/5
XL 9245*
0103/6

0700/14
HP 220
0752/15

---

1. Hut 3 did not know, of course, what was so soon to happen at Oosterbeek and Arnhem, and therefore had no reason to give HP 220 more than modest priority. However, it is likely to have reached SHAEF and 21 Army Group during the afternoon of 15 September—before the operation began, but no doubt too late to affect it.

then corps headquarters had moved from Eindhoven to Doetinchem, east of Arnhem, for instance. More attention might
have been paid to Ultra if we had been able (as so often) to report the number of serviceable tanks (there were only twenty)
in II SS Pz Corps on, say, 12 September, the day when the operation orders for Market Garden were first issued. In all
fairness, this must be admitted. But those who dealt with Ultra
in the field knew from experience that it seldom told everything, and Ultra's long history of proven reliability might have
been expected to ensure that the generals whom they briefed
gave more weight to two successive Army Group B orders
which placed SS Panzer divisions close to the dangerous route
(a single raised causeway) which XXX Corps must follow, and
round Arnhem at the farther end of it. Moreover, the Ultra evidence had been confirmed by other sources (photo reconnaissance and the Dutch Resistance) from at any rate 12 September onwards. Yet the tanks reported at Arnhem were
dismissed as only the battered remnants of exhausted divisions
incapable of putting up serious opposition. Of course these divisions were tired and had lost equipment (Ultra itself had reported this), but German industry was still capable of re-equip-
ping élite SS divisions quickly enough to enable them to crush
airborne troops dropped without heavy weapons; and it was
very unlikely that none of the tanks ordered on 26 August
would have arrived by three weeks later, although no express
notification of delivery had been received.

It should have been no surprise that 9 and 10 SS Pz were encountered somewhere between Eindhoven and Arnhem. Ultra
had placed them in this general area with certainty over ten
days before Market Garden, although it had not located them
precisely. But the front had since stabilized, so they were unlikely to have gone still farther back—particularly as two Ultra
reports (signalled on the 14th and 15th) showed that the Germans were expecting a large-scale airlanding in Holland and a
thrust on both sides of Eindhoven as far as Arnhem.

The Ultra evidence was amply strong enough to shake the
confidence of men with minds as open as they had been on

D-Day.[1] But the high command had lately become so over-confident that it was allowing itself to spend more time in disputes over future strategy than in studying the ground immediately under its feet. Its errors of judgement over Arnhem have often been criticized, but they will be still more severely judged now that it can be shown just how much known risk was disregarded when the operation was launched.

There was less Ultra information about the German troops which fought 82 and 101 US Airborne Divisions at Nijmegen, Veghel, St Oedenrode and Son and delayed XXX Corps as it tried to hasten along the narrow corridor to Arnhem than there was about the subsequently vexed question of 9 and 10 SS Pz Divisions, and it was of less value. It may be dismissed summarily. The route of LXVII Corps could be followed across France and Belgium in the same way as that of II SS Pz Corps until it halted at Esschen (north of Antwerp) next to LXXXVIII Corps and ready to direct operations against the southernmost landings and XXX Corps' first thrust. There were traces of II Para Corps and 3 Para Division (the latter was 'still being set up' on 31 August) which eventually lined the German–Dutch frontier east of Nijmegen, but very little was heard about 1 Para Army as a whole. On 5 September Model ordered emergency measures until it arrived from the central front, but another ten days passed before its Chief Signals Officer was located at s'Hertogenbosch. The static units already stationed in recently peaceful Holland will have had regular land-line communications, and it is not surprising that there was no news of them.

1. An inability to read the evidence in any but a cheerful sense is the most striking feature of the contemporary SHAEF Intelligence Summaries—except, perhaps, the fact that the whole airborne operation is given no prominence at all. Ultra and hindsight throw into lurid relief remarks like '9 SS, and probably 10 SS, has been reported as *withdrawing altogether* to the Arnhem area' (No. 26 of 16 September; my italics) and 'unless [the Germans] hold Arnhem, Holland is lost' (No. 27 of 23 September, when they had already recaptured Arnhem bridge and the seriousness of the situation was at last beginning to dawn on the Allied commanders). Even on 30 September 'The enemy's main effort is being put into exploitation of *the initial success* at Arnhem' (my italics).

On the other hand, information rapidly accumulated about 15 Army's retreat up the coast to hold the estuary of the Scheldt in accordance with Hitler's order, and about the escape of considerable elements of it across the river to the Dutch mainland. The point that the occupation of a bridgehead round Breskens neutralized Antwerp, and that the escaping troops emerged on the flank of the Allied advance towards Arnhem, has already been made; it need not be laboured again, save to underline the value of these items of intelligence. An Army Group B order of 4 September already advised 15 Army units which could not fight their way back by the direct route Louvain–Hasselt to go via Flushing and Breda, and 16 GAF Field Division was being ferried over from Breskens and Terneuzen the same evening. Next day the naval authorities had three ferries working and were hastily improvising more, and on the morning of the 7th they issued elaborate instructions (passed on as Ultra signals the same afternoon) to this end in concert with General von Zangen, commanding 15 Army; LXXXIX Corps and 331 Division were coming up specially to organize the crossings, and artillery protection was being arranged. The location of the ferries was announced, and it was estimated that 25,000 men and 550 vehicles had crossed so far. During the week that had still to elapse before Market Garden, the daily performance of the ferries was regularly reported. In sum, throughout this period Ultra kept 21 Army Group informed of the use 15 Army was making of its only escape route, one which would put it into an ideal position to attack the flank of XXX Corps' salient. Soon after the airlandings we were able to make this intention explicit.

The first reactions to Market Garden showed that the enemy had correctly divined Allied intentions. The main air effort was transferred from Aachen to Holland (Reich defence taking second place in the emergency), panic caused an order (quickly cancelled) for the abandonment of Terneuzen, the ferry port on the south bank of the Scheldt, and OKW hastily authorized the destruction of Amsterdam and Rotterdam harbours. Luftflotte 3 sent fifty-odd guns and a battle group to Nijmegen on the

18th but thereafter tactically useful intelligence (never Ultra's forte) was scarce and sometimes late. Thus Hitler's order for reinforcements to be sent up was not known until 21 September, Goering's assurance to 1 Para Army that he was providing 'tens of thousands of our best people'(!) for the new parachute divisions not until three days after it was issued, nor a shortage of Flak ammunition on the route of incoming gliders until two days after the batteries reported it. Probably the most useful information yet was a summary of 15 Army's ferryings over the Scheldt up to 23 September (82,000 men, 530 guns, 46,000 vehicles, 4000 horses and much equipment) and news of an intended thrust against Veghel which, however, must have arrived after the action began. The steady reinforcement of Holland even after the last survivors were withdrawn from Arnhem on 25–6 September testified to the continuing threat presented by the partially successful operation.

23 September
HP 1019
0347/24

Rundstedt's after-action report on Arnhem, presented on 1 October, pointed in the same direction. It began by admitting that surprise had been secured (one result of which had been heavy casualties among officers), but claimed that the presence of II SS Panzer Corps had in return been an unpleasant surprise for the Allies—a remark which made grim reading after our warnings. The enemy's chief mistake, said Rundstedt, had been to spread the airlandings out over three days, instead of concentrating them into one (this was, of course, to overlook the delays caused by the weather). He did not conclude, however, that Arnhem had probably taught the Allies—as Crete had taught the Germans in 1941—that success is hardly worth buying at so high a price (no further airlanding operation was in fact projected until the Rhine crossing in March, and then it was rather a desirable than an essential element in the battle-plan). Instead, he forecast that similar operations would be attempted in Holland or north Germany, probably in conjunction with a sealanding and probably not just behind the West Wall. He changed the last part of his opinion within a fortnight, warning of probable paratroop action against the Rhine bridges on 15 October and again on 10 November, this time as part of 'a large-scale attack on western Germany which may begin in the very near future'. Airlandings were expected at Aachen in

mid-November, and a Foreign Armies West appreciation of 2
December forecast that the Allied airborne forces would be
ready to operate in a month's time (long before then, of course,
the US 82 and 101 Divisions had played a vital part in the
'Battle of the Bulge'). The persistence of this delusion almost up
to the time of the Ardennes offensive created needless anxiety
in the German command throughout a period when things were
going somewhat better for them, and probably marks the
longest-lasting consequence of the Arnhem operation.

The landing in the south[1]

That the deception plan was nearly as effective in the Mediterranean as in the English Channel was evident from the wildly
fluctuating forecasts of a new assault which circulated between
mid-July and mid-August. There would be a landing in Italy
but not in the south of France; southern France was the target,
but the Adriatic and the Aegean were also possibilities (this
from OKM at the end of July); it would be in the south of
France 'any day' if recent air attacks on railways were anything
to go by; it would be in southern France or on the Ligurian
coast of Italy on 12 or 13 August, with a possible diversionary
attack in the Adriatic; there was still no indisputable evidence,
according to Luftflotte 3 on the 13th, but the target might be
Corsica. Even after the invasion fleet had been sighted and another 'southern France, any time' alert issued, there were lingering doubts whether the landing might not take place on the
Ligurian coast after all.

In spite of this widespread belief that there would soon be a
new landing somewhere in the south, the pressing demands of
Normandy at the time of the Mortain attack and the Falaise
pocket almost robbed Blaskowitz of his only Panzer division
and some useful infantry less than a week before the invasion.
In the event, he lost only parts of each, for on 11 August Hitler
quashed an Army Group B order transferring 11 Pz Division to
Chartres—whereupon Blaskowitz promptly quartered it on both

1. Debated for months under the code-name Anvil, the operation was
re-christened Dragoon just before it sailed.

sides of the Rhône to make up for the expected loss of 338 Division.

Ultra information about the swift southern campaign which began on 15 August was never very plentiful (it is remarkable that it was not far scantier, in view of the relatively undamaged communications in the area), but it was always amply sufficient to keep SHAEF and the invading 6 US Army Group informed about their enemy's plans and to guide them in the drive northwards. As in Normandy in June, we were able to send several advance reports of bomb damage on the railways and to give notice about the success of air-raids on radar installations, and in addition the welcome news that the Air Officer Commanding Fighters South had been bombed out of his battle headquarters at Orange on 12 August. The first situation reports from 19 Army showed two features which were to become regular—that 11 Pz was constantly called on as the maid-of-all-work because it was 'the only effective element in 19 Army', and that its activities were seriously hampered because, the Allied air-raids having destroyed all the bridges, it could not get its tanks across the Rhône (LXIV Corps was ordered to send all its bridging columns to Avignon to remedy this).

By far the most important signals yet were two dispatched with the highest priority on 17 and 18 August. They revealed, only a few hours after he took the decision, that Hitler had ordered the immediate evacuation of southern France: the main body of Army Group G was to disengage and join up with Army Group B on a line Sens–Dijon–the Swiss frontier, while the remainder (i.e. 19 Army) retreated up the Rhône valley, destroying everything as it went, with 11 Pz as rearguard. It soon became plain, however, that 11 Pz (which was being reinforced by seventeen assault-guns and fifty-one Mark IV tanks from Germany) was not finding it easy to assemble for this purpose.

0940/17
XLs 6753,
6919
1408/17

Not until 19 August did 19 Army begin to move off, with the very modest object of passing Avignon in four days, Army Group headquarters transferring meanwhile first to Lyon and then to Dijon. The pressure on it by a better-equipped foe was intense and, because it completely lacked anti-tank weapons, Army Group G appealed to OKW to fly in rocket and grenade launchers. Understandably apprehensive about greater dangers still to come, Blaskowitz impatiently urged 19 Army to make haste. But how safely could the French and American troops of the 6 US Army Group follow, even if their enemy was disappearing in front of them as fast as he could? What chances were there that a counter-attack would be launched from their long Alpine flank by the elements of 19 Army now being isolated along the frontier, or by the considerable German forces in northern Italy? The decoding of the Hitler order for the evacuation of the south gave the desired reassurance[1] that no attack need be feared; the Führer directed that the divisions being cut off in the mountains by the Allied advance should withdraw under pressure across the Alps and join the command of OB South-West, 'who will take over the *defence* of this position'. Subsequent reports showed that the order was being carried out, and in fact the only serious sign of an intention to hold much more than the essential east bank of the Rhône was an order of 21 August that Grenoble should be held until 1 September (the order proved fruitless: the city was taken over by 'terrorists' soon after it was issued). An American after-action report shows the good use to which Ultra's reassurance was put. A task-force pushed ahead quickly, helped by the Resistance, got in front of part of 19 Army, and set up a road-block at Montélimar, some fifty miles north of Avignon; it was no doubt this block which gave 11 Pz and 198 Divisions so much trouble on 25 August.

Rearguard actions and the need to keep ahead of a more fully motorized enemy soon began to take their toll, causing 'great strain to persons unaccustomed to marching, particularly in the present oppressive heat' according to Blumentritt on 25 August. Soon, however, enough progress had been made for Blaskowitz to give directions about the route to be followed farther north and about the use of 11 Pz to prevent outflanking in the Jura on the way from Lyon to Besançon and Belfort, and a temporary blocking position was to be constructed across the Saône valley from Autun through Châlons to Dôle. Army

1. The value of the reassurance was stressed by the Ultra intelligence officer with 7 US Army.

Group G was now getting near enough for Rundstedt to give it positive assistance, so he sent a few second-grade troops to meet it and placed 21 Pz at Langres (north of Dijon) in strategic reserve—welcome news, no doubt, to Blaskowitz, because by now 11 Pz and 338 Divisions were so worn out as to be almost useless. In addition, the frontier area at Dôle was strengthened by 116 Pz on 30 August.

With a safe reception thus assured, Blaskowitz could evacuate Lyon at the beginning of September, set up a protective screen on the plateau north-west of Dijon, and turn his attention to the next stage of the homeward journey by arranging that the Vosges passes, his first direct access to the Reich, should be manned by Home Army units from the Black Forest as a precautionary measure.

At Belfort, which 11 Pz reached on 6 September, rations were short because the crowds of stragglers were eating everything up, but the retreating army had rounded the north-west corner of Switzerland into Alsace and was within sight of home; the weary march was over, and the two separate fronts had been joined into one. Weak and exhausted men were the city's only defence, reported Army Group G; but Belfort was not in fact to fall to the Allies for another two months. There was little that 19 Army could do to protect Belfort, for the moment at least, however; it had got back with nine German and half-a-dozen old French tanks and five 88-mm guns with 400 rounds between them.

On the Allied side the junction between the two fronts had been made symbolically when American troops coming from north and south met near Dijon on 12 September, and more formally when 6 Army Group was subordinated to SHAEF three days later.

Brest and other 'fortresses'

As the ports, harbours and U-boat bases on the Atlantic and Channel coasts of France were cut off in turn by the Allied advance, they were declared 'fortresses' by Hitler and ordered to hold out to the last, often behind a 15-km-deep belt of 'scorched earth'. Once cut off, their only means of communication with the Fatherland was by radio; their normal Enigma keys were naval, but isolation meant that these had to be used to pass military information as well. Much of the considerable amount of Ultra about the fortresses was derived in this way, but by no means all—the remnants of the four or five divisions shut up in Brest, for instance, had brought their army keys with them. Partly for this reason, more news came out of Brest than out of any of the other fortresses, but partly also because of the appointment of General Ramcke (who had led his parachute brigade out of apparent disaster to safety on the field of Alamein two years before) as Fortress Commander by Hitler on 11 August. Ramcke's reports were not as racy as Schlieben's had been at Cherbourg, but he had got the job by proposing himself for it to Goering (although he knew that the quality of the garrison was poor, relations between the three services 'chaotic' and 'the Allies at the door') and he made the most[1] of his brief tenure of command—Brest was besieged on 25 August and captured on 19 September—promising, for instance, that if he had to surrender the town it would only be as a heap of ruins.

Information about the fortresses fell into several well-defined categories:

1. Conditions inside the perimeter, whether among the garrison (for example: an early shortage of anti-tank guns and ammunition at Brest; a ration-strength of 37,000, food for thirty to fifty days and ammunition for twelve days at Brest on 30 August; the report that the Lorient garrison was a motley collection incapable of being trained to fight the American tanks) or among the civil population (draconian measures at St Malo early in August 'so that the people lose the taste for revolt once and for all', announced because the local auxiliaries and gendarmes were refusing to obey orders; or Jodl's recommendations that civilian rations be 'ruthlessly reduced' in order to prolong the siege).

2. Air-drops of supplies, scarce equipment or ammunition, which occurred on most nights. Time and place had to be prearranged in good time, and could therefore often be signalled

---

1. Including a privileged last-minute exchange of personal signals with Hitler about the safeguarding of his family estates.

far enough in advance for the aircraft to be intercepted and shot down. Thus we gave a four-hour advance warning of a sortie by four Heinkels to Brest on 12 August and even more notice of others to Dunkirk, Calais, Boulogne and La Rochelle on the night of 12–13 September.

3. Reports of damage to U-boat pens after bombing raids— or, unfortunately but more frequently, news that the shelter roofs had not been penetrated.

4. Occasional delicate negotiations about possible surrender —with the French and behind the Americans' backs, for instance, at La Pallice on 11 September, because of alleged French fears that the Americans would destroy the only deepwater port which had survived without damage; or discussions at La Rochelle about which General de Gaulle was to be informed.

Information of all these types, but principally advance warning of intended air-supply operations, continued to come through until each fortress in turn surrendered.

6
Deadlock in the autumn

Steadily increasing German resistance, bad weather, supply problems (it was only in mid-November that the artificial harbour in
Normandy gave way to the ports as the main inlet and that the railways were ready to replace the famous Red Ball Express, which
had been bringing up petrol, shells and food to the forward troops
by road for nearly three months) and disagreements over strategy
(which did not reach their peak until the end of November) combined to reduce Allied progress to a slow crawl throughout the autumn. Less ground was gained in the three months between Arnhem and the German offensive in the Ardennes than had sometimes
been won in a couple of days during August. The story is one of
limited objectives and small advances made after hard-fought battles under dreadful conditions which were nevertheless gradually
preparing suitable starting positions for a spring offensive when the
Germans struck on 16 December.

In the northernmost sector of the front the Canadian Army had
secured a great part of the left bank of the Scheldt between Antwerp and the sea before September was out, but the remaining
pocket round Breskens was not mopped up nor Walcheren and
Beveland across the estuary cleared until the first week in November. On the other side of the Nijmegen–Arnhem salient, 2 British
Army did not reach the bank of the Maas opposite Venlo nor the
Roer at Linnich until late November. On its right, 1 and 9 US Armies reached the outskirts of Aachen at the beginning of October
but did not take the city for another three weeks nor get across the
Roer (only fifteen miles farther on, and about the same distance
from Cologne) by the middle of December. Farther to the south, 3

US Army had been close outside Metz for seven or eight weeks before capturing it in late November and pushing on to the West Wall
in the Saar region. The largest advance was made by 7 US Army in
Alsace; it was through the Belfort gap and on the Rhine at Strasbourg by the end of November.

Opposite the quietest sector of the front, from Aachen to the
junction of the Moselle and the Saar between Metz and Trier, and
sheltered by the mountains of the Schnee Eifel, Hitler was meanwhile preparing the surprise blow which shook the Allied command
on 16 December.

The front

It will be convenient to divide the front into five sectors:

1 The Scheldt estuary: 15 Army

The corps and divisions composing the German 15 Army (between the Nijmegen salient and the sea, facing 1 Canadian Army) reported their front lines and the location of their headquarters fairly regularly throughout October and well into November. They did not say much about the progress of the fighting, however; the fear that Walcheren might be cut off, an attempt to prevent this, and its failure were almost the only operational items apart from advance warning that Breskens on the south bank of the Scheldt was about to be evacuated. Soon after 15 Army withdrew across the Maas and Rhine on losing Walcheren and Beveland at the end of the first week in November, information became much scantier, presumably because the Dutch telephone system was used instead of radio. Nevertheless, Ultra identified the new Army Group H almost as soon as it was set up at the beginning of November to control 15 Army and 1 Parachute Army and reported on the 24th that LXVII Corps was being shipped eastwards into Army Group Reserve except for one division, which was going to the Saar front.

The loss of one shore of the Scheldt estuary did not diminish the German command's purpose of preventing the use of Antwerp by the Allies, but changed the means by which it was to

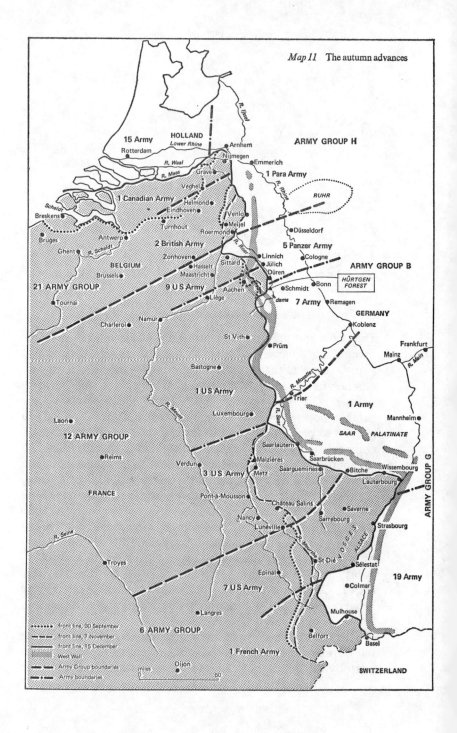

Map 11 The autumn advances

be attained. A number of naval Enigma messages, originating with Doenitz or one of the local naval commands, gave orders for blocking or harassing operations by midget submarines and other small craft. The rocket and flying-bomb attacks which began in October were designed for the same purpose, and Antwerp remained their sole target until Rundstedt tried to get some of them diverted to the Allied supply-base at Liège shortly before the Ardennes offensive.

Two returns, made by 15 Army on the state of its component divisions at the beginning and at the middle of October, gave a great deal of useful information: a comparison of the two shows, for instance, that there was a slight tendency for mobility (whether horse-drawn or motorized) to improve but that nearly all of the divisions were given the third or the lowest of the four possible ratings for fighting value—which meant that they were considered suitable only for defence—and that none was placed in the top category. Towards the end of the month, naval sources endorsed this low opinion of 15 Army's capabilities: one spoke of a 'great decline in fighting strength' having 'a critical effect' on 15 Army, and the other said that the troops round Rosendaal (opposite the Beveland isthmus) were 'tired out' but that no reinforcements could be sent up. A month later, Rundstedt was even more explicit; 64 and 70 Divisions had been so smashed up in the Scheldt battles that they were to be considered as disbanded.

2   South Holland: 1 Parachute Army

On the other side of the Nijmegen salient, 2 British Army's primary objective was to occupy all the ground on the left bank of the Maas in the long bend between Grave and Roermond, and this was in fact all it accomplished in this sector by the middle of December. Ultra's first assistance towards this end was to provide locations of the German forces in the area in the week or two after the Arnhem operation, and to note that although 9 Pz, 116 Pz and a Panzer brigade remained there, I, II and XII SS Corps were to move out, the first two to Germany and the last to the Aachen sector. It was fairly plain that something was brewing when XLVII Corps and 15 Panzergrenadier Division were brought up from Nancy to 1 Para Army on 14 October, but the nearest thing to an explicit warning of the attack on Meijel (aimed at tying down Allied forces and so relieving the pressure on 15 Army farther north) which was launched by these two and 9 Pz on 27 October was the arrival of XLVII Corps in front of the town the previous day. There were several reports on the progress of the fighting during the next four days, until the Flivo of 9 Pz let us know on 1 November that the operation was over and his division preparing to move out of the area. Very little news was received from this part of the front during the next few weeks, and the only item of any significance was an appreciation by Rundstedt in late November that Army Group H's main effort should be concentrated east of the Maas where Allied troops were little more than twenty miles from the industries of the Ruhr.

a.m./26
HP 4592
1450/26

1200/1
HP 5265
1819/1

3　Aachen: 5 Panzer Army and 7 Army

The Arnhem operation and 1 US Army's drive towards Aachen underlined the weakness of the German position between Aachen and the Zuider Zee, and further hasty measures were ordered to strengthen it. Thus 100,000 cubic metres of concrete and a major share in the labours of the Todt organization were to be allotted to OB West in the first fortnight of October, and steps taken to prepare a reserve position along the line of the river Ems (on the German side of the Dutch–German frontier) from Emden on the North Sea down to Emmerich on the Rhine.[1] For Hitler to issue orders like these on 30 September, however, was in a sense to shut the stable door when the horse was no longer trying to bolt, for the Arnhem sector became quiescent as soon as the survivors had been withdrawn. Aachen remained the chief danger-point in the northern half of the front that now ran from the sea to Switzerland, and bitter struggles continued on both sides of the city without much break until the Ardennes offensive opened. Ultra's principal contri-

1. There was some inter-service friction over this position. In early November the navy objected that the defences then under construction were wrongly sited and gave insufficient protection to Emden and Delfzijl harbours. OKW seems to have modified the plan accordingly.

bution here lay in showing the expedients and the changes of plan to which the German command was driven by its anxiety to ensure protection for the communications and industry of the Rhineland. In the last days of September I SS Corps (1 and 12 SS Divisions) was under orders to transfer to Osnabrück in Westphalia to rest and refit under 6 Pz Army,[1] and this was confirmed on 5 October. Within the space of four days, however, the transfer was countermanded, and the corps redirected to Jülich, between Aachen and Cologne, the arrangement being sanctioned by Rundstedt on condition that Army Group B surrendered the corps to 6 Pz Army by 20 October at the latest. The instruction was repeated on 18 October, when elements of 1, 2 and 12 SS Divisions were already being moved away, in accordance with Rundstedt's condition, at the same time as 3 PzGr Division (also under I SS Corps' command) was attacking to close a gap in the line north of Aachen. I SS Corps now disappeared from the battlefield, but XII SS Corps had already taken over a sector of the front extending from Roermond almost down to Aachen. Soon 5 Pz Army was shifted from the Saar (where it had appeared after the great retreat) to take over the front between Roermond and the boundary of 7 Army south of Aachen. Thereby a pattern of command in this neighbourhood was set up which endured even after the fall of Aachen on 21 October.

The long-drawn-out struggle in the Hürtgen Forest and along the Roer around Schmidt which began early in November was reflected in proposals to flood the Roer valley and so transform it into a tank-trap, by attacks on Vossenack by 116 Pz, by renewed demands for Flak to be used in ground fighting, and by alarms about an airlanding.

By 20 November the situation on both sides of Aachen was becoming extremely serious because of the weakness of the German troops. Model remarked on it in a report dated 10 November, and a week later insisted that he could only prevent an Allied breakthrough if he received adequate reinforcements, a better ammunition supply and fighter cover for his operations (the lack of fighter cover was frustrating its every movement,

1. 6 Panzer Army had only just been set up—to prepare the Ardennes offensive, although Allied intelligence did not know this; see p. 192 below.

XII SS Corps complained). In these circumstances, there was
nothing for it but to allow divisions which had been withdrawn
for rest and refit to be sucked back into the fighting: XII SS
Corps was expecting 10 SS Division to return to the Linnich
area on 20 November, and ambulances for it were made ready
close at hand,[1] while at the same time OB West ordered construction work on the West Wall to be speeded up. The Ultra
signals conveying the essential parts of this information bear
the same date as the report in which Rundstedt is now known
to have conveyed his misgivings to Hitler.

The same keynotes were constantly struck by the information which came in during the last three weeks before the Ardennes offensive—the gradual wearing down of the German
troops all along the line of the river Roer and the retention of
at least some parts of the SS armoured divisions on the west
bank of the Rhine as a guarantee against a surprise attack carrying the Allies through in one bound to Cologne, Bonn or
Koblenz.

4 The Saar: 1 Army

At the end of September and the beginning of October the
order of battle of 1 Army, protecting the Saar Palatinate between the Moselle and the Rhine, was already tolerably clear,
and it remained so throughout the autumn. The first information of much immediate operational value came in an exchange
of signals between LXXXII Corps and 5 Jagddivision on 3, 4
and 5 October. The former asked the latter to send its fighters
to attack the airfield at Conflans (between Verdun and Metz),
where American reinforcements were thought to be assembling;
the request was twice refused, the second time on the ground
that there were not enough aircraft available for the task. The
departure of 3 Panzergrenadier Division for Holland was
said on 5 October to have left 1 Army on the defensive east of
Metz, but within a week large-scale attacks were expected a lit-

---

1. Like 1, 2 and 12 SS Divisions (see p. 171), 10 SS had been taken out of
the line to prepare for the Ardennes offensive, which was therefore prejudiced
when the dangerous situation at Aachen called 10 SS back, but this was not
known at the time, of course.

tle farther south, round Pont-à-Mousson and Château Salins. These warnings came from XIII SS Corps, whose Flivo
became for a time one of our most regular and reliable
informants, reporting the battle headquarters of his corps and
its subordinate divisions almost every day.

Although under orders not to provoke a major battle, Patton
was in fact testing out the defences of Metz towards the end of
October, and by the 25th this led the Germans to fear imminent
attack in the Metz–Nancy area. When the assault at last began
on 8 November, we learned almost at once that the headquarters of 17 SS and 48 Divisions had been bombed and put
out of action, and were able to follow the fighting of the next
week or two quite closely through a series of situation reports,
some of them from 11 Panzer Division, which as part of 1
Army's only armoured reserves was once again forced to bear
the brunt of the fighting and move swiftly from one danger-
point to another. Metz fell on 19 November, and soon 3 US
Army's advance from Nancy was threatening to open a dangerous gap between the German 1 and 19 Armies; an urgent call
was sent out for fighter-sweeps to relieve the pressure between
Saarburg and Saverne so that countermeasures could be prepared, and we were able to give notice of this within a few
hours.

1745/22
HP 7489
2256/22

Towards the end of November 21 Pz could be seen playing
the same role as 11 Pz, shifting rapidly into and out of the line
as need arose; thus it was LXXXII Corps' tactical reserve on
24 September, in the front line on the 28th, and being relieved
by 416 Division next day. Both of these Panzer divisions were
taken out of the line on the eve of the Ardennes, but neither
was used in the offensive. In retrospect, a message of 3 December shows up the acute competition for scarce equipment between 1 Army in its endangered sector and the armies secretly
preparing for the surprise assault: on that day thirteen Panther
tanks earmarked for 116 Pz (which led one prong of the attack
a fortnight later) were diverted to 11 Pz, 116 Pz being assured
that it would receive a new delivery in about four days. For by
this time we had pieced together fragments of a 1 Army report
of 25 November which listed the tanks and artillery of some divisions and classified the fighting value of more under the usual

headings. The compiling of it must have been a melancholy task. In LXXXII Corps, 416 Division and 19 Volksgrenadier Division were both assessed in category IV (suitable for static defence), 21 Pz in III (mobile defence) although it only had seven tanks and not much transport; in XIII SS Corps, 347 Division was in category IV, 36 and 17 SS Divisions in III (the last only 40 per cent motorized), and 11 Pz (with only four tanks—hence, no doubt, the need for the new allocation just mentioned—but 90 per cent mobile) in category II (fit for limited offensive operations); in LXXXIX Corps 25 and 256 Divisions were rated III and 361 Division IV; Panzer Lehr Division, which had recently reappeared under its old commander Bayerlein, had thirteen tanks and a number of guns and was therefore rated III, but a final note recorded that 553 Division had been smashed round Saverne and that 462 Division was shut up in Metz. A week later, OB West reported the whole of Army Group G very short of fuel and some types of ammunition.

5 Alsace: 19 Army

Information about the southernmost part of the long front was rather intermittent during the three autumn months, and consisted largely of items which enabled our picture of the order of battle and the positions of the various units to be kept continuously up to date. Thus, for instance, Army Group G and 19 Army headquarters were reported six times and their various components on many other occasions.

The general character of much later news was set in an appreciation of 29 September by Westphal, Rundstedt's Chief of Staff; the whole area from Strasbourg southwards to Mulhouse was weakly held by replacement units from Wehrkreis V (the territorial district on the opposite bank of the Rhine), he said, and in view of the likelihood of airlandings OB West wanted them strengthened (he got a single battalion, and OKW declared that further reinforcement of Mulhouse was out of the question). The weekly report of 30 September by 19 Army on the state of its divisions confirmed Westphal's view. It was no doubt because of this weakness that 11 Panzer Division was several times reported north-west of Strasbourg—a position from which it could as easily move north to the Saar or south into Alsace in case of need—during the next three or four weeks. It finally moved up towards Saarbrücken at the end of October and was replaced by the far less mobile 361 Volksgrenadier Division, at much the same time as XLVII Corps moved north[1] to conduct the Meijel attack and handed over to LXXXIX Corps. A further shuffling of sectors and corps commands succeeded in freeing both XLVII and LVIII Corps from Alsace by early November; the two staffs were needed to control some of the armoured divisions which were to lead the assault in the Ardennes, had we but known this at the time.

Ultra provided very little news of the French and American push towards Saverne and Strasbourg (which fell on 23 November) and in the Belfort gap in mid-November, save for the report (already quoted) that 553 Division had been smashed at Saverne. By the end of the month it was plain that 19 Army was in a bad way; its strength had been still further eroded by the long-drawn-out fighting in the Vosges, reported Army Group G, and the Alsace bridgehead (already reduced to a semi-circle of some thirty miles radius round Colmar) could not be held unless powerful new formations were brought up to strengthen the defence, while attacks on Sélestat (at the northern edge of this perimeter) were already expected. In spite of this, yet another formation was taken away from 19 Army when on 6 December XC Corps (the former IV GAF Field Corps) was transferred to 1 Army—and this notwithstanding Hitler's appointment of Himmler as Supreme Commander Upper Rhine, with the duty of organizing the defence of the German bank of the river for the sixty miles northwards from Basel, an appointment which became known through Ultra the day after it was made.

Recovery and redisposition of the German Air Force

Allied superiority in the air, the petrol shortage of which it was a principal cause, and dislocation resulting from the hasty re-

1. See p. 170 above.

treat had combined to reduce the GAF almost to impotence by the end of August. In contrast, the autumn months saw a considerable recovery, an increase in the number of serviceable aircraft, a major redisposition of figher forces, and the introduction of jet aircraft on a serious operational scale.

Ultra made it possible to follow the steps by which these changes came about, and—again in contrast with the recent past —in October and November this sort of information probably outstripped in value what we learned about operations on the ground. The first indication was a large-scale reorganization of fighter and close-support units at the beginning of October, which was judged to have greatly reduced the number of aircraft available for close support at the front but to have increased the fighter force behind it, particularly in the northern sector. This was no doubt connected with instructions issued by Goering on 8 October that strong forces of fighters should be made ready for the defence of Germany, and it was reflected also in standing orders a week later from Luftflotte Reich to GAF West (its subordinate since the dissolution of Luftflotte 3 in September) that in future the latter's main effort should be devoted to protecting the rear areas and the construction work on the West Wall from interference by Allied fighters and fighter-bombers, and that it should only support the front-line troops in case of emergency.

Behind these shifts of policy there lay the two largest elements in the air situation during the autumn: on the one hand, the strategic offensive of the RAF and the USAAF was being stepped up, both by day and by night, to such an extent that—irrespective of the sometimes fierce disputes over whether its main targets should be oil refineries, communications, or industrial centres—the German economy was being very severely hit; on the other was the paradoxical achievement of Albert Speer, Hitler's Armaments Minister, in greatly increasing the output of fighters. The German reaction to the strategic offensive was revealed in an appreciation circulated by the navy on 18 October: because no large-scale Allied ground attack was likely in the immediate future, fighters were being transferred from the western front to Germany in the hope of inflicting such heavy losses on the Allied air forces that they would abandon 'the systematic destruction of the armaments industry and the communications network'. The defence of the Reich was the GAF's main task 'unambiguously and without reservation', and a reduction of its effort at the front would have to be accepted until the re-equipment of existing units and the establishment of new ones brought about the expected increase in fighter strength, for the results which could be achieved on any of the fronts were slight in comparison with the benefits of successful Reich defence, which would be 'shared by all elements of the armed forces and would affect the whole conduct of the war to a very high degree'—a point which was very soon illustrated by reports that, according to Speer, 30–35 per cent of factories in western Germany were at a standstill because of air attacks.

Less than a month later, this policy was abruptly reversed, and from 8 November evidence of the move of considerable fighter forces to the west accumulated at a great rate. On that day the Luftwaffe ground command in Holland wanted a special allocation of petrol 'for the fighter Gruppen arriving' in its area during the next four days and gave the expected locations of some of them; spoof wireless telegraph traffic was laid on to disguise the move, and a special conference was arranged at Cologne to discuss details. The air of haste and secrecy surrounding the operation was heightened by references in the same context to 'the special contingency known to you', and by a prohibition on using radio communications or displaying the customary unit badges, but within a week the hurry with which everything had been done was causing aircraft to arrive at the wrong airfields and delays in the provision of labour for servicing aircraft and for the construction of runways and parking-places. It was presumably an effort to sort out this kind of problem which gave us a clearer indication of the scale and importance of the operation, for on 16 November the main ground command in the central Rhineland called for daily serviceability returns from all its airfields 'for the type of aircraft intended in the bringing-up of fighters'. Since this rather colourless translation did not convey the full meaning of the original German, a comment took the unusual course of giving the word—*Jaegeraufmarsch*—and of explaining that in military contexts *Aufmarsch* denoted the assembly of forces for a planned

operation, and that it had been used in this sense to describe the
Allied dispositions on the eve of D-Day. Clearly, something big
was afoot, and this signal gave deeper meaning to several others
chronicling the arrival of fighters on west German airfields or
listing the units occupying them which had been transmitted in
the course of the previous four days and were still coming in.
By the 23rd, later information of the same type suggested that
the *Jaegeraufmarsch* was complete, and after another week
Luftflotte Reich admitted that the Allies had recognized the
new concentration of fighters and were trying to lure them into
the air and destroy them by sending large and well-escorted
bomber forces to raid north-west Germany.

p.m./16
HP 7224
1620/20

The reason why so many fighters were suddenly concentrated
behind the front was never even hinted at in any of the decodes,
and there is no sign in any of the Hut 3 signals that it was discovered at the time. What was it? The most likely answer is
that a powerful striking force was being assembled to support
the offensive in the Ardennes. This did not in fact begin for another month, but Hitler is now known to have hoped to launch
it sooner. When detailed planning orders for it were issued in
mid-November, everything was to be in readiness by the 27th,
and it was only at the last minute that a postponement (the
consequence of the acute petrol shortage) until 10 December
was announced. A similar explanation—which incidentally re-
veals how very sudden the postponement on 26 November was
—almost certainly underlay an order of the 25th for GAF West
to release the staff of Fliegerdivision 3 (which had been under
its command since 6 November) at 0700 hours next morning
and put it at the disposal of OKL; no doubt this was to become
the headquarters staff controlling the fighters in the operation
which was then still expected to begin twenty-four hours later.
It seems in retrospect tolerably clear, therefore, that Ultra
threw up plenty of evidence about the air component of the
planned attack (though none about the postponement) but unfortunately not the slightest clue to the purpose behind all the
activity it reported.

The chief reason why no suspicions were aroused at the time
was that the fighters were almost as well placed to deal with the
heavy bombing raids which were now being aimed at the Ruhr

and other industrial centres as they were to support an offensive in the Ardennes; the liberation of France and Belgium had so constricted the area the Germans occupied that it was no longer as easy as formerly to draw strategic deductions from geographical evidence about the placing of troops or aircraft, or to sense from it the kind of distinction which was drawn in the 18 October appreciation just quoted. Another reason was that in the absence of positive news (itself certainly the consequence of Hitler's stringent security rules about the offensive, which allowed only a very small number of senior officers to know anything about it) that a major operation had been postponed, there was nothing to indicate that anything had happened in the last few days of November to parallel the breathless haste which had been so apparent a fortnight earlier. Subsequent airfield returns showed that the aircraft were still in the same places, and it was no more possible in early December than in late November to deduce why they had been put there in the first place. A conference of commanding officers of almost all the fighter Geschwader on the western front was convened at an airfield north of Koblenz on 5 December, but there was nothing to suggest what must certainly have been its agenda—to concert measures for the attack which was then intended to begin in five days' time. Nor was there any reason to attach more than the most general significance to a complaint by Model (who was to command the assault) on 30 November that the Allies' mastery of the air was still increasing and that troops and civilians were undergoing continuous and almost unopposed attacks; what privileged recipients of his message were to understand, no doubt, was that the new fighter forces had not altered the adverse balance of air power from which the Germans had been suffering since June, and that this boded ill for the offensive.

One sizable set of entries stood on the credit side of the rather unsatisfactory Ultra balance-sheet in the late autumn, though its worth was still limited by the impossibility of grasping its full meaning. A newly constituted authority, Jagdfuehrer ('Jafue' in German signals jargon) Mittelrhein (Officer Commanding Fighters, Central Rhineland), kept us regularly informed of the strength and disposition of his forces during the second and third weeks of December, so that when the attack came on the 16th we knew the strength and whereabouts of the GAF fighter formations he controlled better than that of the army divisions they supported. But there was no hint, until then, of why there were so many of them under Jafue Mittelrhein's command.

If the intelligence derived from it at the time fell far short of what might have been secured in only slightly more favourable circumstances, therefore, the episode of the *Jaegeraufmarsch* nevertheless retains interest as an instructive example of the way in which even a great deal of completely accurate information from an absolutely reliable source may not yield up all its secrets if a vital clue is missing. The job of military intelligence is to find the clue, but sometimes the problem is insoluble. There was nothing in the decodes, in the index or in accumulated experience to explain why the fighter aircraft had been concentrated in the west, and this was partly because only a few of those who originated Enigma messages knew the reason themselves. During these weeks Ultra provided if anything more information than usual about the GAF, but by denying knowledge of his plans to all but a few generals Hitler prevented the plans from being mentioned in Enigma and us from understanding what we read. Thus although essential evidence was in our hands, we could not penetrate its innermost meaning nor appreciate the warnings it contained. To read Ultra was not always to read what was in the minds of German generals; sometimes it only told us what junior officers wrote on their signal-pads.[1]

One valuable service performed by Ultra during the autumn was in providing the intelligence and technical sections at the Air Ministry with a steady flow of information about jet aircraft, which were now coming into regular use in the GAF and in consequence were frequently mentioned in Enigma messages. Special importance attached to it because the British and

1. But see the suggestions on p. 202 that the German offensive might perhaps have been deduced if the GAF evidence had been seen imaginatively in the light of that about 6 Pz Army.

Americans were several months behind in this respect (the first Gloster Meteors did not fly on RAF operations until the spring of 1945) and their fastest piston-engined aircraft were 100 m.p.h. slower. Every scrap of news about German progress was therefore precious, and it is now generally recognized that had Hitler hastened the production of jet fighters in the winter of 1943–4—as he could have done, had he not insisted on trying to convert them into bombers—the Allied mastery of the air over France, about which the German army complained so long and bitterly from June onwards, could not have been achieved on the same scale.

Some of the special detachments set up to use jets in front-line operations began to report regularly in October and November, so that evidence of the tasks assigned to them, the success they claimed in performing them and the numbers of pilots and aircraft engaged accumulated steadily. The greatest part of our information concerned the Me 262, but there were occasional mentions of other types, although these were not being manufactured in such large numbers. Two squadrons of the primarily reconnaissance Arado 234 (identified by the names of their commanders, Goetz and Sperling) were known, and a decision about the former made by Jodl on 25 October can perhaps also be seen as explaining the change in fighter policy outlined above:[1] OKL was planning to move very strong fighter forces to the west if the Allies attacked, said Jodl, but shortages of petrol and trained pilots prevented it until then; meanwhile Detachment Goetz was to be given priority in the allocation of new Ar 234s so that it could carry out strategic reconnaissance, though only on a small scale. A report by one of the units operating the rocket-powered Me 163 that it was no longer training pilots implicitly confirmed the suspicion that serious difficulties were being encountered in operating this fast but very unstable aircraft under service conditions. Early in October III KG 2 was identified experimenting with a new propeller-driven type, the Do 335, at a base south of Stuttgart and a description of the aircraft was circulated three weeks later, presumably in anticipation of its widespread appearance.

1. See p. 176.

The lion's share of Ultra mentions fell to the Me 262, which we had already reported in action during the summer.[1] 'Detachment Schenk' of KG 51, based at Rheine in Westphalia, reported its strength from time to time; this rose from ten aircraft and thirteen pilots on 11 October to twenty-seven and forty-seven a month later, and one of the comparatively few urgent operational signals of this period gave advance warning of its intention to raid Eindhoven in support of a tank attack on 27 October.

These paragraphs give some indication of the intelligence received about the development of new aircraft at this time, and are included for that reason, but they do little more than hint at either its volume or its technical content and operational value. But even a large selection from the signals would still give a very inadequate idea of Ultra's contribution in this field. In the first place, many items in the decodes were either almost incomprehensible to all but engineers trained in the newest aircraft technology (of whom there were naturally none in Hut 3) or were plainly not urgent; they were therefore not signalled, but either teleprinted or typed and sent to London by bag—and are consequently not open to inspection in the Public Record Office. Secondly, technical detail requires collation and interpretation before it becomes intelligible to any but the expert. The Air Ministry relied heavily on Ultra, but of course also used other sources when compiling appreciations of German progress with jet aircraft. These appreciations have not yet been placed in the public domain, nor have the Air Ministry signals conveying the most Ultra-based parts of them, which were sent over SLU links and read in Hut 3. Without them, only a very imperfect picture can be given from the direct Hut 3 signals alone—there would be a close analogy in the Ultra material dealing with beam-bombing, radar and the development of the V-weapons at Peenemünde, which was routed by a specialist department in Hut 3 direct to the appropriate section at the Air Ministry without passing through our normal channels at all, had this not lately become public knowledge through Professor R. V. Jones's book, *Most Secret War*.

1. See p. 86 above.

Morale, supplies and reinforcements

Comparatively little information about morale, supply and reinforcements was reported by Ultra during the autumn—the nonurgent and usually lengthy communications involved were naturally among the first to revert to teleprinter links as these were restored—but enough was intercepted to show that the German military economy was increasingly strained as existing tendencies[1] became more marked. Towards the end of October, for instance, OKW noted that further signs of disintegration had appeared and ordered the severest measures, including the immediate execution of officers in front of their own men, against anyone endangering the Wehrmacht's will to fight, while Hitler virtually imprisoned his troops on the western front by reiterating Himmler's former prohibition against crossing the Rhine from west to east.

A single striking ammunition report was curiously reminiscent of Rommel's Mediterranean shipping problems before Alamein—675 tons of shells lost when the supply ship *Wachtfels* was sunk at the Hook of Holland seriously added to the shortage from which Army Group B (and I and II SS Corps in particular) was already suffering on 2 October—but most of our supply information concerned petrol, the shortage of which was now really acute. Goering imposed severe fuel conservation measures on the GAF at the beginning of October (they included an order that cars, driven by producer gas or flyingbomb fuel if possible, should be used to tow trains of supply vehicles); some airfields in southern Germany were told on 13 October that they would receive no more petrol for motor transport until the end of November, and before then one of the fighter divisions engaged on Reich defence had forbidden the use of motorized transport altogether. There were already several signs that air operations were being restricted by the fuel shortage several weeks before Goering issued a comprehensive order on the subject in mid-November: operations were to be ruthlessly cut down, and were only to be undertaken

1. See pp. 143–5 above.

when weather and other conditions made success probable; certain types of activity were to be discontinued altogether—for instance, night ground-attack operations and transport flights (except to supply the Channel Islands and the besieged fortresses). The army was no better off. On 25 October Rundstedt's Chief Quartermaster imposed daily petrol consumption maxima (250 cubic metres for Army Group B, 150 cubic metres for Army Group G), based on his forecasts of the ten-day allocations he expected to receive, encouraged the use of producer gas and diesel as substitutes, and urged even the Panzer divisions to solve their supply problems by establishing horse-transport columns.

The evidence for an acute fuel shortage was overwhelming, but nothing in any of the decodes suggested (what was in fact the case) that current operations were being restricted partly in order to conserve petrol for a special purpose—to build up stocks for an offensive. The natural conclusion was that the restrictions were simply the direct and inevitable consequence of the loss of foreign supplies and the destruction of petroleum plants by bombing. It may well be, therefore, that Ultra inadvertently promoted a recrudescence of the dangerous over-optimism which it had perhaps seemed to encourage in September.[1] In the absence (it was believed) of any other grounds for expecting a German offensive, it could be argued that a prime reason why the enemy could not undertake one was that he had too little petrol. There were serious flaws in the logic of this argument, but it is a great deal easier to see them now than it could have been in late November and early December 1944.

Signs continued to multiply that Allied pressure in the west was drawing troops away from other parts of the contracting perimeter of German-occupied territory. Some transport details strongly suggested that 269 Division was en route from Denmark to 19 Army at Karlsruhe in mid-October, and it was soon identified in that area. The division had come from Norway, the evacuation of which was shortly speeded up at Hitler's order. Several formations which had lately been on the Russian front were discovered in the west, among them 2 Flak Division, 212

1. See pp. 125–6 above and p. 189 below.

Division and artillery and mountain troops from East Prussia, Czechoslovakia and Norway, but there had been such heavy losses among commanders of infantry regiments that in mid-October OKH was forcibly drafting suitable young officers from other units. A little was heard about the Volkssturm, the territorial force raised from the remaining civilian population under the pressure of emergency ('Everyone fit to work is in principle fit to serve'—without medical examination); the third and fourth waves were called up in October, and the organization of the Volkssturm was soon said to be in full swing. Westphal quickly announced OB West's willingness to use it to guard lines of communication and even at the front in quiet sectors, but changed his mind almost at once. The reason for the change came several weeks later in a circular which Keitel sent to theatre commanders on 10 January. The Volkssturm, he explained, consisted of men of all ages who were being called upon to defend their native soil in the hour of its greatest need while also continuing the work of national importance on which they were engaged; it therefore followed that the Volkssturm could not be employed outside the Reich nor take over the Wehrmacht's duty of defending it except when a particular area was under immediate threat. The contrast between Rundstedt's readiness to use the Volkssturm at the front and Keitel's insistence on protecting the industrial labour-force threw into sharp relief the pressing needs of both and the harsh competition for manpower which was now one of the German government's chief worries. Less than a month later, with the fighting now almost everywhere inside the frontiers, Hitler returned to a view more like Rundstedt's, ordering the Volkssturm to be used in mixed battle-groups with the field army, since it was not of much value on its own.

7

The Ardennes offensive

How much forewarning?

The Ardennes offensive was Hitler's in design and execution, and Hitler's alone. Astonishingly, he seems first to have thought of it in the same moment of desperation as the Mortain counter-attack, which it in some ways resembles—a bold idea which could not succeed because the necessary resources were lacking. Outline planning for it began in the second half of August after a conversation with Keitel and Speer, and before long 6 Panzer Army was set up to carry out the attack under the faithful Nazi Sepp Dietrich. This was in mid-September, when Hitler already knew that he could prevent the Allies from exploiting Antwerp fully for several weeks. The target date was at first fixed for late November, partly because that was the earliest moment by which German troops were expected to recover from the exhaustion of retreat, and partly in relation to the probable reopening of the port and the renewed Allied pressure which was bound to follow. The recapture of Antwerp was the primary objective from the start, and success before Christmas would in fact have enabled the Germans to destroy the docks (if they could not hold them) within two or three weeks after the first Allied ships were unloaded.

The forest and mountain region of the Ardennes was chosen for the blow because Hitler was confident that the Allies would refuse to believe that he would try to repeat his triumph of May and June 1940 through notoriously difficult country in the depth of winter, and early in October he ordered the records of the *Blitzkrieg* to be brought out to serve as guidelines. (His confidence was completely justified by the wording of SHAEF intelligence reports in November and December, and by Bradley's action in manning over sixty miles of the Ardennes front with only four divisions—two without experience in battle and two recovering from heavy casualties sustained at Aachen.) An elaborate cover-plan was devised: it was put about that an OKW reserve was being assembled to protect the Ruhr and for an operation called *Wacht am Rhein* (Watch on the Rhine), a name calculated to suggest defence rather than attack.[1] The cover-plan was in the main successful in deluding the Allies. When 5 Panzer Army (the other half of the eventual striking force) moved up from Nancy to Aachen, the chief pieces were already on the board two months before the battle, but 5 Pz Army had to be relieved at the front before it could prepare to attack.

Up to this point, nothing was likely to give the Allies wind of what was brewing—German security was so strict that in the whole of Army Group G, for instance, only the commander and his Chief of Staff knew about the forthcoming offensive. After the middle of October preparations could not remain completely hidden, but Allied intelligence appears regularly to have misinterpreted the information it received about them.

Hitler summoned Rundstedt's and Model's Chiefs of Staff to his East Prussian headquarters on 22 October, and sent them back with an outline plan. The two Field Marshals thought Antwerp too ambitious an objective, and proposed Aachen instead; Hitler rejected their suggestion. Right up to the end, Model continued to point out the risks the Antwerp scheme involved (they included the fact that OKW had never planned a campaign before!), but his final operation orders corresponded exactly with Hitler's outline of 22 October. The two Panzer armies began to concentrate at the beginning of November, but various problems forced repeated postponements of the attack: just before the date (27 November) first announced for the completion of preparations, for instance, it was discovered that sufficient petrol could not be stockpiled until 10 December. Hitler reached his command post outside Bad Nauheim on that day but (again because of the fuel shortage) had to authorize two successive postponements before the tanks rolled forward at dawn on 16 December.

Suspicions that some kind of blow was contemplated were first aroused in the second half of October, when both SHAEF and 12 Army Group said that armour then assembling east of the Rhine

1. Those who were misled did not include the readers of Ultra, in which the cover-name *Wacht am Rhein* did not appear even once.

might be ready to strike by about 1 December. Unfortunately, this possibility was gradually lost sight of during the next six weeks. The armour was at first widely held to be a 'fire-brigade' which would be worn down by attrition as it shifted from one part of the front to another to meet a succession of Allied attacks; a captured document which revealed measures to conserve petrol was taken for evidence of scarcity, not of stocking up for an attack; SHAEF even dismissed the quadrupling of the GAF fighter force in the west[1] as incapable of affecting the military situation because pilots and petrol were both in short supply. All through November there was a widespread illusion, traceable to reports that 6 Pz Army had moved from Westphalia to the west bank of the Rhine about Cologne, that Rundstedt would unleash a counter-attack as the Allies were crossing the Roer (which they had not managed to do by 16 December) but would not attempt anything more ambitious; the prevalence of the illusion testifies to the success of one part of the German cover-plan. SHAEF's and 21 Army Group's Intelligence Summaries lost track of 6 Pz Army during the first ten days of December, but nevertheless discounted rumours that it was about to drive on Antwerp, on the ground that the Germans lacked the means to mount an offensive. By this time something like the buoyant optimism of September was returning; it survived the shocks of 16 December in remarks like Bradley's 'Let them come', Horrocks's 'The farther they come the fewer will get back' and Patton's 'Let them get to Paris, then we'll saw 'em off at the base.'

Just as before Arnhem, counsel was again darkened by more disputes over strategy between Eisenhower and Montgomery. Again, too, a few voices were raised at the last moment in protest against facile optimism, but went unheeded. There were three options open to 6 Panzer Army, General Strong told the Supreme Commander, and one of them was a counter-attack in the Ardennes. His own account does not suggest that he pressed his case hard, and this (as Pogue points out) is the crucial point. Only a week before the attack, an experienced American intelligence officer predicted something not very unlike what was about to happen, but was not listened to because he had a reputation as an alarmist. Otherwise, however, the universal opinion was that the Germans were not in a position to deliver an attack, with the result that surprise was complete on 16 December.

1. The Ultra evidence for this is discussed on pp. 178–80.

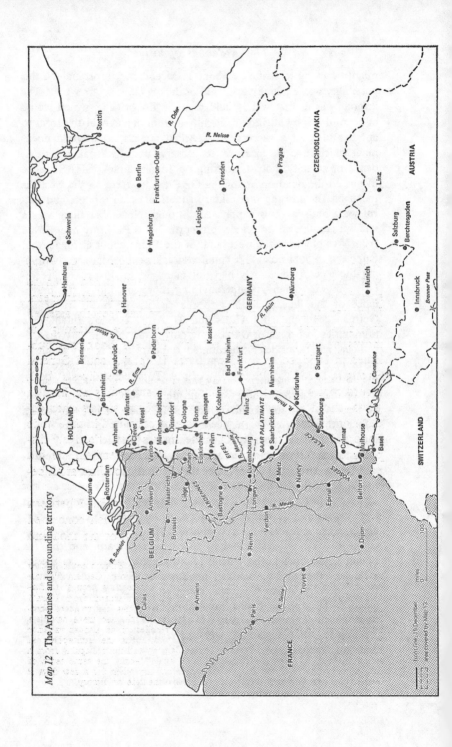

Map 12 The Ardennes and surrounding territory

When post-mortems were held and scapegoats sought, Ultra was blamed (at least by implication) because it had given no specific warning; this is what Tedder's account seems to mean, for instance, and Major-General Belchem has recently asserted that there was 'virtually no signal intelligence indicating the moves of the formations involved'. Tedder's book was published in 1966, so he could not name Ultra; nor could General Strong in 1968, but the identity of the 'Top Secret digests', both record copies of which he claims were destroyed, is not hard to guess—and if, as seems likely, they were Ultra signals, then another copy has survived and can now be consulted in the Public Record Office. Inspection of these signals also effectively disposes of the even wider charge—just as frequently made but even more erroneous—that there was little or no Ultra at all before and during the Ardennes offensive.[1]

In fact, over 11,000 signals were sent out by Hut 3 between 1 October 1944 and 31 January 1945; roughly half concerned the western front, half the Italian front. Five or six thousand

1. The legend that there was little or no Ultra because Enigma could neither be intercepted nor broken was first put about by Group Captain Winterbotham—who was in the Far East at the time. It has recently been given further currency by Mr Lewin ('there were no tell-tale intercepts from Ultra') and others, sometimes with the explanation that land-lines had replaced wireless telegraphy. The numerous signals quoted in this chapter are a complete refutation of the legend in all its forms. My recollection is also at variance with what Mr Lewin has apparently been told about the atmosphere at Bletchley in December 1944. I remember no flagging and no 'collapsing from a simple inability to face "going through it all again" '—only the same sense of fury and frustration as was felt by the whole country when for a few days it seemed that the Germans might still turn back the tide of victory.

signals (an average of between forty and fifty a day) cannot be dismissed so lightly. So far from conveying little intelligence, these signals had a great deal to say about German movements in and near the Ardennes during the weeks preceding 16 December. The information they contain is not wholly free from ambiguity, and hence easily lends itself to hindsighted interpretation which would do grave injustice to those who handled it operationally at the time; but when all due allowance has been made it does seem to point much more convincingly towards a coming attack than it was then held to do.

The day after the Arnhem landings, SS Operations Headquarters ordered a rest and refit of the SS Panzer formations in the west; it was to begin with the transfer of 1, 2, 9 and 12 SS Pz Divisions, three heavy tank detachments, and the corps troops of I SS Pz Corps to 'the staff of 6 Panzer Army, the setting up of which has been ordered under Oberstgruppenführer Sepp Dietrich'. Various bases were assigned for the purpose, including Sennelager near Paderborn. It was only a few days since Hitler had created 6 Pz Army, the existence of which was made known to Allied intelligence by this signal.

18 Septembe
HP 1378
1626/27

Further details of the rest and refit programme followed within a week. I SS Corps (1 and 12 SS Pz Divisions) was to use the Münsterlager training ground near Osnabrück, Pz Lehr (now first mentioned in this connection) was to join the divisions at Sennelager, and 6 Pz Army's headquarters was also somewhere near Osnabrück. Soon we had two more locations— 9 and 12 SS near Hanover. An important communication from Keitel about the middle of October explained what was going on: 6 Pz Army was designed as OKW reserve; it was to control the rest and refit of the divisions already mentioned, but progress would depend upon how soon various battle groups now engaged at the front could be pulled out and sent to their new bases. On the same day OKH added a few administrative details about Pz Lehr, which was to be ready again by 31 October (sooner, it was implied, than the SS divisions). At the same time it became clear that the rest and refit had been ordered by

14 October
HP 3693
)002/18

Hitler himself and that generous allocations of tanks and guns were being made to the SS divisions.

The full scale of the programme was revealed in a message of 5 October which we were not able to decode and signal until the 20th. According to SS Operations Headquarters, reporting the result of discussions with OKH, 1, 2, 9 and 12 SS Pz Divisions and Pz Lehr were originally intended to rest and refit in October, 10 SS and three army Panzer divisions[1] in November. OKH had ascertained, however, that 9 SS could not rest and refit until after the end of October, and the whole November plan was still undetermined. Manning and equipment levels were next laid down: 1, 2 and 12 SS would be brought up to full strength and would each have 134 tanks (including twenty-eight Mark IV, twenty-eight Panthers, about forty Tigers and twenty-one tracked anti-tank guns), 135 armoured troop carriers, 1750 lorries and a full complement of heavy weapons.

Keitel's concern about making the necessary withdrawals was evidently in further elaboration of OKH's doubts about the feasibility of parts of the programme. Both were soon underlined by events. The Aachen battles held I SS Corps in their grip, and Pz Lehr, 1 and 12 SS were not expected to get free until towards the end of October; only 2 SS began to move east at the middle of the month and was receiving rations near Paderborn early in November. An air of uncertainty clung to both 9 and 10 SS, which had so often been grouped together in II SS Corps. They were linked again on 11 October—clothing issues for both divisions were being directed to points not far from Osnabrück, in the 6 Pz Army area—but 10 SS's fighting elements remained near Aachen for the greater part of November and moved no farther away than a position opposite Venlo at the end of the month. At about the same time II SS Pz Corps was on the move, but when it shortly turned up just outside Bonn it had no troops under its command and intended no operations.

After the issue on 22 October of a long list of report centres (all in the Osnabrück–Hanover area) for the divisions already

---

1. The German was ambiguous here, and could also be translated to mean '3 Pz Division'. The version given above seemed the more likely, because 3 Pz Division was known to be in Russia.

known to be connected with 'SS Panzer Army 6' (as it was called on this occasion—the use of the 'SS' prefix was not regular until later on), several weeks now passed without mention of divisional movements. Instead, we could report the allocation of a dozen howitzers (but only in default of Panzer howitzers) to each of 1, 2, 9 and 12 SS Pz Divisions, and of a 'winter issue' for their tanks, guns and transport (deficiencies were to be reported to OKH), and the provision of more rocket batteries as army troops. A reference on 11 November to a 'short-term repair scheme', important enough to be given a code-name, which affected 2, 9, 11, 21 and 116 Pz Divisions, 17 SS PzGr and 12 Volksgrenadier Division, gave a hint that these too might perhaps be involved in the same forward planning for which there was now so much evidence although its purpose was still obscure.[1]

Meanwhile, however, it was clear that there were heavy troop movements from east to west across the Rhine: it was a fair inference that they concerned 6 Panzer Army, although no link between it and Army Group B was positively established until a fortnight after the movements began. On 2 November Army Group B called for fighter protection for the unloading of important troop transports during the next two days at various points in an arc of some twenty miles radius from northwest to south-west of Cologne; the request was signalled with high priority at dawn on the 3rd. This was the first of thirty or more similar signals sent during the remaining forty-five days before the German attack—that is, an average of two signals every three days. The requests always came from Army Group B, never from its subordinates, and always spoke of either railway transports or unloadings; we could seldom connect either with specific units, but one major and several minor exceptions to this rule will be discussed shortly. Two general areas were constantly in question. One was the Cologne–Aachen–München-Gladbach triangle, but this appeared comparatively seldom; the other, which was mentioned with steadily increas-

---

1. The fact that 2, 9 and 116 Pz Divisions were engaged in the December offensive while 3 Pz Division stayed on the Russian front gave subsequent confirmation to the translation 'three army Panzer divisions' in HP 3935 on p. 193, above.

ing frequency and sometimes almost shrill urgency, was based on the Rhine crossings from Bonn to Koblenz and lay between the Cologne–Aachen railway and the Moselle valley, with a growing emphasis on the southern half of the area—that is to say, the portion directly behind the Ardennes from which the attack was later delivered. No connection was established between the institution of these patrols and the move of fighter aircraft westwards from Germany which has already been noted,[1] and in any case the fighters did not begin to arrive until some time after the patrols began.

A third phenomenon coincided with the others. Throughout November and December the German State Railways key was broken; the somewhat cryptic information it carried only yielded up its full meaning when consignment-numbers could be linked with individual field units and when the figure-code which disguised the identity of the various transport control offices was understood. Even then, it was much more often possible to determine where a train had come from than where it was going to, save that in the case of the large number reported passing through Bentheim (where one of the main east–west routes crosses the German–Dutch frontier) a destination somewhere between (say) Cleves and Roermond could safely be presumed.[2] From about the beginning of November, however, more details began to come to light about some of these transport movements, particularly when they were on a large scale. For instance, one of two movements of 3 November, consisting of forty-one and twenty-eight trains respectively and both to be unloaded in Cologne, had come from Hamburg and Schwerin, the other from the Wehrmacht Transport Office in Berlin; the first carried 352 Volksgrenadier Division (which later guarded the southern shoulder of the 'bulge'), the contents of the second were not stated but its arrival was notified to 7 Army and 5 Panzer Army. A week later another railway movement conveyed the command echelon of 6 Panzer Army from its training area, a third brought 12 SS Pz Division westwards, and seven-

---

1. See p. 178 above.
2. Most of the Bentheim trains were westbound. The occasional mention of eastbound trains loaded with 'evacuation goods' suggested the looting of Holland.

teen more trains (contents unknown) were delivered to 7 Army and 5 Pz Army. In a yet further case it was possible to determine that troop transports were to be given priority, that railway bridges over the Rhine were involved, and that the four armies in the centre were concerned but not 15 or 19 Armies at the northern and southern extremities of the front. On two out of the three separate days on which these movements took place, requests for fighter protection for railway transports were intercepted.

The last example of this sort of thing was also by a long way the most informative. On 2 December Army Group B asked with special urgency for fighter protection to be given to troop movements mainly in the Moselle valley area, and a little later in the day GAF West reported what they were: a total of nearly 200 trains carrying a dozen different formations, almost half of which took part in the Battle of the Bulge a fortnight later (they included the Führer Escort Brigade, which formed one of the armoured spearheads), were to be unloaded in the Eifel and Saar districts, while a further forty were destined for Alsace.[1]

2 December
HP 8448
0842/2

The huge scale of a transport programme designed to move an army staff and half-a-dozen tank divisions over 150 miles and across the densely packed industry of the Ruhr under almost continuous air-raids soon caused problems. On 10 November, only a week after it started, the Director-General of Transport was demanding that 6 SS Panzer Army tell all its formations to ensure strict punctuality, as otherwise the prescribed time-table—which already provided for the maximum possible number of trains per day—could not be observed nor delays made good. Only the previous day, he went on, the Kassel Transport Office had complained that 2 SS Pz Division had fallen thirty-six hours behind schedule, Pz Lehr twenty-four, and 12 SS about twelve so far as could be ascertained. This illuminating insight into the movements of the best of the German armour was signalled with the highest priority as soon as it was received on 12 November.

10 Novembe
HPs 6372,
6377
0602/12

---

1. According to Schramm 438, about 800 trains were used in November and early December to move 6 Pz Army westwards. A total not far short of half that number can be accounted for in Ultra signals.

Despite these difficulties, several divisions reached their appointed places during the second half of the month: 9 and 10 SS were round Euskirchen (a few miles south-west of Cologne) on the 21st, 2 SS at München-Gladbach on the 24th, I SS Corps also south-west of Cologne on the 26th and 27th and apparently preparing to take command of Pz Lehr, 1, 2, 9, 10 and 12 SS Pz Divisions, 116 Pz in association with the SS divisions but still on the east bank of the Rhine outside Cologne where it took delivery of a few Panther tanks on 1 December. Ammunition and spares for 6 Pz Army reached dumps south-west of Cologne during the first days of December, but the most spectacular of the comparatively few items of information about equipment concerned an evidently quite elaborate scheme, sponsored by OKW, for the surrender of lorries (over 1000 were accounted for) to 6 Pz Army by Kesselring's command in Italy.

There was still one more noticeable development in the last week of November (the recurring coincidence of date now seems unmistakably striking)—a series of orders for aerial reconnaissance which repeatedly directed attention to the same two areas and which, like the railway patrols, betrayed an increasingly urgent note. Both areas first appeared in a pressing Army Group B request on the evening of the 24th: one (the Eupen–Malmédy area) covered the direct approach to Liège, which the Germans knew to be an important Allied supply centre; the other was along the Prüm–Houffalize axis, which they later used as their main route towards the Meuse crossings at Dinant and Givet, fifty miles farther upstream. Occasionally varied by requests for reconnaissance in the area of what Army Group B called 'the third defensive battle of Aachen', this pattern was repeated almost daily for the next three weeks. By 29 November the call was for reconnaissance of the Meuse crossings from Liège to Givet, and this now became a regular daily event. It was soon being carried out by night as well, and one unit was told precisely what to look for: Were reinforcements being brought up? Where were the Allied tank concentrations and supply dumps? Soon the day flights were entrusted for safety and as 'a matter of the greatest urgency' to the fast Arado 234 jets of Detachment Sperling, which on 8 December

was told to secure good photographs of the same Meuse crossings and of the road-junction at Ciney (a fortnight later Ciney
was to be the westernmost point reached by 5 Panzer Army).

Finally, a big conference of the commanding officers of
fighter squadrons was convened for the evening of 5 December
at an airfield outside Koblenz. The purpose of the meeting was
not stated, but summonses were sent to all the main fighter formations—Jagdkorps I, Jagddivisionen 1, 3 and 5, and Jafue
Mittelrhein. A day or two later Jafue Mittelrhein's latest
strength return (we were decoding them almost every day now,
and continued to do so for some time to come) showed thirty-
five Me 109s serviceable out of sixty, and about seventy Fw
190s out of 108. On the 10th, the figures suddenly rose, and on
the day before the offensive began—with the increase still unexplained—they stood at 164 aircraft (almost equally divided
between Fw 190s and Me 109s) serviceable out of 340, with
crews for half as many more. This one fighter control, then, was
capable of putting upwards of three hundred planes into the air
if its repair and recovery services exerted themselves—a larger
number than had operated over a single section of the front for
a long time past.

The signals have so far been presented without commentary in
order to limit the advantages hindsight confers. It is impossible
now to forget what happened ten days before Christmas 1944
or to read the story of the previous weeks in any other light,
but those who had to make up their minds that autumn about
the likelihood or otherwise of a German attack had nothing to
go on but the inconveniently ambiguous clues they could find in
Ultra and other sources. One advantage of hindsight cannot be
discarded, however. Historical investigation always telescopes
events, making them appear closer together than they really
were. Juxtaposition may suggest links between them, patterns
and perspectives which it would have been difficult or impossible to detect at the time. The evidence from which an offensive
in the Ardennes might have been deduced took three months to
accumulate, but it can be examined in a day or two. In consequence, it probably makes a different impression on the histo-

rian today from that which it made on the intelligence officer
thirty-five years ago. By the time the Germans struck, some of
the October signals had evidently either receded into the background of memory or had been accorded only transient
significance and banished from it altogether. In any case, military intelligence officers are more accustomed in wartime to
dealing with short-term problems than to forecasting the re-
moter future from slender evidence scattered over a long period.

Even so, it remains extraordinary that Ultra did not arouse
more forebodings. The signals point at least as plausibly towards a coming attack as in the opposite direction; at worst,
they should have been enough to prevent the comfortable view
that the enemy was not contemplating offensive action from
being so lightly preferred. A curious feature of the SHAEF Intelligence Summaries in November is their tendency to discuss
Allied rather than enemy intentions—and thus to see the future
in terms of an Allied attack provoking a German counter-
stroke, to the exclusion of all other possibilities.

The first Ultra news about 6 Panzer Army was also the
clearest indication that its purpose was offensive. The decodes
underlying HP 1378 of 18 September did not explain why the
new army had been set up; but the aggressive character of its
Nazi commander, its apparent monopoly of the SS Panzer divisions and their restoration to fighting efficiency, and the fact
that it was plainly not intended as the instrument of a quick reaction to the Arnhem landings but for some larger purpose—all
this strongly suggested preparation to attack at a place and
time unknown. SHAEF was evidently of this opinion in October, but gradually changed its mind as the weeks passed without positive confirmation. Yet the absence of confirmation did
nothing to weaken the logic of the original conclusion, and
there were two simple explanations for it: the random selection
of intercepts which land-lines enforced, and the certainty that
the Germans were no less bound than the Allies had been
before D-Day to mask an attack (if they planned one) with security precautions. No news therefore was not bound to be
good news. It has never been authoritatively stated, though
sometimes hinted, that intelligence staffs had by now come to

rely so heavily on Ultra that they took the absence of unequivocal evidence that an attack was planned to be proof of the
contrary, and therefore reassured themselves that none was intended. The charge is unconvincing unless fully substantiated,
because it ascribes intellectual naïveté to men sophisticated
enough to know the danger of arguing from the negative and
well enough versed in Ultra to realize that it provided absolute
certainty only on rare occasions like Rommel's Alam Halfa attack before Alamein or Hitler's order for the thrust from Mortain to Avranches. However, a recurrence in other quarters of
the complacency and over-confidence of September may have
made some of them forget that (for instance) 352 Division had
been waiting on Omaha beach and two SS Divisions at Arnhem, although Ultra had said little on the first occasion and
they had disregarded its warnings on the second. A similar state
of mind may have induced others to look in vain for a new and
unambiguous statement of German intentions rather than to
keep prominently in mind the one piece of evidence that ap-
proximated to it—HP 1378—even though time might seem to
have tarnished its value. Had all subsequent information been
analysed in the light of two alternative hypotheses—that an attack was, or was not, planned—and had the results been compared, then the conclusion could hardly have been avoided that
both hypotheses were tenable but that the former was a shade
the more convincing.

There is no sign that such impartial comparative studies, if
undertaken, had much influence upon final conclusions, and
during November the Intelligence Summaries put out weekly by
SHAEF and the two Army Groups committed themselves to
the view that the enemy lacked the resources (particularly the
petrol) for an offensive and that he was concentrating his armour for nothing more ambitious than a counter-attack as soon
as the Allies unbalanced themselves by striking out for Cologne
and the Ruhr. It was ironic that, just as in September the Germans were convinced that Montgomery's habitual caution ruled
out an air-drop at Arnhem, so the Allies now argued that a soldier of the old school like von Rundstedt would not be so rash
as to begin an attack which he lacked the resources to sustain.
Memories of Mortain might have suggested that there was a fal-

lacy in this argument, and so might HP 3693 of 14 October: for if the whole 6 Panzer Army rest and refit programme originated with Hitler personally, then it was quite on the cards that he might once more want to direct the tactical employment of the armour as well.

Speculation apart, moreover, a great deal of the Ultra intelligence received in November and early December accorded very ill with the comfortable conclusion that the German command was reconciled to being permanently on the defensive. Why, for instance, was it a matter of concern to Berlin that a single division had fallen a mere twelve hours behind schedule a week after the transport of 6 Panzer Army to the west bank of the Rhine began? Would so tiny a hitch deserve so much attention if the armour was only being moved forward to meet a contingency (an Allied attack across the Roer towards Cologne) which had not yet arisen and obviously would not arise for some time? But if the movement was so precisely timed that even the slightest delay was of great moment, might this not be because it had to be completed by a certain date? In that case, did it not probably follow that 6 Panzer Army was being assembled for some deliberately planned operation in the not very distant future? And what could this be but a large-scale attack?

Another look at the surrounding circumstances would have given some confirmation to this idea. As soon as the 6 Panzer Army transports began to roll about 2 November, Army Group B demanded air cover for them. But the fighters which provided it did not come from units which had moved westwards for the purpose: the *Jaegeraufmarsch* only began a week after the transports started. If the fighters did not come west to protect the trains, then, why did they come at all? And why did they stay, when they were badly needed at home as defence against the raids which were crippling German industry? Why had the policy of concentrating fighters in Germany, adopted two months previously,[1] been reversed now although the raids by Allied heavy bombers had increased during the autumn? Perhaps the fighters were coming west to support some future ac-

1. See p. 176 above.

tion by 6 Panzer Army? On its own, the GAF evidence does not positively suggest an offensive, but it begins to point in that direction as soon as it is seen in the context of 6 Panzer Army's activities. This does not seem to have been realized at the time.

In late November some of the evidence could still be read either way. The 'winter issue' would be needed in attack or defence. Divisions detraining west of Cologne would block a drive on the Ruhr from the Roer valley sector, where the Allies had been threateningly aggressive throughout the autumn. Concentrations farther south were well placed for counter-attack either on the Roer or towards Metz and the Saar, the other dangerously active part of the front. Even the priority given to the armies of the centre over those at the ends of the line could be explained in this way (the appointment of no less a figure than Himmler to defend the Upper Rhine, however, was a reminder that this too was a sensitive area and that the enfeebled 19 Army had a strong claim on the reinforcements which were for some reason now being deliberately denied it).

But although some of the evidence can easily be squared with the 'no attack' hypothesis, the rest hardly suggests it. There were enough straws in the wind to attract more than a glance or two in the opposite direction. Why should the Führer Escort Brigade, the mobile and fully armoured praetorian guard, be suddenly committed to the western front, unless to serve as the spearhead of an important attack? Did the close links between the transport arrangements for 5 Panzer Army, 6 Panzer Army and 7 Army portend a future operational link between them? Why was the hard-pressed Italian front being made to give up a thousand lorries, unless the west had some specially urgent reason to increase its mobility? (Did it occur to anyone to wonder whether this was yet another case where Ultra had got hold of one copy of a circular sent to many addressees, and whether other fronts were also being scoured for vehicles—as was in fact the case?) Should not Ultra have suggested that the opinion advanced in successive SHAEF Weekly Intelligence Summaries (those of 10 and 17 December) that armour was being withdrawn for rest and refit needed modification, whatever its source, because Ultra not only said nothing about it but had given several hints to the contrary?

Were not some of the trains for which fighter protection was required unloading parts of 6 Panzer Army a good deal too far forward to satisfy the theory that they were a counter-attack force? Troops who detrained on the general line Kall–Gerolstein–Bitburg (place-names which appeared in the first of Army Group B's requests and recurred frequently thereafter) were within ten or fifteen miles of the front in a sector held only weakly by 1 US Army, and well forward of the best north–south roads and railways nearer the Rhine which they would need to use swiftly if (in accordance with the prevailing theory) they were being held ready to be switched at a moment's notice to the Aachen or Saar fronts to meet a sudden Allied thrust. Was it not at least as likely that the positions they were taking up indicated an intention to make a sudden attack somewhere along the Ardennes front? Yet even in early December SHAEF believed that 'none of the divisions is in the line, or even known to be close up', and prefaced this opinion with a rhetorical phrase which betrays the deep roots struck by the theory that the Germans could not attack: 'The outward surface remains comparatively unchanged, but there has been quite considerable stirring within the sepulchre.' Ultra could not be mentioned directly, of course, but it in no way authorized an outlook like this, which it is therefore surprising to find expressed so firmly.

Bradley took his 'calculated risk' in the face of evidence which showed that there were strong enemy forces close to the most thinly held section of his line. By reading railway Enigma and the Army Group B requests for fighter protection, Ultra had penetrated the veil of secrecy the Germans had hoped to draw over their preparations for attack, but full advantage was not taken of its success.

The reconnaissance orders which were decoded and signalled almost every day between 24 November and the opening of the offensive are a striking illustration of this. Liège was a supply distribution point for the Roer sector, and reconnaissance of it was an obvious defensive precaution. But the Meuse crossings upstream to Givet led the Allies nowhere but into the difficult terrain of the Ardennes behind a quiet sector of the front. So consuming an interest as the Germans showed in these crossings and in the country between them and their own lines suggested not that the Germans feared what might come over the river and through the mountains against them but that they planned to force a passage in the opposite direction themselves and wanted daily reassurance that the area was still too weakly held to cause them much difficulty. It was against reason and logic to concentrate so much reconnaissance effort by the best available aircraft upon that part of the front where least danger was to be apprehended—unless the intention was to take advantage of this fact and attack through it (in fact, of course Hitler intended to use the crossings on either side of Namur for a curving drive on Brussels and Antwerp).[1] In the light of this chain of reasoning, the fighter conference on 5 December might have suggested an attack even before the 16th, and so might the announcement by Jagdkorps II on 10 December that all the SS units were observing wireless silence; but without it neither item would have appeared specially significant.

Ultra intelligence was plentiful and informative, but it did not point conclusively towards an offensive in the Ardennes. Had it done so, the right decisions would undoubtedly have been taken at the time and there would be no room for argument now. But it lent itself much more readily to interpretation in that sense than to support for the prevailing view that the Germans would remain quiescent until the next big Allied attack. Ultra provided ample ground for questioning this view and for urging the operational commanders to bear constantly in mind that to act upon it might be to expose themselves to very great danger. In so far as they were not firmly warned of this possibility and did not guard against it, the Ultra evidence was misread and misused. Properly understood, it was more than enough to prevent the complete surprise the German offensive achieved, and to prompt a disposition of the Allied forces less calculated to invite disaster than that which actually prevailed on the morning of 16 December.

1. Yet even on the day after the offensive SHAEF was still puzzled: 'The area of operations offers little in the way of strategic objectives except Liège.' Compare Ehrman vi. 68: on 20 December 'aided by recent Intelligence, Montgomery decided that the enemy's first target would be the stretch of the Meuse between Liège and Namur.' The Ultra evidence for the same thing began almost a month earlier.

The Battle of the Bulge

The offensive opened along a fifty-mile front from Monschau to Echternach at dawn on 16 December. The main blow was to be struck by 6 Panzer Army, which was to aim for the Meuse by the shortest route, cross the river at Liège and Huy on the first day, and drive straight for Antwerp. On its left, 5 Panzer Army would also cross the river on the first day, but at Dinant and Namur as the initial stage of a more curving route to Antwerp via Brussels, while 7 Army protected its flank and rear from Echternach to Givet. Though surprise was gained and confusion caused, the plan went wrong from the start, principally because 6 Panzer Army failed to overcome stubborn American resistance at St Vith, round Stavelot, and along the Elsenborn ridge. When it became clear that Dietrich, the old Nazi, was held up, Hitler allowed von Rundstedt to put his main weight behind von Manteuffel (a young professional soldier with a reputation earned by defensive successes in Tunisia and Russia), whose 5 Panzer Army was making better progress along parallel axes which led through Houffalize and Bastogne. This shift of emphasis meant that the German thrust pointed west rather than north-west and became considerably less dangerous. Eisenhower blocked one of von Manteuffel's lines of advance in the nick of time on 19 December by rushing 101 US Airborne Division into Bastogne (the most important communications centre in a district with few good roads), where it was almost immediately besieged. Bradley had already halted Patton's intended drive eastwards; he now ordered 3 US Army to turn at right-angles, face north, and advance to the relief of Bastogne. But the German thrust towards the Meuse had by now cut Bradley off from contact with Hodges and 1 US Army as they strove to hold back the other arm of the assault and keep it away from Liège; 9 US Army, farther north, was still more remote. To make the control of operations in this region simpler and more effective, Eisenhower therefore transferred 1 and 9 US Armies from American to British control, placing them under Montgomery and 21 Army Group. As a precaution, Montgomery had already halted his own British XXX Corps as it moved up to the attack farther north, and had positioned it between Brussels and Liège behind 1 US Army.

One or two small parties of Germans came within sight of the Meuse near Dinant on 23 December, but that was the farthest they got. The weather, which for the past week had been too bad for flying, now improved enough for the Allies to reassert their supremacy in the air. The advance was halted and the siege of Bastogne raised on Boxing Day. Rundstedt advised that the offensive be called off, but Hitler refused, ordering in addition a diversionary attack in Alsace to relieve pressure on the Ardennes salient. By the New Year the initiative was gradually changing hands, although the fighting remained evenly balanced for another week as the Germans tried to recapture Bastogne, mounted a showpiece thousand-fighter raid on New Year's Day, and by their Alsace attack nearly caused the Allies the acute political embarrassment of evacuating Strasbourg. But by the end of the first week in January the Alsace attack had petered out and Hitler had permitted a withdrawal in the Ardennes. An Allied counter-blow began on 13 January, and before the month was out it had regained the front line of mid-December. Hitler signalized the end of the Ardennes offensive by ordering 6 Panzer Army to the Russian front on 20 January.

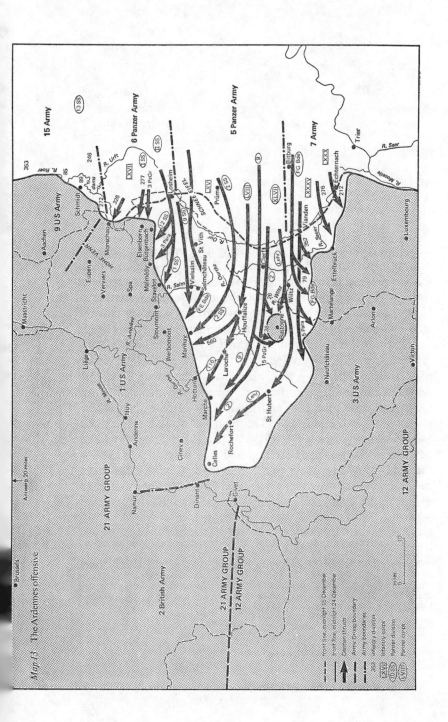

Map 13 The Ardennes offensive

There was no Ultra news about the fighting until the evening of 16 December, and not very much until the following morning: the Germans evidently maintained wireless silence throughout the day (I SS Corps did not cancel it until shortly before midnight), and the timing of our signals strongly suggests that the Red was not broken until much later than usual. Neither the lateness nor the scarcity of information prevented Ultra from rendering two useful services, however. Between ten and eleven o'clock that evening we were able to tell commands that Jagdkorps II had just been ordered to 'support the attack of 5 and 6 Armies' next morning[1] and at dawn we transmitted Rundstedt's Order of the Day: 'The hour of destiny has struck. Mighty offensive armies[2] face the Allies. Everything is at stake. More than mortal deeds are required as a holy duty to the Fatherland.' Together, these two signals made it quite clear that a major operation was under way, and from the time that commands in the field had received and considered the second (say

1945/16
HP 9600
2241/16

16 December
HP 9629
0617/17

1. Read in conjunction with HPs 9267 and 9333 of 12 December, this message also gave away a good deal of the air–army co-operation plan for the attack.
2. Approximately 900,000 men were engaged, together with 80,000 horses. Army Group B's ration-strength (which covered non-combatant staffs, etc., as well as the fighting troops; divisional battle-strengths never rise as high as half the ration-strength in a 5 Army return of 6 January and are frequently much lower) on 1 January was

15 Army	205,193
6 Panzer Army	319,031
5 Panzer Army	187,769
7 Army	170,567
	882,560

by about 9 a.m. on the 17th) there should have been no doubt about German intentions or the seriousness of what was happening—as there is sometimes said or implied to have been even on the second and third days of the offensive.

Nor was Ultra without success in identifying at least the outlines of the German tactical plan almost as quickly. It was plain even on the 16th that I SS Corps (consisting of 1 and 12 SS Pz, 277 and 12 VG Divisions, with 3 Para attached) was directing a major thrust from a command post opposite Elsenborn (midway between Monschau and Malmédy), although it was nearly another twenty-four hours before we could exactly locate its two Panzer divisions close up in the same area. This was in fact 6 SS Panzer Army's attempt to drive straight for Liège and Antwerp. Another signal sent on the afternoon of 17 December placed Pz Lehr and 2 Pz on one side of an evidently important boundary-line (it turned out to be that between 5 Pz Army and 7 Army) running from Bitburg to Wiltz, and LXXXV Corps on the other side; the two Panzer divisions, though not precisely located, were evidently somewhere in the neighbourhood of Clerf. Here the outline of the other major thrust, the 'left hook' by 5 Panzer Army on Namur and Brussels, can already be traced. LXVI Corps near Prüm and 21 Pz, in reserve but asking for news of the battle (we already knew that it had recently been relieved on the Saar front), seemed destined to be drawn into the fighting before long, but II SS Corps had evidently been set to protect Cologne and the Ruhr against the anticipated Allied attack from the Roermond area.

Information was rather more plentiful on 17 December, and it was available much more quickly. By mid-afternoon we knew the roads along which I SS Panzer Corps was approaching the Elsenborn ridge (with 12 SS held up by American artillery there but 1 SS nearing Malmédy) and LXVI Corps advancing on St Vith from the north-east. A few hours later a converging movement on St Vith from the south-east was reported, while farther south still German spearheads were across the river Wiltz on their way to Bastogne. Jagdkorps II announced that it would put up between one and two hundred aircraft next day to support 6 Panzer Army's operations, but on both days it betrayed Model's anxiety to protect his flanks (particularly the northern)[1] against Allied forces moving up either from Aachen across the Hohe Venn or from the direction of Luxembourg. Aerial reconnaissance of these areas and of the Meuse crossings ahead of the developing salient was called for, but it appeared that Detachment Sperling with its Ar 234s was the only long-range reconnaissance unit at GAF West's disposal to meet the demands of all three services. Apart from a few messages concerned with these topics, Ultra information on 18 December was again subject to delay, and could not be signalled until the early morning of the 19th. The first items that came to hand showed II SS Panzer Corps about to come south from the Roermond area to reinforce 6 Panzer Army (just twenty-four hours later there was good evidence that both the Corps and 10 SS Pz Division were under the orders of 6 Army) and Pz Lehr advancing between Wiltz and Clerf. As the day wore on, we discovered that the Führer Escort Brigade was directed on Vielsalm by a route north of St Vith[2] and learned the latest whereabouts of 12 SS Pz and five other divisions. Other items showed 15 Army moving its left-hand boundary as far south as Eupen and Euskirchen (before long there were signs that its place in Holland was being taken by 25 Army), and gave enough corps and divisional boundaries to make the outline of the German command structure tolerably clear.

1730/18
HP 9790
0257/19

2100/18
HP 9826
1458/19

Thus by the time Eisenhower held the conference with Tedder, Bedell Smith, Bradley, Patton, Devers and de Guingand at Verdun on 19 December at which he demanded 'only cheerful faces round this table' and gave Montgomery control over 1 and 9 US Armies and all operations north of a line from Givet to Prüm, all the senior commanders already knew from Ultra how much importance the Germans attached to the offensive, the direction of their main thrusts, and the identities of fourteen (out of about twenty) of the divisions engaged. His in-

1. Several other messages showed that the Allies were expected to react to the offensive by counter-attacking due southwards from Aachen towards Malmédy rather than northwards from Luxembourg and Metz against Bastogne. An analysis of Allied reactions, dated 16 December but not decoded until 8 January, shows this very clearly, and by implication suggests that 3 US Army's later thrust towards Bastogne may at first have been a considerable surprise; but see also p. 211 below.
2. Hitler only released the Brigade to von Rundstedt in the course of 18 December, in a renewed effort to beat a path to the Meuse quickly.

telligence staffs would have learned a good deal more of a tactical nature from prisoner interrogation and other sources, but
there was amply sufficient Ultra to provide a firm and reliable
basis for the assessment of conflicting news and rumour in a
fluid and potentially very dangerous situation and—still more
important—for the planning of suitable counter-measures. In his
Crusade in Europe Eisenhower indeed said that he knew
enough for this purpose by the previous night, but he did not
set out the sources of his knowledge. It is also perhaps worth
pointing out in passing that Ultra also refutes the suggestion
which is sometimes made that at this juncture only Montgomery, through his liaison officers, really knew what was going
on—for it was precisely 6 Panzer Army's front, the most accessible to Montgomery's inquiries, about which Ultra had so far
given most information.

In contrast to the last three days, almost all the noteworthy
items on 19 December concerned the southern part of the front.
Inadequate bridges, a shortage of heavy weapons, and strong
Allied resistance were blamed for slow German progress across
the river Sauer. This was welcome confirmation that the southern shoulder of the salient was holding firm, but it was a great
deal less satisfactory to learn that 7 Army's Y-Service had detected two American divisions being withdrawn from the
Metz–Longwy sector and suspected that they might now advance on Bastogne via Virton. It was by no means the first time
that Ultra had shown up the poor state of American signals security (nor was it anything like the last) and it meant that 3 US
Army's sharp left-wheel had already been betrayed by this
means—a particularly unfortunate loss of the element of surprise in view of Model's initial expectation that the chief Allied
reaction would come from the north.[1] In addition XC Corps
headquarters was found to be leaving Alsace for Bitburg, and
several useful identifications were made in the area south of
Bastogne which 7 Army was anxious to occupy as soon as possible in order to prepare for 3 US Army's expected onslaught.

It was on 19 December, too, that there was one of the few
Ultra references to either of the two peculiar features of the Ar-

1. See pp. 209–10 above.

dennes offensive. Jagdkorps II's intentions for the coming night were to harass movements across the Meuse and to 'supply Battle Group Heydte'. Oberst von der Heydte, who was known to have commanded 6 Para Regiment in Normandy, had in fact been dropped, along with the few remaining genuine parachutists in the Luftwaffe, on high ground between Monschau and Eupen, but had been cut off—hence the air supply—without accomplishing much. The other (and better-known) special feature—the activity of a group of English-speaking Germans in American uniforms, who caused confusion behind the Allied lines quite incommensurate with their small numbers—was only mentioned once during the fighting. There had been several references during the autumn to a detachment under the command of SS-Obersturmbannführer[1] Otto Skorzeny (who had led the party which rescued Mussolini from the Gran Sasso the previous autumn), but the only one which probably referred to the present operation was a simple statement of little intelligence value about the allocation of 150 vehicles to him at the end of November. Ultra was thus unable to give any warning of an enterprise which caused much annoyance and delay but brought no noticeable military advantages. At the end of their operation, Ultra reported the survivors of Skorzeny's party (under the innocuous disguise of Panzer Brigade 150) moving back to St Vith on 26 December.

Should there still have been any lingering doubts in anyone's mind about the Germans' objectives or about their determination to pursue them in spite of initial checks, they will have been dispelled in the early hours of 21 December by the news that on the previous morning the Luftwaffe had been forbidden to attack the Meuse bridges west of a line between Verviers and Bastogne even when Allied troops were crossing—clearly in order to preserve them intact for German use. Just twenty-four hours later this was fleshed out by a report that on the 22nd 6 Pz Army was to continue its thrust towards the Meuse, part of its forces passing through Elsenborn on their way, while 5 Pz Army took St Vith and pushed on to Marche, and 7 Army (taking over 5 Para Division and the Führer Grenadier Brigade

0900/20
HP 9982,
BT 62
0720/21

2100/21
BTs 70, 87
0557/22

1. A rank equivalent to Lieutenant-Colonel.

to block a break-out from Bastogne) advanced south-west as far as Arlon. All three armies were evidently now expected to dispose in a moment of the resistance which had already wrecked their whole time-table by holding them up for five or six days, so that these signals also conveyed the intelligence that an ominously wide gap was opening up between the enemy's intention and his performance. (This gap was, of course, once more the result of Hitler's interference, and belated comparison with previous examples of it may by now have suggested as much at SHAEF and elsewhere. Model had in fact telephoned Rundstedt and Jodl as early as the 18th to say that the offensive had failed. Rundstedt agreed, but Hitler refused to call it off, released more troops to take St Vith and Elsenborn, only permitted Rundstedt to switch emphasis from 6 to 5 Pz Army, and planned a diversionary attack in Alsace to draw Allied troops away from the Ardennes.)

Meanwhile, 6 Panzer Army's difficulties were becoming clearer than ever in a series of messages the most dramatic of which was a cry of alarm which we transmitted in just under three hours from the moment when it was uttered at midday on 20 December: tanks of 1 SS Pz Division[1] were without petrol and ammunition at Stoumont, with Allied armour closing in on them. By the middle of the evening we had passed on three situation reports explaining why the Führer Escort Brigade had failed to take St Vith on two successive days, and had reported the loss of Stavelot by the enemy and their capture of Houffalize; however, it is unlikely that any of these signals did more than dot the i's and cross the t's of what field commands already knew. The move of II SS Pz Corps towards the Elsenborn sector was further charted, Pz Lehr located within ten miles of Bastogne, and 21 Pz shown to be moving past Saarbrücken on its way north, with 11 Pz following behind it. By the following day the GAF was trying to drop supplies to the detachment of 1 SS Pz isolated just east of Stoumont, but was beaten by the weather, while II SS Corps had reached the battle area and taken over command of 12 SS Pz Division.

1. They no doubt belonged to Battle Group Peiper (although the name did not occur in Ultra messages until later) which had shot over a hundred American prisoners of war on 17 December.

(margin) 00/20 Ps 9926, 34 59/20

Perhaps the most valuable single piece of intelligence of the
21st could not be signalled for another five days because of
decoding difficulties. It gave the complete tank state of Army
Group B that evening; such reports were made at regular intervals, and this rare example must have come our way either because a well-placed bomb or shell had cut the land-line by
which it would otherwise have been sent, or because some
quirk of cryptography made this particular day's army supply
key more vulnerable than others. In sum, it showed that Army
Group B had 288 serviceable tanks, with another 115 undergoing short repair, out of a total of 462 (only six total losses were
reported—presumably the sign of an efficient repair and recovery organization); of the 288, 144 were Panthers and thirty-
seven Tigers (out of 236 and 145 respectively), and the Army
Group possessed in addition 146 assault guns and tracked anti-
tank guns (nineteen of them on either Panther or Tiger
chassis). Only in one or two cases was it possible to identify the
units or formations for which individual figures were given; of
the possible explanations—code-groups corrupted in the course
of wireless transmission, or unidentifiable cover-names—the latter seems the more likely.

The only other comparable document of the early Ardennes
campaign may best be grouped with this, although it originated
two days later and was not decoded until 2 January. It was a
report on the current state of seven out of the ten divisions in 5
Panzer Army. The overall picture it presented cannot have
been very reassuring to Model and Rundstedt, for its main
points may be summarized thus: after no more than a week's
fighting, only two (2 SS Pz and Pz Lehr) of the four armoured
divisions listed were rated as fully capable of offensive operations, only they were more than meagrely provided with anti-
tank weapons, and only seven battalions out of a total of forty-
six were classed as 'strong' (seven were 'weak' and two 'exhausted'). In some ways the most striking feature of the report,
however, was the revelation that even the two favoured Panzer
divisions were not completely motorized and that two other divisions (26 VG and 560 VG) which had formed part of the
striking force and were now deep in the salient beyond Stavelot
and Bastogne depended partly on horse-drawn transport.

The now really acute petrol shortage which accounted for this was soon driven home by an order from Goering for the Luftwaffe to immobilize all motor transport not required for the conduct of battle in order to economize fuel. The situation was in fact worse than we knew. Early in the new year Oberst Polack of the quartermaster's department of OKH presented a report in which he said that air attacks on the hydrocarbon industry ever since the opening of the Ardennes offensive had so reduced petrol supplies that 'it may be necessary to de-motorise the army, even Panzer Grenadiers moving on foot or by bicycle and only the Panzer brigades remaining fully motorised.' Ultra gave a partial glimpse of the same thing in an extraordinary joint inquiry by Rundstedt and Kesselring: Panzer divisions operating on the eastern front had been ordered, they understood, to have two sixty-ton horse-drawn transport columns each,[1] in order to economise fuel. Was this to apply to their commands too?[2]

In spite of their increasing difficulties, the Germans' objectives remained the same for several more days—7 Army would advance towards Luxembourg while 5 and 6 Panzer Armies enlarged the salient, eliminating resistance at St Vith on the way, and the GAF still refrained from damaging the bridges over the Meuse at Liège. Among useful battlefield details were successive reports on the movements of the detachment of 1 SS Pz Division still isolated between Stoumont and Stavelot, and its eventual break-out, and a pin-point location of Panzer Lehr Division's headquarters at Château Losange near Bastogne. The dispatch of an envoy demanding the Bastogne garrison's surrender and the Americans' refusal both found their place in Ultra, but not General McAuliffe's famous reply 'Nuts'.

The defenders of St Vith were finally overwhelmed on 21 December; the garrison of Bastogne held out until it was relieved. The part played by each in delaying the German advance while counter-measures were prepared is of course well known. But it is worth recording the impression that the con-

---

1. As already foreshadowed in October: p. 184 above.
2. At the end of the month stocks of heavy diesel oil in German naval bases were 'practically exhausted', and such supplies as there were came straight out of current production.

stant Ultra references to both places as obstacles to be eliminated abundantly confirms this view and suggests that it would
be difficult to over-estimate the extent to which their defenders
frustrated Hitler's plans and brought about the failure of the
offensive.

With the weather beginning to clear on 22 December, GAF
West expected a resumption of Allied air operations, the relative absence of which hitherto had greatly facilitated the German advance (in the hope of assisting in the resumption we had
signalled a number of GAF weather reports during the last few
days), and ordered all units to prepare for 'air battles on the
grand scale'. The tide began to turn as soon as Allied air superiority could make itself felt again, although two or three more
weeks' bitter fighting were necessary to make victory secure.
There was already an unreal and almost frantic note about
Army Group B's intentions for the 24th: 6 Pz Army would 'at
all costs' push across the river Salm beyond Stavelot (but 2 SS
Pz was still on the banks of the river next morning) and 5 Pz
Army to the Meuse, which it claimed to have reached on
Christmas Day.

Up to a dozen corps and divisional locations were being signalled every day at this period, and advance warnings of raids
and reconnaissances were more plentiful than they had been for
some time, as were records of sorties flown and serviceability
rates. The value of the last two can be faintly discerned between the lines of a Joint Intelligence Committee paper of 27
December on the German capacity to maintain the offensive,
which estimated that the GAF was using 1800 aircraft, 1250 of
them single-engined fighters. But the merely tactical usefulness
of Ultra was once more declining[1] as the German impetus
failed and the initiative gradually passed back to the Allies. The
change in the GAF's outlook was very sharply marked. On 19
December General Peltz, at this time commanding both Jagd-

1. Save in cases like the confirmation that a raid by 100 four-engined
bombers on 26 December had completely blocked St Vith to all traffic, or the
perfect scenario for intercepting and nullifying a GAF attack which was signalled on 27 December: at one minute past midnight that morning 3 Jagddivision announced that formations of thirty aircraft flying at a height of 500
metres would make raids in the Dinant–Marche–Rochefort area at five-minute
intervals from 0630 hours—two hours after the Hut 3 signal was dispatched.

0001/27
BT 454
0437/27

korps II and Fliegerkorps IX, pronounced himself pleased with the way air operations had been conducted on the first two days of the offensive, but barely a week later he was complaining about pilots breaking off attacks without good reason, jettisoning their extra fuel tanks and making for home, while the Kommodore of JG 27 estimated that 20 per cent of his pilots had behaved like this on the 23rd and threatened to court-martial any who did so in future.

Two reports of 27 December, both signalled a few hours after they were made, demonstrated the enemy command's loss of confidence very clearly. In the small hours 7 Army recognized that because the Allies now had 'material superiority over the whole front' it would have to confine its efforts to defending

0100/27
BT 479
1656/27

the north bank of the Sauer until it was possible to take the offensive again, and ended with the words 'situation particularly critical on both flanks', while soon after dark Dietrich and

1915/27
BT 526
0157/28

Manteuffel put out a joint called for the heaviest possible airstrike on a wood north of Bastogne. The second of these reports showed how fatally the Bastogne garrison's heroic resistance was slowing the German advance, and confirmed the wisdom of placing 101 US Division there to deny the

1200/29
BTs 663, 669
1553/29

road-junction to the enemy. A renewed attack on Bastogne by 167 VG and 3 PzGr Divisions having failed, further air attacks (of which advance warning was given) were made on 29 December, but 5 Pz Army was already being forced to accept LVIII Corps' plea to be allowed to withdraw under pressure

2000/29
BT 763
1804/30

outside Rochefort, only ordering certain strongpoints to be held at all costs.

The immensely destructive effect of air power upon the enemy's capacity to bring up reinforcements and supplies to maintain the impetus of the offensive was strikingly portrayed in a series of messages at the turn of the year. Heavy bombing raids had caused such chaos on the railways on both sides of the Rhine from Koblenz to Karlsruhe and Stuttgart that re-routing was impossible and armament production was being crippled, said the local Home Army Territorial command to Reichsminister Speer in an appeal which it sent by wireless in Enigma code because 'telephone facilities hardly exist'. Rundstedt's Director of Transport added that there would be delays of up to a

week before some routes were open again, and Army Group B
summed up the transport and supply situation bleakly: Allied
air power dominated the skies, bent on the systematic destruction of all traffic centres; the GAF gave only slight relief, even
when making maximum effort; the progressive destruction of
railways in the Eifel meant that supplies had to be unloaded
along the Rhine and were subject to serious delay in reaching
the front. The only solution Army Group B could suggest was
to commandeer 10 per cent of each subordinate formation's
transport, but that this would bring little relief was shown
when, on 4 January, 6 SS Pz Army reported that its only two
available supply-routes were completely blocked by stationary
lorries. A later report showed that there was still chaos on railways in mid-January. Air-raids on Mainz had caused traffic-
jams at junctions and overloaded such marshalling-yards as
were still in operation, so that 'goods traffic is only possible on
a small scale'; on the same day Frankfurt was accepting no
goods trains at all and Saarbrücken only a few.

The thousand-fighter raid on New Year's Day, which was the
Luftwaffe's last despairing effort to regain for a moment the
mastery of the air it had lost long ago, did not figure prominently in Ultra. A forecast of good weather with little cloud, and
a mysterious message from 3 Jagddivision to four fighter
Geschwader 'X-time for Hermann 0820/1', were signalled with
maximum priority soon after 3 a.m., but there was no way of
knowing what the code-name Hermann signified.[1] After the
raid, 3 Jagddivision claimed 398 aircraft destroyed on the
ground plus ninety-three probables, and three shot down plus
one probable, but admitted 'considerable own losses' out of the
622 planes it had put up for 'the annihilation of the Allied air
force in Holland and Belgium'. Whatever the exact figures, the
Luftwaffe had lost more men and machines than it could afford.
Within a very few days there was a call to speed up the repair
of aircraft urgently needed both at the front and for Reich

1830, 2330/1
BTs 878, 879
0308, 0329/1

---

1. Hermann was presumably the signal for these four Geschwader to be airborne for the raid. The whole operation was known as Bodenplatte, but this
word seems never to have appeared in Enigma traffic.

defence, and OKL was concerned to make good heavy losses among day fighter formation-leaders. Other evidence permitted some of the details to be filled in: thus Jafue Mittelrhein's serviceability fell from 192 on 31 December to 116 on 3 January, the whole fighter strength in north-east Germany could be signalled next day and the calculation made that 221 pilots had been posted to the western front during the first fortnight of the offensive.

All three German armies were by now plainly dragging their heels, and the word 'defence' was beginning to occur with increasing frequency in reports from their front-line units, but Ultra gave no hint during the first week in January of any intention on Rundstedt's part to abandon the dangerous salient into which he had been forced to drive his troops. Rather did the constant insistence (which continued throughout the week) that air attacks should be concentrated on Bastogne, and signs of considerable regrouping of armour in the same area, suggest the contrary—that he would persist in trying to remove this obstacle to a resumption of the advance while at the same time meeting the counter-attacks which began on 3 January. Only once was serious danger apprehended: an unknown authority pointed out on the 3rd that the whole southern flank would be seriously weakened if the Allies enlarged their bridgehead across the Sauer near Wiltz. The first hints of a German retreat came during the afternoon of 8 January, with 9 Pz's announcement that it had withdrawn the previous night to a line east of Rochefort and Marche, and the division was soon still farther back. On the southern flank of the salient 7 Army, which had intended that same night 'to defend what has hitherto been the sector of attack', was withdrawing next day (at two hours twenty-one minutes, our signal was near the record for speed of retransmission), and by dawn on 11 January 5 Panzer Army in the centre revealed the scope of the rearward movement by reporting that it had withdrawn along its whole front 'according to plan' on the 10th. Four days later it had come to a complete standstill round Houffalize because of Allied air attacks; in response to an urgent appeal for protection, Jagdkorps II sent out its whole force, 216 aircraft.

0900/8
BT 1641
1415/8

2030/9
BT 1800
2251/9

Thus Ultra was as quick as ever to detect signs of retreat—
Hitler had only sanctioned the first stage of it in the early hours
of 8 January. But there now ensued a frustrating fortnight during which items of first-rate importance were late in arriving
and often badly out of time-sequence, so that their meaning was
obscured and interpretation made hazardous. This period was
heralded by two messages which had an air of mystery about
them once they were read in the context of the withdrawal
which was already in progress: LVIII Pz Corps, hitherto under
5 Pz Army in the centre, had taken over another sector
(thought on fair evidence to be that of I SS Corps farther north
and under 6 SS Pz Army) on 11 January, and a division (very
likely 2 SS, but the evidence was again maddeningly uncertain)
had been taken out of the line 'for new tasks' and was just
south of St Vith at midday on the 13th. Until this moment there
had been no recent evidence about 6 Army and its SS Panzer
divisions, nor any hint either of how far Hitler would allow the
retreat to go or whether he would now sacrifice the west to protect the Reich (and particularly the industries of Silesia)
against the offensive which the Russians launched along the
whole front from the Baltic to Budapest on 12 January. Stalin
later alleged that he brought forward the planned timing of this
attack to relieve the pressure in the Ardennes, and Tedder was
in Moscow to co-ordinate strategy. It was likely that Hitler
would at last realize the risks he had run by using up the best of
his armour in a fruitless endeavour to punch a hole in the
Anglo–American front and would now send it to the east, re-
versing the tendency (detectable in Ultra over the last few
weeks)[1] to give the west priority.

To discover Hitler's next move was in any case of the highest
importance, but the more so at this moment because the Allied
command was over-compensating for its carefree mood of early
December by a nervousness far greater than the transient emergency warranted; it tended to 'see burglars under every bed'
and to fear that the Germans would renew the attack with every
division they could muster, and had lately been acutely embar-
rassed by the unhappy press conference at which Montgomery

1230/11
BT 1979
1738/11

1200/13
BT 2209
2327/13

1. See p. 185 above.

had appeared to say that only his intervention had saved the Americans from disaster. It was therefore unfortunate that Ultra could not immediately give clear and unequivocal answers to the questions being asked of it and only arrived at them more stutteringly than usual and with greater hesitation and delay.

In the present state of public knowledge, no certain reason can be assigned for this. Nevertheless, a plausible hypothesis may be advanced to explain it: small amounts of traffic in army keys were identified and intercepted (most army communications were now going by land-line). Granted the greater security of army signals procedure, its small quantity would normally have made this traffic unremunerative (in terms of bombe-time) or impossible to break. But the high value of the intelligence it might contain, and recent increases in the number and sophistication of the bombes, might now render at least some of it decodable if enough bombe-time could be spared from the regular daily tasks of breaking the Red and Light Blue and keeping abreast of the various naval keys. Time was found after these tasks had been accomplished, but lower priority on the bombes and the relatively clumsy cryptographic methods imposed by the paucity of material caused inescapable delays and brought a few days' keys out in the wrong time-sequence. If all this is true (and, in the total absence of accessible evidence about the internal history of Hut 6, it must be stressed that it is no more than intelligent guesswork) then there is more ground for thankfulness that the cryptographers were able to provide us with any information at all about major changes in OB West's dispositions than for regret that much of it was late and at first difficult to interpret. The incident does, however, illustrate with particular clarity two intermittent occupational hazards in the use of Ultra—late decoding, and evidence which, because it stopped just short of being explicit, held out an invitation to conjecture which had to be firmly resisted.

A great deal of circumstantial evidence that the bulk of the German armour might be on its way out of the salient gradually accumulated in mid- and late January, but to begin with much of it was hazy and inconclusive. Thus 1 SS Panzer Division was to assemble on the 15th near St Vith, behind the sector where it had been fighting. No reason was given, however, either on this occasion or when the Flivos attached to Pz Lehr, 1, 2, 9 and 12 SS Divisions and 3 PzGr Division were ordered back to their companies the same day. (The presumption, of course, was they would not be needed for air liaison duties in the immediate future because the divisions would not be in action, but presumption was not proof.) Next—a whole week later—came the announcement by Army Group B that on or before 10 January Hitler had ordered all the SS Panzer divisions to be released for employment 'elsewhere', any elements remaining in their present theatre of operations to be engaged only on express Army Group order and only if an Anglo–American breakthrough threatened. This was more definite, but evidence that any of the divisions had actually moved was hard to come by for the next three days, and indications that 10 SS was in Baden proved in the end misleading because this division reappeared in the Saar and Alsace, as already forecast, and remained there for another three weeks. Late at night on the 21st we signalled an order issued by Model the previous afternoon which seemed to confirm the execution of Hitler's directions. Model set out certain arrangements which were to come into force at midday on 22 January, but it was typical of the frustrations of this period that parts of a vital sentence had been lost at the moment of interception. All efforts to reconstruct it failed to make this sentence read better than '6 Panzer Army will be [pulled out?] and given command . . . divisions including Corps HQs I and II SS.' The rest was clearer and more informative: Model promised to send orders later for 9 SS and the two Führer brigades, which would 'still be operating', and instructed 5 Pz Army to take over all the troops in 6 Pz Army's sector at once 'except the SS formations which will be pulled out'. This made the evacuation of the salient tolerably plain, and Model's anxiety that Pz Lehr should transfer as quickly as possible to the focal point of the fighting in 7 Army area (other formations were even ordered to help it out with tanks and petrol) suggested a fear that 3 US Army's northwards drive might cut his escape route; but no hint of the departing divisions' destination came our way for another three more days.

Light began to dawn at last on 25 January, when the com-

11 January
BT 2590
2056/17

mander of Jagdkorps II announced that some fighter Gruppen were being transferred to the eastern front to meet the situation there and bleakly informed the remainder that they would have to cope with the Anglo–American air forces on their own. This was followed at twenty-four-hour intervals by two pieces of information which were plainly connected. First came the proclamation of a route 'for the march of the SS formations' of 6 Panzer Army which took them almost to Cologne on their way to being 'loaded' north-west of the city, and after it the decoding of a week-old order from SS Operations Headquarters, Berlin, about the extreme urgency of providing men and materials 'for O'. In view of the Jagdkorps II news in particular, it was reasonable to suggest that 'O' stood for *Ost* (that is, east), but this was a flimsy basis for notionally wiping half-a-dozen SS Panzer divisions off the strength of Army Group B and counting them instead among the forces facing the Russians. Fortunately, confirmation came within six or seven hours. The Berlin message had been dated 19 January; now it was discovered that on the 22nd the same authority had again referred to 'O' when posting an officer to Deutschkrone near Schneidemühl, 150 miles north-east of Berlin and close to the pre-war Polish frontier, and that on the 26th the Flivo of I SS Panzer Corps (mercifully he had not been silenced along with his divisional colleagues!) had said that his corps was being transferred to the eastern front.

26 January
BT 3470
0509/27

If this seems to place the issue beyond doubt, it will be regarded as excessive caution[1] which kept us from drawing the apparently obvious conclusion for another twenty-four hours, but it must be remembered that even now the evidence was still only fragmentary and that a move by the whole of 6 Panzer Army to the Russian front was not much more than a very plausible deduction from it. New material arriving on 28 January came nearer to positive proof. On the previous evening 3 Jagddivision issued its complete plan for providing fighter cover

p.m./27
BT 3553
0654/28

1. This caution can now be seen as additionally justified by the fact (of which of course no one was then aware) that Hitler's decision was taken in three stages: on 8 January to withdraw 6 Panzer Army from the salient and hold it ready to meet Allied counter-attacks; on 15 January to rest and refit I and II SS Corps on OB West territory between 20 and 30 January; and on 20 and 22 January to send 6 Panzer Army to the Russian front.

for unspecified army movements which had started on the 25th and were likely to go on until 3 February—long enough, that is, to be accounted for by a whole army in transit. Protection was to be given to very much the same area as that of the SS march-route, but with the addition of the railway lines on both sides of the Rhine between Boppard and St Goarshausen (a short distance south of Koblenz). This information was, of course, signalled at once with the highest priority in order that the Allied air forces might take maximum advantage of it to disrupt the railway transports and road convoys it implied. When further details linking 1, 2 and 9 SS Divisions and II SS Corps with the move came in during the morning, they were signalled with the comment that both the War Office and ourselves felt that they clinched the move of 6 Panzer Army eastwards, and before midnight we had further confirmation in a long list of consignments addressed to 6 Panzer Army at Gueterglück south of Magdeburg on the Elbe—but it was in keeping with the circumstances which had made this one of the most long-drawn-out pieces of detective work in the history of Ultra that this was another delayed decode (it was already three days old) and that the consignments were so trivial in themselves that they would have solved nothing had they not come at the end of a painfully constructed chain of reasoning. The move of the armour eastwards was now clear, but it was more than a fortnight since the first hints that some of the Panzer divisions might be pulling out of the salient. Positive proof that the Russian offensive was drawing the best of the German armour away from the western front simplified the Allied commanders' task in planning and conducting the assault on the Rhine and the final offensive; but victory in the Ardennes was already certain long before this proof was obtained at the end of January, and final victory had again become only a matter of time as soon as the German advance was halted before Christmas. It may therefore well be that at the turn of the year Ultra rendered an equal or even greater service by continuing to supply the bomb-damage assessment teams with regular evidence about the destruction of German factories and other economic matters on the one hand, and with indications of the steady erosion of the army's fighting strength on the other: for the one might assist in forecasting a date for final industrial collapse and the other in estimating how long it would take to pierce the remaining crust of resistance and penetrate into the heart of Germany.

The first was perhaps the more valuable of the two (the decline of the Wehrmacht was well established by now) because Ultra records of raid-damage could be used to cross-check photographic reconnaissance and ensure the most effective target-selection for the bombing offensive. However, a mere recital of separate accounts of damage to factories and estimates of how long production would be interrupted in each case tells little without the contemporary statistical analyses of the specifically Ultra evidence—which are not available. Two reports about coal supplies were more generally informative. On 30 December the Director of Transport West announced his January allocations of coal: a paltry 33,100 tons was the month's ration for the army of occupation in Holland and all the fighting troops from the Dutch coast down to 6 Panzer Army, whose quota was to be delivered to Bonn, and all were told to use water-transport to the utmost in order to save coal. A few days later an electricity works at Herford (between Hanover and the Ruhr) was said to have been out of action since 17 December; coal stocks in the area were only enough to cover civilian needs for three days, and industry was at a standstill. A set of instructions issued on 19 January by Albert Speer, Minister for Armaments and War Production, to the presidents of the Armaments Commissions immediately behind the eastern front about steps to be taken when evacuating territory shed a bizarre light on the mental attitude of Hitler and his entourage, because of the implication that even at this late date they still cherished a belief in eventual victory. Speer's keynote was a Hitler order 'Render unusable, do not destroy', and he made two points: (a) there was no need to bring tools or machinery back, because there was plenty of both in Germany; preference was to be given instead to finished or half-finished articles and raw materials; (b) factories were not to be destroyed because they would then be useless in the event of recapture, and 'in view of German military counter-measures' this was 'entirely to be reckoned with'. Certain installations in the Saar had only been put out of action, were subsequently recovered and got going again, and were now doing valuable work.

The army reports gave more specific information: 6 Panzer Army had very low petrol and diesel stocks at the beginning of January, partly because its only two supply roads were still completely blocked by halted vehicles. The supply situation was just as critical with 5 Panzer Army, which received no allocation of petrol at all on 7 January (some arrived three days later, however) and whose consumption of ammunition was outstripping the rate of replenishment. Another 5 Pz Army return showed only the Führer Escort Brigade fully fit to operate in an attacking role (Pz Lehr, 9 and 12 SS Pz were only limitedly capable of taking the offensive), and the army's tank holdings as fifty-eight IVs, sixty-four Panthers and four Tigers, with apparently another 133 of mixed types undergoing repair. This return was made about the time when many of the divisions concerned were being taken out of the fighting line; on 27 January, when 6 Panzer Army was on its way eastwards, 1, 2 and 12 SS Divisions could muster only 128 tanks (fifty IVs, sixty-five Vs and thirteen VIs) between them (two months earlier they were intended to have 134 tanks *each*,[1] but all three divisions were now rated as only fit for defensive action). A far larger number of tanks was shown in a quartermaster report from Army Group B which complained that existing stocks of final drive assemblies were not enough to keep some 700 tanks in action, and requested immediate delivery of 200 in order to get as many now immobilized tanks moving again; we had, however, some reservations about the accuracy of this figure. (For the sake of comparison, it may be noted that according to the OKW War Diary seventy-seven IVs, 132 Vs, and thirteen VIs were lost between 16 and 31 December and that through Ultra 1 SS Division reported losses of eighteen, twenty-nine and thirteen respectively during the first ten days of January.)

The desperate straits the German armies were in for ammunition was revealed in an OKW circular of 10 January: because of the scarcity of raw materials, the decline in production and transport difficulties, it was only possible to meet the demand for shells and mortar-bombs during periods of heavy fighting by

1. See p. 194 above.

restricting supplies to focal points and by stringent economies in quiet sectors; yet so much was being expended in spite of warnings that it was proving impossible to build up any kind of a reserve. Two sets of operational orders by Doenitz showed that the manpower situation was as threatening as the material. On the 19th he called for a 5 per cent reduction in the staffing of all naval commands without exception, in order to release men to boost the army's combat strength, and he repeated the instruction on the last day of the month in view of the 'serious crises' on the Russian front and in spite of Hitler's order for the intensification of submarine warfare.

8
Closing to the Rhine

A series of small attacks on several parts of the front during the second half of January showed that the initiative had returned to the Allies even before they had quite regained all the territory lost during the Ardennes offensive; they took place just to the north and just to the south of the main battle area, on the Saar and in Alsace (where Colmar was captured on 2 February and the German bridgehead west of the Rhine eliminated). A larger-scale operation (Veritable) by 1 Canadian Army began on 8 February; it pointed south-eastwards from Nijmegen and aimed at clearing the Reichswald forest area between Maas and Rhine. It was to have been co-ordinated with a drive (Grenade) by 9 US Army north and north-east across the Roer, but the Germans blew the dams and flooded the Roer valley on 9 February, so that the American attack had to be postponed until the 23rd. The British and Canadians made slow but steady progress against heavily reinforced German resistance in difficult country; the Americans (still under 21 Army Group control) were able to move more quickly once the water-level dropped enough for them to make a start, and the two met at Geldern on 3 March. Soon the whole west bank of the Rhine from Nijmegen to Düsseldorf and Cologne was in Allied hands.

Farther south, 3 US Army's capture of Trier on 1 March gave Patton the chance to exploit the huge breach which had been made in the West Wall by a bold dash up the Moselle valley to Koblenz, which he reached on 7 March, just twenty-four hours after 1 US Army's scarcely less rapid advance enabled it to rush the Rhine bridge at Remagen and gain a foothold on the east bank.

Meanwhile Montgomery was preparing to cross the river at Wesel, north of the Ruhr, where Eisenhower had decided to make his main effort. The crossing was made on 23 March, but 3 Army had got across at Oppenheim, south of Mainz, the day before.

Strasbourg and Colmar: 6 Army Group

The secondary attack in northern Alsace which Hitler launched to divert some of the American troops away from the Ardennes so that he might regain the initiative there led—like the main offensive itself—rather to the eventual loss than to the recapture of territory as well as to the squandering of irreplaceable reserves, and its failure in fact consolidated the first stage in the Allied occupation of the west bank of the Rhine, the essential prerequisite for an advance to final victory. Hitler dictated the outline plan on 22 December, when German impetus in the Ardennes was already beginning to fail; the objective (to recover the high ground between Saverne and Pfalzburg) and the timing (it was to begin an hour before midnight on 31 December) were set in the course of the next few days. Ultra knew nothing of all this, but in the week preceding the attack it provided reasonable cover of enemy activity in the threatened area. Several reports gave information about the divisions in 1 Army each side of Saarbrücken (although they left the order of battle a trifle confused), showed that replacements for 17 SS's casualties were being sent by express transport to the area north of Wissembourg, and revealed that 21 Panzer Division (which was still deep in the Ardennes salient on 23 December) was moving four days later to Pirmasens, close to what was to be the attackers' start line.

By the evening of 1 January only slow progress had been made on 1 Army's front against stiff resistance between Saar-

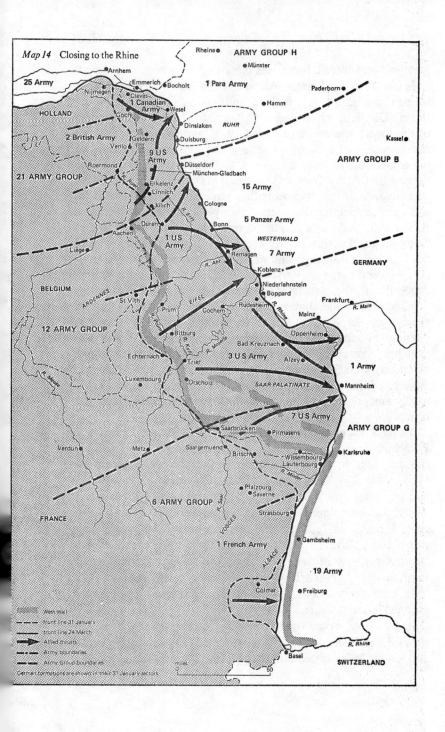

Map 14 Closing to the Rhine

ARMY GROUP H

Rheine ●
● Münster

25 Army
● Arnhem
● Emmerich ● Bocholt
1 Para Army
● Paderborn

● Nijmegen
Cleves
1 Canadian
Army
Goch
● Wesel

HOLLAND
Dinslaken *RUHR*
● Hamm
● Kassel

2 British Army
● Geldern
● Duisburg

● Venlo
9 US
Army
● Düsseldorf
ARMY GROUP B

● Roermond
München-Gladbach

21 ARMY GROUP
Erkelenz
Linnich
15 Army

● Jülich
● Cologne

● Düren
● Bonn
5 Panzer Army

● Aachen
1 US
Army
WESTERWALD

● Liège
● Remagen
7 Army
GERMANY

R. Ahr
● Koblenz

BELGIUM
● Niederlahnstein
● Boppard

ARDENNES
● St Vith
EIFEL
● Cochem
● Rüdesheim
● Frankfurt R. Main

● Prüm
R. Rhine

12 ARMY GROUP
● Bitburg
● Mainz

R. Prüm
R. Kyll
R. Moselle
● Bad Kreuznach
● Oppenheim

● Echternach
● Trier
3 US Army
● Alzey
1 Army

● Luxembourg
● Orscholz
SAAR PALATINATE
● Mannheim

● Saarbrücken
7 US Army
ARMY GROUP G

● Verdun
● Metz
● Saargemuend
● Pirmasens
● Karlsruhe

● Bitsch
● Wissembourg
Lauterbourg
R. Moder

● Pfalzburg
● Saverne
6 ARMY GROUP
R. Saar
● Strasbourg

FRANCE
VOSGES
1 French Army
● Gambsheim

ALSACE
19 Army

● Colmar
● Freiburg

West Wall
front line 31 January
front line 24 March
Allied thrusts
Army boundaries
Army Group boundaries
German formations are shown in their 31 January sectors

miles
0   50

R. Rhine
● Basel
SWITZERLAND

gemuend and Bitsch, but it was clear that the attack would nevertheless be pressed home. Air protection for an advance southwards from Bitsch by mobile units (evidently including 21 Panzer Division, which had been keeping wireless silence north of the town) was to be provided on 3 January, but no striking results were claimed. At no time during the first three days of the attack—or, indeed, later—was there any Ultra evidence to suggest that Army Group G was looking for a swift and extensive advance or that it expected the capture of Strasbourg to result from a junction between 1 Army's southward drive from Bitsch and 19 Army's combined operation across the Rhine at Gambsheim. To this negative extent, therefore, Ultra should have provided a background of reassurance to the politico-military decision taken at Versailles on 3 January—not after all to proceed with the plan to evacuate Strasbourg which had so infuriated de Gaulle, but to achieve the same object (that of shortening the line in Alsace to release troops for the Ardennes) by minor readjustments in several sectors. It was presumably these readjustments which led Army Group G to infer erroneously on 5 January that the Allies might be abandoning Alsace, and raised hopes of success which made Hitler abnormally anxious to receive immediate reports direct from the front.

To lend more weight to the assault, 10 SS Panzer Division, 7 Parachute Division and others entrained for a move south by rail, but they took several days over the journey—not surprisingly, since they had to traverse the area where so many lines had just been cut by air attack and so much congestion caused.[1] About the same time 11 Panzer Division came out of reserve to protect the Trier–Saarbrücken sector where 3 US Army had just begun a limited attack on the 'Orscholz switch position' between the rivers Moselle and Saar; the quick transmission of the boundary between it and 416 Division on 18 January may have been useful, since both these divisions were prominently engaged in the struggle.

Apart from some quartermaster returns (one of which showed the combat strength of 198 and 708 Divisions to be only about 2000 apiece and that of 269 Division—under orders

2036/2
BT 1067
0332/3

1. See p. 218.

for the eastern front—not much greater), there was no news from 19 Army, and hence none about the Franco–American attacks which eliminated the Colmar pocket at the beginning of February: presumably operation orders and situation reports were conveyed back and forth across the Rhine by telephone, but there were no teleprinter links for the long lists of figures required in ammunition and full stock returns.

Between Maas and Rhine: 21 Army Group

After 'vehement disagreements' among the Allied Chiefs of Staff at their meeting in Malta, and the unusual spectacle of Tedder and Montgomery taking the same line at a SHAEF conference, it was decided at the beginning of February to resume the interrupted advance by seizing the west bank of the Rhine above Nijmegen as a preliminary to the encirclement of the Ruhr. In two converging attacks, 1 Canadian Army would drive south-eastwards through the Reichswald (Veritable) on 8 February and 9 US Army north-eastwards across the Roer between Venlo and Jülich (Grenade). Ultra showed that Model and von Rundstedt expected both attacks (Berlin, however, was in some doubt about 21 Army Group's intentions), but in the prevailing rather scanty state of Enigma traffic little intelligence could be gathered about their preparations for resistance. In an evident attempt to position an armoured reserve to the best advantage, XLVII Panzer Corps was placed under 1 Parachute Army round München-Gladbach; it consisted of 116 Pz Division (at nearly full strength in men but with only seventy-three tanks) and 15 PzGr Division, but there were no reports from the front line. The tremendous artillery barrages which the Allies could afford in the coming battle were in sharp contrast with the severe ammunition shortage which was now afflicting the Germans. All Army Group commanders were informed by OKH on 3 February that production had been so much interrupted that current allocations of shells would be 'considerably less' than in January, and for some calibres[1]

---

1. No doubt light and medium field howitzer. 1 Parachute Army's supplies of these types were not keeping pace with expenditure a week after Veritable began, and complaints about them recur with great regularity in Ultra during the next three months.

would only be made known ten days in advance instead of the usual four weeks. The seriousness of the situation was underlined by the news that 476 Division—coming into line along the river Erfft as defence in depth against 9 US Army—would have had only ninety shells for its four infantry guns had not fifteen tons of ammunition been rushed up to it just before the battle started, by a report through Nazi Party channels asking that Hitler's attention might be drawn to the fact that in the last fortnight Army Group North (on the Russian front) had received 7600 tons of ammunition but fired off over 19,000 tons, including its last reserves, and by Jodl's refusal to let Kesselring have any more shells even though a large-scale battle was expected in Italy towards the end of the month.

These and other similar difficulties were monitored through a series of returns rendered at intervals by the quartermaster's department of 1 Parachute Army during the next three weeks; they were set out according to a standard pro-forma, unintelligible to the casual reader of the signals which passed them on to 21 Army Group but now as well understood by the logistics specialists there and in Hut 3 as by the German officers who compiled them. They were sometimes subject to late decoding, which mattered more in the case of the operational signals which were often affected by similar delays until the end of February. Within twenty-four hours of the start of Veritable for instance, von Rundstedt appreciated that Montgomery intended to press on to the lower Rhine 'come what may' and that the Americans would cross the Roer as soon as the water-level dropped (the dams had been blown that day to delay them), but this was not known until nearly a week later. The Intelligence branch of 1 Parachute Army was some way short of the truth when it first identified the British objectives as Goch and Gennep and then forecast an armoured thrust to Wesel; on the other hand there was almost a note of panic in the reiterated warnings about probable airlandings issued by commanders at all levels: most of them pointed to the Rhine bank between Wesel and Duisburg as the likely target area—except von Rundstedt, who forecast a descent on the Ruhr, to protect which Hitler had just ordered the development of a 'Rhine position' between Emmerich and Königswinter. The capture of Cleves on

1420/14
BT 4821
1707/14

11 February provoked XLVII Pz Corps into a plan to regain the town with fourteen hastily assembled tanks and assault guns, and we were able to give advance warning of a night ground-attack raid on Cleves by Jagdkorps II in quite the old style. Save for keeping track of the movements of XLVII Pz Corps, giving grounds for the surmise (it was subsequently confirmed by other sources) that Westphal's order for 8 Para Division to leave the Erfft sector might herald its transfer to the Canadian Army's front, noting the arrival of 245 Division on the east bank of the Rhine at Bocholt and locating the headquarters of 1 Parachute Army on the west bank opposite Dinslaken on 3 February, however, Ultra provided very little operational intelligence during the Veritable action. On the other hand, as the British and Canadians approached their junction with 9 US Army, a report of 28 February showed how the fighting had eroded German strength: three battalions of 15 PzGr and two of 7 Para had been wiped out, and the two divisions mustered barely 5000 men between them, while though 116 Pz was stronger than both together and had plenty of guns, it was only rated, like them, as fit for defensive operations.

The armour facing them was closely observed during the fortnight's wait imposed on 9 US Army by the blowing of the Roer dams on 9 February. Thus Pz Lehr was identified in the general Grenade area five days before it appeared between Euskirchen and Brühl, and all the formations already in this sector had been traced by the time evidence forecasting the arrival of

1215/24
BT 5586
1614/24

9 Pz and 11 Pz round Düren and Erkelenz came in shortly before the American offensive opened on 23 February. Almost at once an unspecified authority reported 'state of crisis at Bridgehead Linnich' and 9 Pz was reported in the woods to the east of Jülich, but the full seriousness of the situation was not apparent until a delayed decode of 25 February from Army Group B explained that the elements of 9 Pz and 11 Pz which had so far arrived were quite insufficient to cover a weak section of the line between Linnich and Jülich and asked for Pz Lehr to be sent forward to prevent a breakthrough. Lehr had arrived on both sides of Erkelenz by early morning on the 27th, and 338 Division had been ordered up to the same area from quiet billets near Freiburg in the Black Forest. The list of reserves

signalled on 1 March was not impressive, and did not prevent that collapse of the defences on the west bank of the Rhine which von Rundstedt proclaimed it his intention to avert if he could. His failure (for German troops were withdrawn across the river everywhere north of Cologne by the end of the first week in March) was followed by his dismissal and the appointment of Kesselring to succeed him as OB West on 10 March. News of the change was immediately released at corps level, but on Kesselring's orders was for security reasons not to be passed lower down the chain of command, and he did not make his appointment public until he issued a resounding Order of the Day on 1 April in which he called upon his soldiers to become 'a sworn brotherhood of warriors rating honour more highly than life.'

Remagen and Koblenz: 12 Army Group

While the battle of attrition ground on between Maas and Rhine, the 12 Army Group front was relatively quiet for the greater part of February, until 1 US Army began to advance from Düren and 3 US Army through the Orscholz switch position during the last week of the month and the restless Patton broke loose from restraint and seized Trier on 1 March. Ultra was correspondingly sober in both sections, and the best of its intelligence was confined to order-of-battle items (the most notable of which was an up-to-date list of all the divisional and corps headquarters in 15 Army and 5 Panzer Army, the most complete such list of the whole war) and assessments of strength which enabled accurate estimates to be made of the opposition which would face the coming drive to complete the occupation of the west bank of the Rhine by capturing the remaining central sector between Cologne and 7 US Army's positions on the southern edge of the Saarland.

An admission by Army Group B on 11 February that the troops round Echternach (formerly the southern bastion of the Ardennes salient) were 'exhausted' was followed during the next couple of weeks by estimates of the battle-worthiness of most of the divisions in 5 Panzer Army and 7 Army (opposite 1 US Army); the greater number were rated fit only for defensive operations, strikingly few tanks and anti-tank guns were listed among their equipment, and Manteuffel himself (commanding 5 Panzer Army) put the fighting value of several of them at only one or two battalions' worth and complained that petrol for transport was very short. Several quartermaster returns in early March told the now familiar tale of low fuel and ammunition stocks.

Almost the only operational item of much value was Model's urgent order to 5 Panzer Army to send Pz Lehr to Bonn along the *Autobahn* soon after midday on 6 March. This evidently sounded a note of alarm about 1 US Army's thrust across from Euskirchen and up the Ahr valley which resulted in the seizure of Remagen bridge next day, but both Lehr and 11 Pz Division (which was given a similar order on the morning of 7 March but could not move until it received enough petrol) arrived too late to prevent the establishment of the first Allied bridgehead across the Rhine.

In view of the relative inactivity on 3 US Army's front until the second half of February, it was probably of little importance that an extremely long and detailed report on the state of every division in 1 Army (holding the Saar Palatinate) as at 3 February could not be signalled for another week. Only two of its fifteen divisions were judged capable of taking the offensive and the total fighting strength of them all combined was no more than some 45,000 men: the two Panzer divisions in the list, 11 Pz (which had not yet moved north to counter the threat of Grenade at this date) and 10 SS Pz, were credited with eighty-three tanks between them (thirty-one IVs and fifty-two Vs), both were rated fit for defence only, and the effect of the petrol shortage could be clearly detected in the bald words '30 per cent motorized, one battalion on bicycles' entered against 10 SS Panzer. A couple of days later 10 SS was relieved by 257 Volksgrenadier Division (one of the two thought capable of conducting an attack) and two more divisions were drafted in as reinforcements. The battlefield picture was shortly completed by a list of locations and a description of the chain of command in Army Group G and by another 1 Army return (signalled on 2 March, just before the American advance) which revealed its whole complement of assault guns and anti-tank guns on 21

1400/6
BT 6543
1117/7

February. The two Panzer divisions had now gone (17 SS's two tanks were the only ones in the whole army) and several artillery and anti-tank units had arrived, but otherwise the order of battle was much the same in both returns. It appeared that on 21 February 1 Army held 128 German and seventy-six Czech assault guns and that it was better equipped to withstand an armoured attack than in any other respect—146 75-mm anti-tank guns and eighty-three 'Jagdtiger' (self-propelled 88-mm anti-tank guns on Tiger chassis). Costly fighting in the Orscholz section of the West Wall had reduced 256 and 416 Divisions to no more than a battle-group apiece (they had lost 73 per cent and 81 per cent respectively of their men in a week), reported Army Group G, and Foreign Armies West predicted 3 US Army's advance on Trier and up the Moselle valley the day before it began.

Both these reports were overtaken by events, but it must have been heartening for Patton, as he planned 'the boldest and most insolent armoured blitz of the western war', which took 3 US Army from the environs of Trier to Koblenz and the Rhine in a single bound on 6 and 7 March, to know that Army Group G had just been ordered to extend its sphere northward and take over command of 7 Army (their headquarters were at Bad Kreuznach and in the hills above Cochem respectively on 3 March), and that his advance would therefore be astride the new boundary between Army Groups B and G, where co-ordination of the defence was likely to be at its weakest. Bradley and the whole of 12 Army Group, on the other hand, stood to benefit from the complete list of all corps and divisional battle headquarters in Army Group B which was intercepted and signalled just as Patton reached the Rhine.

1300/3
BT 6241
0750/4

Preparing to cross

Although they scented victory, the Allies had still to cross the great water-barrier of the Rhine. On the far bank, Kesselring had of course no secret plan for averting defeat when, on taking over as OB West, he hid real misgivings under false jocularity and greeted his staff with the words 'Well, gentlemen, I am the new V3', but he was expected to put up fierce opposition to the crossing which Eisenhower had decided to make north of the Ruhr and for which Montgomery was now preparing with his accustomed thoroughness and caution. In the event, the opposition was less than had been anticipated. The energy which Kesselring injected into his new command was apparent almost at once, however, in an upsurge in the volume (and to some extent also in the currency) of Enigma traffic, which may also have been due in part to some delay in setting up land-line connections between his headquarters outside Bad Nauheim and the three different command posts of Army Group B in the Westerwald which were reported inside a few days. This traffic gave abundant evidence that 21 Army Group's attack was expected at the time and place at which it eventually occurred, but there was surprisingly little about preparations to oppose it. Warnings of possible airlandings were so frequent that they ended by seeming like cries of 'Wolf, wolf', and on the eve of the operation Jodl and the local naval command grew suddenly agitated about a landing in the Ems estuary. By far the two most valuable items were both dated 13 March, and in spite of some delay in decoding were available at 21 Army Group well before its troops began to cross the Rhine.

The first was an order from Jodl for the construction of a 'blocking position' east of the river which, by reiterating the order Hitler had given a month earlier,[1] suggested that the intervening weeks had been wasted. The second (it arrived in successive fragments which amounted in the end to an exceptionally long message) was a comprehensive Parachute Army supply return which not only revealed the full order of battle in the Emmerich–Wesel–Duisburg sector, where 21 Army Group was to cross the Rhine, but betrayed the fact that even in this known danger-spot petrol was 'so short that even the supplying of the troops is jeopardized' and ammunition so scarce that the immediate delivery of 150 tons of certain specified calibres was deemed essential. An artillery return from the same source amplified another issued four days earlier and could be read alongside evidence that 15 Army, 1 Para Army's southern neighbour, was suffering from similar handicaps and had so few

1. See p. 234 above.

jerricans that it could not unload a fuel tank-train which had just arrived. (This was evidently a widespread problem. So many empty containers had been left behind in the retreat that the factories could not turn out new ones quickly enough, complained Kesselring, and ordered an immediate 'large-scale barrel-collection scheme' round Cologne.)

The disarray into which 1 US Army's capture of Remagen bridge threw the enemy was starkly revealed in the twenty-five or thirty messages describing his frenzied efforts to restore the situation which were intercepted during the next fortnight. Taken together, they convey such an impression of panic and unpreparedness to meet the emergency that Eisenhower's refusal to let Hodges exploit the advantage his soldiers' enterprise had won appears regrettable. To come to this conclusion on the Ultra evidence would be to make the old mistake of seeing strategy solely in terms of intelligence, however. By deliberate previous decision, the bulk of SHAEF's forces were committed north of the Ruhr, and the complicated movements of men and equipment for the Rhine crossing at Wesel were already under way. To switch several divisions right across the front would have thrown his whole force off balance, and Eisenhower did not dispose of sufficient reserves to exploit both opportunities at once. His order to Hodges not to advance more than a thousand yards a day was therefore unavoidable, although he, Bradley and Hodges all knew through Ultra that Kesselring could not have enforced such slow progress against their will.

From the immediate and tactical point of view, the Ultra account of the Germans' plight at Remagen was not altogether satisfactory, for only some items were available at once. Rundstedt's appreciation on the evening of the capture was not among them, but it was still informative forty-eight hours later: 'Situation must be cleared up tonight and the bridge destroyed. 11 Pz to be used. Bridge to be bombed from the air and naval special detachment to come from Army Group G. Investigate the neglect of duty.' On the other hand some warning could be given of suicide attacks on the bridge by volunteers from KG 51 flying Ar 234s and Me 262s at low level on 10 March. Then there followed a serio-comic tale of naval misadventure. Swimming saboteurs found only two warheads for their human torpedoes. Mines, which were to be used if they could be procured in time, were sent to the wrong place, so the attack was put off until the 20th, by which time only a 'mass operation' was thought to stand much chance of success. Some of the men and some of the mines were unfortunately captured on their way to the bridge, and bad feeling resulted between army and navy. Finally, there was no fuel for another attempt.

Reinforcements for the troops endeavouring to rope off the American bridgehead on the east bank (some of them under the redoubtable General Bayerlein of Panzer Lehr) were clearly being raked up from anywhere and committed piecemeal. They early included a Tiger tank company, and Hitler demanded that another be employed as well. Kesselring, however, admitted to Model on 14 March that this was not enough to wipe out the bridgehead (11 Pz was only 5000 strong) and that the only feasible course was to prevent its extension, although Hitler believed it could be stunned by heavy artillery fire and pinched out by flank attacks. By the 18th there were signs of a carefully considered counter-attack organized by Army Group B, and a zzzzz signal was sent in the hope of giving sufficient warning of it. A week later further reinforcements were reported and the strength of 11 Panzer and Panzer Lehr (respectively 2150 men—a reduction of more than 50 per cent in ten days—four Panthers and five anti-tank guns, and 3180 men, four Tigers and eleven Jagdtiger), together with their locations, were signalled within twenty-four hours, just before even more urgent needs forced Kesselring to move 11 Panzer to a new danger-spot south of Frankfurt and to let Panzer Lehr be drawn northwards into what was shortly to become the Ruhr pocket.

There was much less news from 3 US Army's front in the fortnight after Koblenz and Remagen fell on 7 March, but almost all of it could be signalled with far greater currency. A routine instruction for the preparation of defences along the Rhine bank between Koblenz and Boppard was followed on 15 March

0700/12
BT 6986
1327/12
2200/18
BT 7684
1422/19

12 March
BT 7104
1741/13

p.m./18
BTs 7674,
7678
1224/19

by an order signed by Kesselring's Chief of Staff telling 7 Army
to hold its ground because 'any retreat would lead to unforeseeable consequences' and to collect reinforcements by
makeshift methods in order to prevent an American crossing
between Niederlahnstein and Rüdesheim. This was the sort of
invitation Patton was not likely to decline, so he aimed his
main thrust some twenty miles farther south, where 7 Army
soon recognized a danger-spot round Alzey and dispatched 47
Volksgrenadier Division to deal with it. Was it perhaps the signal informing him of this which gave Patton the 'intuition' that
a German counter-attack was coming, and enabled him to react
so quickly that he 'beat Montgomery to it' by crossing the river
at Oppenheim on 23 March?

p.m./15
BTs 7375,
7381
1709/16

2030/18
BT 7709
2132/19

A declining Wehrmacht

The diminution in the scale of German air activity, which had
become progressively more apparent as the months passed
(GAF West's *total* effort on 9 March was 171 sorties, thirty-
five of them by bombers, at a time when the RAF and USAAF
were sending out a thousand bombers a day against German
towns, not to mention the fighters escorting them or engaged at
the front), showed up in two different ways during the spring.
Jodl informed all theatres of war on 13 February that flying
must be ruthlessly restricted to save petrol and that no operations were to be undertaken except those considered essential at
points of danger. A few days later OKL instituted new economy measures for jet fuel, which elicited the Air Ministry comment that this was the most striking evidence of its kind yet received and was likely to have a considerable effect on the scale
of jet activity (nevertheless, I KG 51 at Rheine was expecting
soon to have forty serviceable Me 262s). It was a logical consequence that some training Geschwader were dissolved in
March. Recruiting for the Luftwaffe and Kriegsmarine had
ceased in February, and all conscripts were now destined for
the army—itself now so short of men through casualties and
capture that Hitler authorized the use of specialists in particular
weapons as ordinary infantry and called for the 'formation of
reserves' by the setting-up of 10 and 11 Parachute Divisions in

Holland. A further decline in GAF training standards was suggested by Fliegerdivision 15's orders on two successive nights for raids on the Allies' Rhine crossing-places, since they ended with the words 'Load—high explosive for good bomb-droppers, fragmentation bombs for the rest'.

At first sight some extraordinary figures in a Hitler order communicated to OB West on 20 March seemed to offset this picture of a Wehrmacht in decline. The order promised the delivery of 1125 armoured fighting vehicles to OB West from the factories' March output in addition to 205 already announced—145 tanks Mark IV, 113 Mark IV with long-barrelled gun, 180 Mark V, seventeen Mark VI, 222 assault guns and 380 self-propelled anti-tank guns.[1] Next day Kesselring passed on the glad news to Army Group G with an instruction to have crews ready for 325 armoured fighting vehicles during the next three weeks. It was difficult to credit these figures, in view of the damage caused to armaments production by bombing, but there was no Ultra warrant for not doing so until 5 April, when Kesselring had to tell all his army group commanders not to expect more than 75 per cent of the promised allocation. Even this, of course, was pure fantasy. A couple of days after the interception of the original order, Speer attended an armaments conference at which Hitler 'frivolously ignored the realities . . . discussed totally nonexistent steel production' and expected five new models of tank to be demonstrated shortly. A truer scale of values was provided by the four tanks which Pz Lehr fetched to contain the Remagen bridgehead in mid-March, by the motley collection of men and tanks listed as reserves and reinforcements for 5 Panzer Army and 15 Army at the end of March, and (later on) by the seven tanks which Army Group Centre lent 7 Army for a single day to enable it to make an attack on 28 April and the very modest figures in two returns made by 7 Army about the same time.[2] Moreover it was noticeable that the same two or three Panzer divisions were always used when an armoured counter-attack was needed.

Signs of lowered morale and confusion behind the lines

1. These figures total 1057, not 1125; the discrepancy is unexplained.
2. See pp. 254–5.

began to be frequent in February and March. The Gestapo were called in to deal with unrest among civilian workers at a naval supply base near Frankfurt early in February, but there was unfortunately no Ultra reaction to the Dresden raid a few days later. Stragglers and refugees were an increasing problem. Gauleiters in the country between Moselle and Rhine were told to maintain morale by courts-martial but not to allow large-scale evacuation of civilians for fear of blocking the roads. Despite these and similar orders, both OKW and OB West were concerned about the way operations were being impeded in early March; OKW urged the drastic use of courts-martial, remarking that behind the eastern front a few executions had worked wonders. As 3 US Army approached the Rhine, the retreating troops were so demoralized that a court-martial had to be set up on the bridge at Mannheim. Kesselring laid the blame upon officers who lessened their own authority by questioning the orders of their superiors, and bade them raise the morale of their men by giving an example of obedience and discipline; in the same spirit a circular he sent to all Army Groups prohibited hasty and unplanned withdrawals which were sometimes carried by their own momentum farther than intended. A propaganda directive for the guidance of Luftwaffe commands on the Russian front was even more indicative of the fighting man's preoccupation with saving his skin rather than defending the Fatherland.[1] 'Some people say', it ran, that an Anglo–American occupation of Germany would be the lesser of two evils and that all efforts should be concentrated on keeping the Russians out. This was wrong, and bad for morale. There was only one principle—not to surrender one square metre of German soil—and all talk of an Anglo–German rapprochement was to be suppressed. Nevertheless the military bureaucracy was unperturbed: in the short interval between the Remagen crossing and those at Wesel and Oppenheim, OKH announced that it was prepared to accept nominations of suitable reserve officers for General Staff careers.

1. At an OB West conference on 7 February which was attended by all Army and Army Group commanders Rundstedt's opinion was that *'Der Soldat hat im allgemeinen die Schnauze voll'* (The troops are pretty well fed up to the back teeth).

9
Drive to victory

A general advance began in the last week of March from all three bridgeheads, and a fourth was added when 7 US Army crossed the Rhine near Worms. Quickest to move were 1 and 3 US Armies: when they met at Lippstadt on 1 April they had surrounded the Ruhr, and they at once set about besieging it. (At this point 9 US Army reverted to American command under 12 Army Group.) The isolation of Army Group B in the Ruhr left a huge gap in the centre of the German line (over 300,000 prisoners were taken in the Ruhr in the next three weeks), and 11 Army was hastily brought in to plug it. For a few days 11 Army managed to put up some resistance in the Harz, but before the end of April three American armies had swept round it and taken up positions on the north–south line of the rivers Elbe and Mulde, well beyond the limits of the occupation zones assigned to the western powers in the agreement recently made with the Russians.

The British 2 Army was also on the Elbe outside Hamburg by 20 April, but with Bremen still in German hands it was facing north as well as east when the Canadians began the liberation of Holland on its left flank. By 2 May it had sealed off Denmark by capturing Kiel and Lübeck, and met the Russians at Wismar on the Baltic.

Eisenhower's telegram to Stalin on 28 March was the first serious attempt at co-ordination with the Russians, who were on the Oder forty miles east of Berlin in February but did not get much closer until after the western Allies were on the Elbe (about the same distance away from Berlin on the opposite side), and they themselves had taken Vienna. The first contacts were made when Russians and Americans met at Torgau, south-west of Berlin, on 25 April.

Hitler committed suicide on 30 April as the Russians fought their way into Berlin and American troops occupied Munich, the capital of the Nazi movement. The general surrender came on 7 May.

Productive to the end

In retrospect, it is easy to see that the character of Ultra began to change soon after the Ardennes battles. Ever since D-Day its main strength had been immediate and operational—tactical moves in the front line and in the air over it, or hints that reinforcements in men and materials were on the way—and Hut 3's most important signals had usually been dispatched only a few hours after the German originals. Battle targets like petrol dumps or Panzer divisions on the move could still sometimes be notified to commands during the spring and so could an increased number of stock-returns, but there were now many more high-level appreciations with a bearing on strategy rather than tactics; they ranged over subjects as various as the separation of the Berlin headquarters into northern and southern staffs (and hence raised the spectre of an 'Alpine redoubt')[1] and estimates of how long the Wehrmacht's petrol and ammunition supplies would last. There were many more messages signed by Keitel, Jodl and others in Berchtesgaden or Berlin—presumably because bomb-damage denied them their usual telephone circuits during these last weeks—and many more concerning the Nazi party and its leaders.

The interval between German and British time of origin fluctuated more widely than in the past, and delays of three or four days were at some periods nearly as common as speeds of three or four hours had once been. The explanation lies, it is safe to

1. See p. 257 below.

speculate, somewhere in the struggle perpetually going on in Hut 6 between improved bombes and improvements in the Enigma machine, the details of which are still secret. Enlarged bombes could now decode practically anything, given the time required to test a vastly greater number of possible solutions, yet the increased cryptographic complexity of which the latest Enigma machines were capable sometimes made the new bombes slower in the end than their predecessors had been in accomplishing what were by comparison easier tasks. However, the volume of intercepted and decoded traffic was remarkably constant and surprisingly large, given the steady contraction of the area from which it came, although it too was more subject to sudden fluctuations than of old. Considerably more traffic was decoded on most days in March than on any day in February, for instance, and—astonishingly enough—the third week in April 1945 was almost as busy as any in the whole campaign except for the hectic period of German retreat the previous August.

On both counts, then—content and volume—there is no truth in the assertion that Ultra had shot its bolt by the time of the Ardennes offensive and was not of much importance thereafter. The assertion has already been contradicted for the winter months, and the contradiction is valid until the bitter end. The balance of the information conveyed undoubtedly changed, but there is no reason to believe that its value declined; certainly the only accessible estimates[1] of its usefulness in combat make no such suggestion but quote several examples to the contrary from the last three months of the war. It is of course true that, at any rate from the moment they crossed the Rhine, the Allies enjoyed such a preponderance of power that they could largely disregard the intentions, even when they knew them in advance, of an adversary who on military grounds should have given up the fight long ago. (This applies with particular force to the GAF, which had been reduced to impotence by now.) It is for just this reason that the change in the character of Ultra intelligence was so opportune. Better things than battle tactics could

1. Written in May 1945 by Ultra officers at the various US Army and Air headquarters on the western front.

now be derived from a source of Ultra's quality: news of the plight of the Dutch, of risings in Munich and Prague (the former involving old party members), of what was going on inside Germany, of the whereabouts of the Nazi leaders, of the way prisoner-of-war camps were being shifted to keep them clear of the western Allies' advance, perhaps above all information about the Russian armies. One of Hut 3's last signals, dated 9 May, will not have been the least useful we sent; it was a long one which rounded off a series conveying the German view of the Russian order of battle.

Some features of the advance

As Hitler himself said, by the beginning of April the western Allies were behaving 'as though the resistance of the Wehrmacht and the German people had already collapsed', pushing forward armoured spearheads in a fashion determined rather by considerations of topography, politics and supply than by the opposition encountered and moving so quickly that no intelligence service operating outside the battle area could keep up with them. His generals had implied as much already: on 28 March Fliegerdivision 15 did not know the strength and direction of the Allied penetrations between Sieg and Lahn or across the Main because there had not been enough patrolling, and Army Group B, commenting on the same two thrusts, appreciated that 1 US Army was directed on Kassel and 3 US Army north-east from Hanau. Most of the tactical information provided by Ultra in March and April—and there was an astonishing amount of it—is consequently not worth recalling, but a few notable features deserve mention.

When 21 Army Group moved out of the bridgehead which it secured across the Rhine on 23 March, 9 US Army followed the course of the river Lippe along the northern edge of the Ruhr. Hitler tried to halt it by ordering an attack on its flank round Haltern and Dülmen (where efforts to concentrate troops had already been made), and this was known almost at once. Reinforcements were scraped up and a staff improvised for a blow which General Student planned to deliver on the evening of 2 April: Ultra revealed his purpose eight hours be-

2100/31
BTs 9068,
9081, 9083
0459/1

2200/1
BT 9189
1103/2

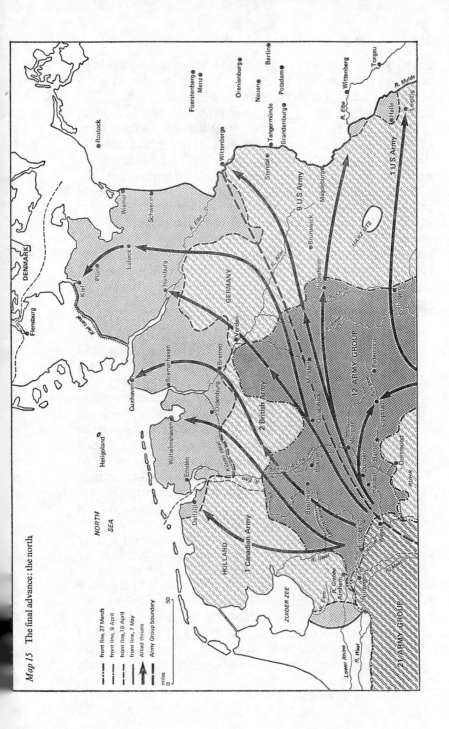

Map 15 The final advance : the north

front line, 27 March
front line, 9 April
front line, 19 April
front line, 7 May
Allied thrusts
Army Group boundary

miles
0   50

DENMARK

Flensburg

NORTH
SEA

Heligoland

Rostock

Kiel
Plön
Lübeck

Wismar
Schwerin

R. Eider

Cuxhaven

Bremerhaven

Hamburg
Verden
Bremen
Oldenburg

R. Elbe

Wittenberge

Stendal
Tangermünde
Brandenburg
Magdeburg

Fuerstenberg
Menz

Oranienburg
Nauen
Potsdam
Berlin

R. Elbe

Torgau
Wittenberg

R. Mulde

Halle
Leipzig

9 US Army

HARZ TS

1 US Army

GERMANY

Wilhelmshaven

Emden

Delfzijl

HOLLAND

ZUIDER ZEE

Lower Rhine
R. Waal
R. Ems
R. Grebbe
Arnhem
R. Ijssel

2 British Army

1 Canadian Army

12 ARMY GROUP

21 ARMY GROUP

Brunswick

Hildesheim

Münster
Dortmund
Lippstadt
RUHR

forehand. Lack of petrol caused it to be postponed until the afternoon of 4 April, and then cancelled before it could begin because of a threat from the north to Student's own flank. The operation had, however, in any case probably never been more than another of Hitler's fantasies: three days before he ordered it, Army Group H had reported its fighting strength so much reduced by heavy casualties and a widening front that the Allies would be able to break through wherever they chose. At the end of March, too, there was a good deal of agitation about defences along the Dortmund–Ems canal, the Weser and as far south as Würzburg (these defences had been planned as long ago as 1936, and had already been photographed). When it appeared that the forces available could not hold enough of this line to protect the naval bases at Emden and Wilhelmshaven and also cover Holland at the same time, Westphal decided that Holland should if necessary be sacrificed. By some curious chance, Holland almost monopolized Ultra news in the north from that moment on: there were enough men to defend it, but too few weapons, so Hitler ordered extensive flooding, and there were regular stock returns from the quartermaster branch of 25 Army, the occupying force. Still more interesting were several reports which kept the British and American governments abreast of the deteriorating situation behind the lines. Police authorities told Himmler on 24 April that food for the civil population would run out by 10 May, that German morale in Holland was low, and that police headquarters had moved to The Hague. Finally, there was a report which gave the German view of the meeting between Reichskommissar Seyss-Inquart and General Bedell Smith on 30 April to discuss relief for the starving population; it ended 'the course of negotiations so far could serve, if OKW deems it necessary, as a basis for further contacts', thereby suggesting a greater willingness to surrender than had been evident at the meeting itself.

The three weeks' death agony of Army Group B in the Ruhr pocket could be followed in some detail through a series of situation reports and supply returns, which began with a long list of the reduced forces composing its two armies (5 Panzer and 15 Army) as they were on the point of being surrounded. Just before the ring closed, Model told Kesselring that he would

1600/2
BTs 9279,
9302
0557/3

a.m./1 May
KO 1844
2352/1

give Bayerlein command of an attack designed to reopen communications with the east; if cut off, however, Army Group B could hold out for two or three weeks, but 'relieving attack must come from outside'—yet none knew better than Model how impossible the isolation of his two armies had made the gathering of forces sufficient to mount such an operation. He weakened his Rhine defences to reinforce Bayerlein, and Hitler ordered a thrust from Kassel westwards, but to no avail. Kesselring regretted that because petrol was so short he could not manage more than 32 tons of supplies a day by air, and inquired what Model needed most; the answer was 'small arms ammunition', and landing places for transport aircraft were arranged between the two commanders. Soon 5 Panzer Army estimated that its ammunition would run out in forty-eight hours and its petrol inside a week, but Model was still hoping to gain time for a relieving attack from outside on 11 April and still urging his troops on (although by now only 20 per cent had weapons) in the last messages from him that were intercepted.

As soon as the Allied advance began, both Kesselring and Hausser (commanding Army Group G) were quick to appreciate the acute danger which threatened them in the sector south of Frankfurt. Army Group B and the Remagen front were weakened in its favour when 11 Panzer was ordered south on the night of 24–5 March,[1] and reinforcements were directed to guard the line of the river Main between Aschaffenburg and Miltenburg to halt 7 US Army's drive eastwards from Worms and Darmstadt (among them was an SS training battalion which had no weapons heavier than small arms, no ammunition, five lorries powered by producer gas, two cars, three motor cycles, fifteen horses and two carts!). Two orders from Kesselring[2] to Army Group G on 31 March and 1 April made the sensitiveness of this area very plain, and they were decoded and signalled in reasonably good time. The first was designed to stop the American drive towards Eisenach (sufficient forces were available for this, he said) and the second to ensure that

1. See p. 241.
2. From late March until the end of hostilities, the location of Kesselring's headquarters was reported every few days as it moved from Bad Nauheim through Fulda, Ohrdruf and Augsburg to the Salzburg–Berchtesgaden area.

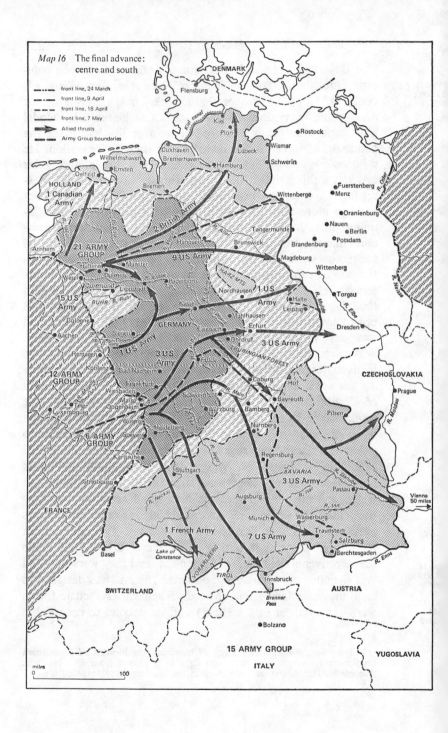

Map 16 The final advance: centre and south

- ···–··· front line, 24 March
- ········ front line, 9 April
- – – – front line, 18 April
- ——— front line, 7 May
- ⟶ Allied thrusts
- — ·· — Army Group boundaries

DENMARK
Flensburg
Kiel canal
Kiel
Plon
Rostock
Lübeck
Wismar
Schwerin
Cuxhaven
Wilhelmshaven
Bremerhaven
Hamburg
Emden
Bremen
R. Oder
Fuersterberg
Menz
Wittenberge
HOLLAND
1 Canadian
Army
Delfzijl
Oranienburg
Nauen
Berlin
Tangermunde
Brunswick
Brandenburg
Potsdam
2 British Army
Hanover
R. Aller
21 ARMY
GROUP
Arnhem
Münster
9 US Army
Magdeburg
Wittenberg
Wesel
Dülmen
R. Lippe
Paderborn
HARZ Mts
Torgau
Dortmund
Lippstadt
Nordhausen
1 US
Army
Halle
R. Neisse
15 US
Army
RUHR R. Ruhr
Cologne
Mühlhausen
Leipzig
R. Mulde
Aachen
Siegen
GERMANY
Erfurt
Dresden
R. Elbe
Remagen
1 US Army
Kassel
Ohrdruf
3 US Army
12 ARMY
GROUP
Koblenz
3 US
Army
Fulda
THURINGIAN FOREST
CZECHOSLOVAKIA
Trier
Bad Nauheim
Coburg
Hof
Prague
Luxembourg
Frankfurt
Wiesbaden
Mainz
Schweinfurt
Bamberg
Bayreuth
Pilsen
R. Moldau
Oppenheim
Würzburg
Worms
Nürnberg
6 ARMY
GROUP
Speyer
Heidelberg
R. Regen
Karlsruhe
Regensburg
R. Danube
BAVARIA
3 US Army
Strasbourg
Stuttgart
R. Neckar
Augsburg
R. Isar
Passau
R. Inn
Vienna
50 miles
FRANCE
1 French Army
7 US Army
Munich
Wasserburg
Traunstein
Basel
Lake of
Constance
VORARLBERG
Salzburg
Berchtesgaden
R. Enns
SWITZERLAND
TIROL
Innsbruck
AUSTRIA
Brenner
Pass
Bolzano
miles
0   100
15 ARMY GROUP
ITALY
YUGOSLAVIA

the line of the rivers Jagst and Tauber (between Stuttgart and Würzburg) was held 'at all costs'. Their purpose was made explicit during the next two or three days as Kesselring announced that the high ground in the Thuringian Forest was the best place for a stand to inflict casualties on the advancing enemy and to protect several strategically important features—the Halle–Nürnberg railway which links Berlin with south Germany, certain 'industrial installations' at Nordhausen (plainly the underground V2 rocket factory), the centre of the German ball-bearing manufacture at Schweinfurt (to guard which a battle-group was shortly withdrawn from the Russian front), and the Zeiss works at Jena. An order to concentrate troops in preparation for a counter-attack from Mühlhausen towards Eisenach on the 6th or 7th was signalled in time to give due warning.[1] The maintenance of communications from north to south across the Thuringian Forest—7 Army's headquarters was at Coburg, south of it—was also stressed when 11 Pz Division was set to guard the supply route through Ohrdruf. (With only four assault guns and ten Jagdtiger under command, 11 Pz was far from strong, but it was still one of the best remaining formations.)

Soon after Model told Kesselring that he was ordering Bayerlein to reopen communications between the Ruhr pocket and the east but that real relief must come from outside,[2] 11 Army (a new command) was instructed to assemble north-east of Frankfurt and regain contact with Bayerlein through Korbach. This proved impossible, and a couple of days later Kesselring shifted 11 Army eastwards to prepare a blocking position in the Harz and gain time for 'new measures'. The nature of the new measures was not stated, but protection of the railway through Halle was again stressed and one of 11 Army's strong-points was to be at Nordhausen. If Kesselring's aim was to use the Harz as a bastion to cover Berlin, events once more outstripped his plans. By 12 April, when he warned 11 Army to maintain liaison with Magdeburg in its rear and to bear the operations of 85 Division in mind, 9 US Army had been on the

.m./5
T 9610
145/6

---

1. This warning was useful to 3 US Army which, however, had sufficient strength forward to meet it without a change of plan.
2. See pp. 250–1.

banks of the Elbe north and south of Magdeburg for almost
twenty-four hours. Ultra had already shown that 85 Division
was to be the main strength of another new army, 12 Army,   1430/9
which Hitler had first ordered to assemble in the Harz. Circum-   KO 62
1450/10
stantial evidence suggests that 12 Army's original purpose—
which may also have been Kesselring's 'new measures'—was to
relieve the Ruhr; instead it was to be intimately concerned with
the fate of the Führer in Berlin.

As the rapid American advance swept 11 Army into obliv-
ion, however, it became clear that its short life had spanned the
transference of attention from western Germany to the Russian
front. On 12 April OKW ordered the Elbe defences as far upstream as a point just north of Dresden to face west; just a
week later Kesselring wanted them turned to face east if the situation south of Magdeburg deteriorated, so long as westward-
looking defence could be provided in case of need. Signs became common that the two fronts were now so close together
that the few remaining battle-worthy formations could be
switched from one to the other; thus 11 Panzer Division was
under OB West and 7 Army at Leipzig on 16 April, under
Army Group Centre to block a Russian threat five days later,
and back fighting the Americans north of Regensburg on the
23rd. How long could this kind of thing last, or any effective
resistance be maintained? When Keitel reallocated a little over
2500 tons of fuel from OKW's 'last stocks' on 16 April,
explaining that all new production had been lost, and when a
separate item in the same signal showed that shortage of petrol
was preventing even tactical battlefield moves by some units of
Army Group G in Bavaria, the answer was clear. From mid-
April, too, front-line reports from the German armies facing
the Russians become suddenly much more common among the
Ultra signals, clearly because of a directive to keep British
and American field commanders informed about events in
which they might find themselves suddenly embroiled even before the western and eastern Allies formally met.

For some reason not now apparent 11 Panzer Division's activities along the Danube occupy the stage in most of the remaining Ultra reports on the southern part of the front. They illustrate the conditions to which Hitler's army was reduced in its

last weeks. On the day the Americans reached the Danube (21 April) a 7 Army return showed that 11 Pz Division had twelve tanks (ten IVs and two Vs) and ten self-propelled anti-tank guns—more than the rest of the army put together. Meagre as this holding was, it was enough to earn the division the title of 'by far the prime unit' in 7 Army and to bring it the task of keeping the Allies out of south Germany although it had very little petrol for its tanks. A thrust it was to make across the Czech border was at first prevented by weakness (its personnel consisted mainly of stragglers) and by the breakdown of improvised means of securing petrol, and only went ahead when 7 Army gave up all its fuel stocks to the division. On 26 April it was still trying to counter-attack the Allied advance towards Passau with seven extra tanks borrowed for the day from Army Group Centre to increase its striking power. Its last recorded Enigma message, timed at 1600 hours on 27 April, told 7 Army that the division was barely mobile, was tied down by a superior enemy, and would only be able to move off southwards if hostile pressure eased and petrol could be provided.

Through Ultra, the Allied commanders were kept remarkably well informed about the drama being played out round Berlin; signals were sent with high priority in spite of the fact that they could be of no direct operational value. By 23 April 12 Army, under the command of General Wenck, had escaped encirclement in the Harz and was assembling a striking force thirty or forty miles west of Berlin for a thrust north-eastwards towards the capital, having denuded its westward-facing lines along the Elbe and Mulde for the purpose. During the afternoon of 24 April the Russians forced 12 Army back again through Oranienburg and Nauen across the northern face of Berlin as far as Brandenburg forty miles to the west and thus made impossible that 'speedy intervention on the north wing of the battle for Berlin' which Krebs, Chief of Staff of the Army, called for from Hitler's bunker on the 25th, lamenting that he 'still' had no word from 12 Army. He and Hitler were already out of touch with everything except the fighting in the streets around them and did not know that Wenck had already begun to move his forces off to the south-west and had got almost as far away as Tangermünde on the Elbe by the time Hitler called,

1500/23
KO 1216
0234/24

very late on 26 April, for Army Group Centre to attack towards Berlin in concert with 12 Army and for 9 Army (south of Berlin) to 'do its duty'. Hitler's despairing telegram to Jodl (on the way north with the A echelon of OKW) just before midnight on 29–30 April was a late awakening to reality from the dream-world in which only the previous day he was insisting that all decisions by commanders on the southern front should be submitted for his approval thirty-six hours before coming into effect, and had a little earlier been hoping for the completion of a railway line a few miles east of Berlin by 15 June. His telegram was timed 2300 hours 29 April and was intercepted as it was being transmitted—the text of the Ultra signal is identical with that in the OKW War Diary: 'Where are Wenck's spearheads? When will they advance? Where is 9 Army?' Keitel's reply two hours later that Wenck was stuck fast south of Potsdam and could not attack eluded Ultra. It was the sign that all hope was gone, and Hitler committed suicide twelve hours later during the afternoon of 30 April. The anxiety of his adjutant to arrange air transport out of Berlin that evening was no doubt because the 'important order' he bore was Hitler's appointment of Doenitz as his successor.

'Scorched earth'—or not?

At the Nuremberg trials and in the book he published after his release from Spandau prison, Albert Speer made much of the way in which he silently sabotaged Hitler's 'scorched earth' decree of 19 March 1945. Ultra told enough of the story at the time to show the Allies that there were two opposing views about the extent to which retreating troops should destroy factories, railways and bridges when they evacuated Reich territory; certainly, Speer's milder view loomed the larger and seemed to hold the field at the time of the last Ultra signal on the subject in late April.

　　Until mid-March Hitler's previous decree—'Render unusable, do not destroy'[1]—remained in force. The strongest of several pieces of confirmatory evidence was Model's record of a con-

1. cf. p. 225 above.

ference with Speer about demolitions in the Ruhr on 9 March,
to which Speer refers in similar terms in *Inside the Third Reich*.
It had been agreed between them, Model reported to OB West,
that railways and canals should be made unusable but not destroyed (for instance, railway and *Autobahn* bridges would not
be blown up, nor barges sunk in canals), and requested an appropriate OKW order to authorize him to carry out this policy.
Just over a week later a harsher note was struck by a request
for a special engineer detachment to prepare all nine hundred
Ruhr bridges for demolition, and this fits well enough with
Speer's account of how his attempt to get the kind of authori-
zation Model needed was blocked by Keitel and Hitler. The
'scorched earth' decree which Hitler issued on 19 March to end
the discussion was intercepted and signalled less than two days
later. There ensued a confused period of struggle within the
German government (according to Speer, twelve contradictory
decrees were issued in nineteen days), only faint echoes of
which reached Ultra. On 2 April OB West reproduced an order
from the Director-General of Transport for the creation of a
'transport wilderness', but the effect of Speer's countermeasures
was visible in orders from Luftflotte Reich and the north German territorial command during the next fortnight which required heed to be paid to the national economy and civilian
needs when demolition was being contemplated—power installations were not to be totally destroyed, water supplies and
drains to be left alone.

An 'Alpine redoubt'?

When the Russians began to threaten Berlin, and when the encirclement of Army Group B in the Ruhr removed 300,000 irreplaceable men and their equipment from the centre of the
German line in the west, it became clear to both sides that the
Reich might soon be cut in two somewhere about a line between Frankfurt and Leipzig, and that it might shortly be impossible to conduct operations from a headquarters in Berlin. If
further resistance were contemplated (and by 15 April SHAEF
thought it would be 'senseless') two general areas suggested
themselves: north Germany, Denmark and Norway on the one

hand, and the mountainous southern region between the western, Italian and Russian fronts which enclosed Hitler's favourite retreat at Berchtesgaden on the other. Little was heard at first about the former (although SHAEF was reluctantly girding itself to face the prospect in mid-April), but the idea that the Nazi might finally turn at bay in a 'National Redoubt' in the Bavarian and Austrian mountains gained a firm hold on many among the western Allies: SHAEF was taking it seriously in mid-March, Churchill was concerned about it, and in Eisenhower's telegram to Stalin on 28 March it was one of the bases of strategy.

Two issues therefore presented themselves, and both sides could envisage them with almost equal ease: the division of OKW and other headquarters between the two areas, and the preparation of a 'last ditch' stand in the south. The two issues were not necessarily very closely connected, for either could be realized without the other—the staffs might be divided to ensure separate surrender negotiations, for instance, and fanatical Nazis might well fight to the end without any previous plan— but in the heat of the moment it was easy to take signs of the former as implying the latter also. Belief in the redoubt was for a time stronger than any evidence warranted. The Ultra evidence, which accumulated in great volume in late March and throughout April, was confined to the division of the Berlin headquarters until the very last days, and therefore lent no support to aerial photographs of defences being built in the Tirol or to the rumours emanating from other sources, both of which were still holding SHAEF's attention in late April. Ultra in fact gave a very fair picture of the situation, although of course no one could be sure about this until after the end of hostilities: there is no mention whatever of a National Redoubt in an order Hitler issued on 15 April which envisages the possibility that land connection between north and south Germany may shortly be interrupted and lays it down that if this happens Doenitz will take over in the north if Hitler himself is in the south, and Kesselring in the south in the reverse case, but does not even hint at which course Hitler will adopt. Only on the 24th, a week before his suicide, did Hitler order the stockpiling of supplies and the building of arms factories in an 'inner fortress'; post-war investigation detected no signs of earlier preparation for defence.

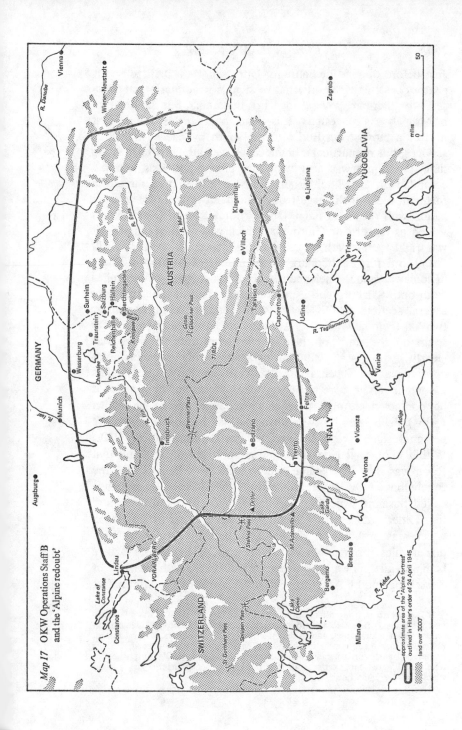

Map 17 OKW Operations Staff B and the 'Alpine redoubt'

Vienna

R. Danube

Wiener-Neustadt

GERMANY

Augsburg

Munich

R. Isar

Wasserburg

Chiemsee

Traunstein

Reichenhall

Surheim

Salzburg

Hallein

Berchtesgaden

Königsee

R. Inn

Innsbruck

Brenner Pass

TIROL

Gross Glockner Pass

R. Enns

R. Mur

AUSTRIA

Graz

Klagenfurt

Villach

Tarvisio

Caporetto

Udine

R. Tagliamento

Trieste

Zagreb

YUGOSLAVIA

Ljubljana

Bolzano

Ortler

Stelvio Pass

M. Adamello

Feltre

Trento

Venice

Venice

Vicenza

ITALY

R. Adige

Verona

Lake Garda

Brescia

Bergamo

Lake Como

R. Adda

Milan

SWITZERLAND

St Gotthard Pass

Splugen Pass

Lake Constance

Constance

Lindau

VORARLBERG

approximate area of the 'Alpine fortress' outlined in Hitler's order of 24 April 1945

land over 3000'

miles
0   50

Just before the end of February Ultra reported OKL to be urgently constructing an alternative signals headquarters at Wasserburg (there are several towns of this name, but the one east
of Munich was suggested). It is clear now that this was the first
hint of a move from Berlin to the south by one of the three
services, but no particular significance was attached to it at the
time—the signal was sent with low priority, as was another,
compiled on 20 March from scraps of information already a
fortnight old, which suggested a similar move by OKH to a location with the cover-name Olga. Within a week Olga was revealed as Ohrdruf in Thuringia, which was soon evacuated (it
was right in the path of the rapid advance which took 3 US
Army to Erfurt and Coburg by the middle of April), in favour
of somewhere in the neighbourhood of Traunstein (twenty miles
from both Salzburg and Berchtesgaden), and at the same time
several sections of OKL were also found to be in Thuringia,
two of them at Weimar. A large-scale but piecemeal move
south by the staffs of the German army and air force was
clearly in progress, with Thuringia apparently a staging-point
on the way to Bavaria. By 10 April we knew that OKH's
mountain refuge bore the cover-name Roon and that it could
be contacted through a signals exchange known as Alpen
(Alps) near Salzburg, where we had just identified Himmler's
personal signals regiment and several departments of OKL.
Within another ten days there was good reason to think that
Roon was Bad Reichenhall, where what were being called the
B echelons of OKH were housed, that it also used an exchange
called Susanne which was probably in or near Salzburg, and
that Hitler's office at Berchtesgaden used another called Hagen
which was probably at Hallein (all these places are within a
dozen miles of one another).[1] Explicit proof that the staffs were
being divided, not moved south en bloc, came with an order of
Kesselring for 11 Army to send officers from its quartermaster

1. It is worth drawing attention here to two points: (a) Ultra was of course
in a particularly favourable position to acquire the information on signals procedure from which these moves by Wehrmacht headquarters were deduced;
(b) the Allies made a practice of taking cover-names, when needed, from a
prepared list of words arranged in random order. Olga = Ohrdruf, Roon =
Reichenhall, etc., are examples of the dangerous penchant for giving clues
which the Germans never lost.

branch to both Potsdam and Traunstein, and by 22 April we knew that the main body of OKL had gone south, part to Berchtesgaden, part to Wasserburg.

Several more pieces of the jigsaw puzzle came to hand in a rush during the afternoon and evening of 25 April, and although some were as much as six days old all were processed with urgency (7 US Army had meanwhile been dispatched to deal with the 'National Redoubt'—if there were one—since Eisenhower had agreed with Strong that after the surprise in the Ardennes it was better to take no more chances). The first new part of the jigsaw was the discovery that Susanne and Alpen were the same and were at Surheim near Salzburg, that the battle headquarters of OKH was at Reichenhall, and that billets had been arranged for the OKW Operations Staff in the same district by 19 April. A few hours later we learned that transport for both northern and southern echelons of OKH and OKW Operations Staff had been made ready for a move on the 20th,[1] and that the Nazi Party directing staff with the army was also splitting up, its leader travelling with the south-bound group. Between these two there arrived three inscrutably cryptic messages from the GAF liaison officer with Hitler, one of which (dated 22 April) ordered aircraft of Hitler's communications flight not to go to Berlin. Lastly it appeared that the B echelon of OKW Operations Staff had been ready for work on the 23rd but that Kesselring (who, its head recommended, should make his headquarters near Salzburg) had so far given them nothing to do, and that American tanks between Salzburg and Regensburg were causing some alarm.

Although a little in arrears of events, then, Ultra was making tolerably clear what was happening to the main German service staffs. The OKW War Diary confirms that the B echelon left Berlin on 20 April and reached Berchtesgaden on the 23rd; when it left, Hitler was expected to rejoin it in the south, but he suddenly changed his mind two days later and decided to await the end in the Reich Chancellery; hence, no doubt, the message about the aircraft.

There had so far been more news of the south than of the

1. The two did in fact separate that day.

north, but the balance was now redressed. Early on 25 April we learned that OKH had moved from Berlin to Menz, fifty miles to the north, on the previous day, and soon afterwards that the A echelon of OKW was close by at Fuerstenberg, so that there were now clearly two separate command complexes, each resembling the former set-up in Berlin. Later news from the north showed OKW moving to Wismar by midday on the 30th in company with Himmler, and Naval War Staff going from its regular base at Plön near Kiel to Murwik on the outskirts of Flensburg, where it was eventually taken prisoner.

The new situation was made plain (and the detective work of the last few days shown to have been not far wide of the mark) by an order Hitler issued at dawn on 25 April which was decoded in time for a signal to be transmitted the following afternoon.[1] It set out the military subordinations in the northern and southern command areas, but held the assumption of responsibility by Doenitz (who had left Berlin for the naval headquarters at Plön near Kiel on the 22nd) and Operations Staff A in suspense for the moment (Doenitz received full powers very shortly afterwards, however), and laid upon OKW the mammoth task of regaining contact with Berlin by converging attacks from north-west, south-west and south.[2]

0500/25
KO 1444*
1452/26

early/25
KO 1452
1646/26

There was no mention of an 'Alpine Fortress' until a message of 29 April in which Winter (in the south) asked Jodl (in the north) to approve orders he had given about transport priorities in spite of the fact that they might delay the carriage of food into the 'Alpine Fortress' from Bohemia. This was soon followed by another (originated two days earlier) announcing the appointment of a commander for the northern front of the fortress with the duty of holding the approaches to it south of Munich and defending a semi-circle round the north of Salzburg. (This was partly a repetition and partly an extension of Hitler's 24 April order which first sketched the outline of the 'fortress'.) It was far too late, of course, for an effective defence to be improvised, and although a number of other signals told

2130/29
KO 1814
1403/1

---

1. The text is almost identical with that which Winter (Deputy Chief of OKW Operations Staff South) gave to Koller, Chief of Staff of the Luftwaffe, twelve hours after Hitler signed the order in Berlin.
2. These were the abortive attacks discussed on p. 256 above.

the American commanders, as they drove on, that ammunition was running short in the mountains, that they would find a lot of SS and Gestapo in the Tirol and Vorarlberg, that the population inside the fortress area was turning anti-Nazi and that they might catch Kesselring between Berchtesgaden and Zell-am-See, these will have done little more than add a garnish to an advance that was 'not even pursuit warfare any more; it was more a motor-march under tactical conditions'. Salzburg and Berchtesgaden fell without serious fighting on 3 and 4 May; OKW Operations Staff B was planning a getaway into the upper Enns valley above Zell-am-See as the American tanks rolled in, but did not get much beyond the Königsee and was very likely already 'in the bag' before the signal revealing its intention was delivered.

A brief chronology of the Western Campaign, 1944-45

1944

6 June	D-Day. Allies land in Normandy, but the Fortitude deception plan persuades the Germans that this is a secondary operation and that the main assault will be in the Calais area
19–22 June	Gale destroys one Mulberry harbour and delays unloading of men and supplies
25–30 June	Epsom: British attack across the river Odon, west of Caen
26 June	Americans capture Cherbourg
1 July	Von Kluge succeeds von Rundstedt as OB West
10 July	Caen captured
17 July	Rommel wounded
17–19 July	Goodwood: British attack east and south of Caen
20 July	Plot against Hitler fails
25 July	Cobra: the American break-out through Avranches
7–11 August	German attack at Mortain
15 August	Anvil/Dragoon: Franco–American landing on the French Riviera
13–20 August	The Falaise pocket
25 August	Paris liberated
25 August–4 September	The great Allied advance
1 September	Eisenhower assumes direct command of the Allied armies. Von Rundstedt again OB West

4 September	Antwerp captured. Allies on the general line Antwerp–Aachen–Luxembourg–Nancy
15 September	Anvil/Dragoon forces under Eisenhower. A single front from the North Sea to the Swiss frontier
17 September	Airborne attacks on Nijmegen and Arnhem
21 October	Aachen captured
23 November	Strasbourg captured: Allies on the Rhine
28 November	First convoy up the Scheldt enters Antwerp
16 December	German offensive in the Ardennes
26 December	German offensive in the Ardennes halted

1945

8 February	Veritable: British/Canadian drive through the Reichswald forest. Grenade: US drive across river Roer
3 March	Allies on the Rhine from Nijmegen to Cologne
7 March	1 US Army crosses Rhine at Remagen. 3 US Army reaches Rhine at Koblenz
10 March	Kesselring succeeds von Rundstedt as OB West
22 March	3 US Army crosses Rhine at Oppenheim
23 March	2 British Army and 9 US Army cross Rhine at Wesel
1 April	The Ruhr surrounded
25 April	First US–Russian contacts at Torgau, east of river Elbe
30 April	Russians enter Berlin. Hitler commits suicide
7 May	General surrender

A note on the Wehrmacht

Organization

Army groups (consisting of two or more armies) were designated by letters, armies (two or more corps) by arabic numerals, corps (two or more divisions) by roman numerals, and divisions by arabic numerals again. (Thus for instance II SS must be distinguished from 2 SS, for the former is a corps and the latter a division.)

Nominal strengths were 12,500 all ranks for an infantry and 15,000 for a Panzergrenadier division. Most army Panzer divisions were about 15,000 strong, but SS Panzer divisions could have as many as 20,000 men. Panzer divisions had about 160 tanks each, divided fairly equally between types IV and V.

Luftflotte (Air Fleet) 3 controlled all air operations in the west until September 1944, when it was downgraded to GAF Command West and subordinated to Luftflotte Reich (the air defence of Germany). It included Jagdkorps (Fighter Corps) II, Fliegerkorps (Air Corps) II (close support), IX (bombers) and X (anti-shipping). Jagdkorps II directed Jagddivisionen 4 and 5, and later also Jafue Mittelrhein (Officer Commanding Fighters Central Rhineland).

The GAF was organized into Geschwader (arabic numerals) of 100–120 aircraft, each consisting of three or four Gruppen (roman numerals) of 30–35 machines. The basic unit of operation was the Gruppe, not the Geschwader, and Gruppen were often detached from their parent Geschwader.

Equipment

Leading features of the main tank and aircraft types were as follows:

Tanks

Type	Main gun	Maximum speed	Weight
IV	75 mm	25 m.p.h.	25 tons
V (Panther)	75 mm	34 m.p.h.	45 tons
VI (Tiger)	88 mm	25 m.p.h.	54 or 68 tons

Self-propelled anti-tank guns (Jagdpanzer) mounted larger-calibre guns on a tracked chassis, and were called by the equivalent names—e.g. Jagdpanther had 88-mm guns, Jagdtiger 128-mm.

Aircraft: piston-driven
Messerschmitt (Me) 109   Single-engined, single-seat fighter
Focke-Wulf (Fw) 190   Single-engined, single-seat fighter
Me 110   Twin-engined night-fighter
Dornier (Do) 335   Twin-engined fighter/bomber

Aircraft: rocket-propelled
Me 163   Single-engined, single-seat fighter

Aircraft: jet-propelled
Me 262   Twin-jet, single-seat fighter or bomber
Arado (Ar) 234 Twin-jet (reconnaissance) or four-jet (bomber)

Personalities

Most of the German generals whose names occur in the text are either mentioned only on one occasion (when their significance is sufficiently described) or held high command and can therefore be found in Figures 1, 2 or 5. The following additional notes may, however, be useful.

Bayerlein, Generalleutnant Fritz. Commanded Panzer Lehr Division during the summer of 1944, LIII Corps opposite Remagen in March 1945 and a composite force in the Ruhr pocket later

Dietrich, SS Oberstgruppenführer Sepp. Commanded 1 SS Panzer Division in Normandy and later 6 SS Panzer Army in the Ardennes

Eberbach, General Heinrich. Commanded Panzergruppe West 5 July–10 August 1944, 'Panzergruppe Eberbach' for the Mortain offensive 10–21 August, 7 Army 22–31 August

Guderian, Generaloberst Heinz. Inspector-General of Panzer Troops 1944, Chief of the General Staff of the Army 21 July 1944–28 March 1945

Himmler, Heinrich. Reichsführer SS (i.e. head of the SS). In addition became Commander of the Home Army on 21 July 1944, directly after the plot against Hitler. Briefly OB Oberrhein 2 December 1944–24 January 1945, then commanded an army group on the Russian front

Kesselring, Generalfeldmarschall Albert. OB South-West 1943–10 March 1945, when he became OB West

Seyss-Inquart, Dr Arthur. Reichskommissar (i.e. governor) for the Netherlands 1940–45

Speer, Dr Albert. Reichsminister for Armaments and War Production 1942–5

Student, Generaloberst Kurt. Commanded 1 Parachute Army 1944, and assembled scratch forces to halt the Allied advance on the Belgian–Dutch frontier in September. Commanded Army Group H November 1944–April 1945

Glossary and abbreviations

Abteilung	Section, detachment
Abwehr	Secret Service
Flivo	*Fliegerverbindungsoffizier* (air liaison officer)
Flak	Anti-aircraft (regularly used in this general sense. Originally an abbreviation of *Fli*eger*a*bwehr*k*anone, anti-aircraft gun)
Foreign Armies West	Intelligence department of OKH responsible for estimating the strength and order of battle of the British and American armies
FUSAG	First United States Army Group. An imaginary army group which was part of the Allied deception plan
GAF	German Air Force (Luftwaffe)
JG	Jagdgeschwader (fighter aircraft)
KG	Kampfgeschwader (bombers)
Kriegsmarine	German navy
Luftgau, -en	GAF administrative ground commands in Germany and occupied territories
NCO	Non-commissioned officer
OB West	Commander-in-Chief West
OKH	Supreme Command of the Army
OKL	Supreme Command of the Air Force
OKM	Supreme Command of the Navy

Ultra in the West

OKW	Supreme Command of the Armed Forces
Pz	Panzer (armoured)
PzGr	Panzergrenadier (lorried infantry)
Pz Lehr	A Panzer division originally formed by amalgamating training (Lehr) units
SHAEF	Supreme Headquarters Allied Expeditionary Force
SLU	Special Liaison Units (see p. 9)
Stuka	Dive-bomber (*Sturzka*mpf)
V1, V2	Vergeltungswaffe (revenge weapon); V1 —flying bombs, V2—long-range rockets
VG	Volksgrenadier. VG divisions were introduced during the autumn of 1944; they were somewhat smaller in size than infantry divisions, and had a lower standard of equipment
Wehrkreis, -e	Territorial base and recruitment areas of the army in Germany
Wehrmacht	Armed forces
Werfer	Rocket discharger
Y-Service	The study of the external features of undecoded wireless traffic

Bibliography

Records

The Ultra signals between January 1944 (the opening of the service to Supreme Headquarters) and the end of the war are bound up in nearly 200 volumes of class DEFE 3 in the Public Record Office. Each series of signals was distinguished by a two-letter prefix and each series (with two exceptions) ran to 9999 signals; signals to Western and Mediterranean command were included in the same series.

Series	Dates of issue
VL 4789–VL 9750	26 January–29 March 1944
KV 1–KV 9999	30 March–28 June 1944
XL 1–XL 9999	29 June–13 September 1944
HP 1–HP 9999	13 September–21 December 1944
BT 1–BT 9999	21 December–9 April 1945
KO 1–KO 2089	9 April–15 May 1945

The addresses to which it was sent are contained in a panel at the head of each signal: SH for instance, stands for SHAEF, AG for 21 Army Group. The double brackets which mark off this panel and some words of the text are a coding device for burying the address in the text for security reasons, and may be disregarded. Phrases in single brackets like '(strong indications 21 Panzer Division)' or '(fair indications Aachen)' reproduce agreed conventions conveying degrees of uncertainty about the bracketed words. The word 'Comment' separates a summarized translation of the German original from Hut 3 comment upon it.

There is in addition a single roll of microfilm (DEFE 3/573) containing the c series of teleprints between September 1942 and the end of the war. Items concerning named personalities (e.g. German generals implicated in the 20 July plot, or escaped British and American prisoners-of-war) were put into this specially confidential series.

Non-Ultra records which I have consulted in the Public Record Office include WO 219/1920–1932 (SHAEF Weekly Intelligence Summaries, June 1944–May 1945) and PRO 31/20 (reports on the operational use of Ultra by Ultra officers with American Army and Air commands in the field, May 1945).

Printed books

P. Beesly, *Very Special Intelligence,* Hamish Hamilton, 1977.

C. Bekker, *The Luftwaffe War Diaries,* Macdonald, 1964.

D. Belchem, *All in the Day's March,* Collins, 1978.

E. L. Bell, *Ultra as an American Weapon,* TSU Press (Drawer F), Keene, New Hampshire, 1977.

*M. Blumenson, *Breakout and Pursuit,* 1961.

O. N. Bradley, *A Soldier's Story,* Eyre & Spottiswoode, 1951.

A. Bryant, *Triumph in the West* (*The Alanbrooke Diaries*), Collins, 1959.

P. J. A. Calvocoressi, 'The Secrets of Enigma', *Listener,* vol. 97, pp. 70–71, 112–14, 135–7.

A. Cave Brown, *Bodyguard of Lies,* W. H. Allen, 1976.

A. Cave Brown, *The Secret War Report of the OSS,* University of California Press, 1976.

W. S. Churchill, *The Second World War,* vol. vi, Cassell, 1954.

*H. M. Cole, *The Lorraine Campaign,* 1950.

*H. M. Cole, *The Ardennes,* 1965.

†J. Ehrman, *Grand Strategy,* vols. v and vi, 1956.

D. D. Eisenhower, *Crusade in Europe,* Heinemann, 1949.

†L. F. Ellis, *Victory in the West,* vols. i and ii, 1962, 1968.

* indicates a volume in the series *The United States Army in World War II,
European Theater of Operations,* Department of the Army, Washington D.C.
† indicates a volume in the series *History of the Second World War,* United
Kingdom Military Series (ed. Sir James Butler), HM Stationery Office

M. R. D. Foot, *History of SOE in France,* HM Stationery Office, 1966.

F. W. de Guingand, *Operation Victory,* Hodder & Stoughton, 1947.

*G. A. Harrison, *Cross-Channel Attack,* 1951.

B. G. Horrocks, *Corps Commander,* Sidgwick & Jackson, 1977.

D. Irving, *The Trail of the Fox,* Weidenfeld & Nicolson, 1978.

B. Johnson, *The Secret War,* BBC, 1978.

R. V. Jones, *Most Secret War,* Hamish Hamilton, 1978.

D. Kahn, *The Code-Breakers,* Macmillan, 1967.

R. Lewin, *Montgomery as Military Commander,* Batsford, 1971.

R. Lewin, *Ultra Goes to War,* Hutchinson, 1978.

B. H. Liddell Hart, *History of the Second World War,* Cassell, 1970.

*C. B. Macdonald, *The Siegfried Line Campaign,* 1963.

*C. B. Macdonald, *The Last Offensive,* 1973.

J. C. Masterman, *The Double Cross System,* Yale University Press, 1972.

B. L. Montgomery, *Normandy to the Baltic,* Hutchinson, 1946.

B. L. Montgomery, *Memoirs,* Collins, 1958.

*F. C. Pogue, *The Supreme Command,* 1954.

E. Rommel, *The Rommel Papers* (ed. B. H. Liddell Hart), Harcourt Brace, 1953.

C. Ryan, *The Longest Day,* Gollancz, 1959.

C. Ryan, *A Bridge Too Far,* Hamish Hamilton, 1974.

P. E. Schramm, *Kriegstagebuch des Oberkommandos der Wehrmacht* (War Diary of the Supreme Command of the German Armed Forces), vol. iv, Bernard and Graefe, Frankfurt, 1961.

A. Speer, *Inside the Third Reich,* Weidenfeld & Nicolson, 1970.

H. Speidel, *We Defended Normandy,* Herbert Jenkins, 1951.

W. Stevenson, *A Man Called Intrepid,* Macmillan, 1976.

K. W. D. Strong, *Intelligence at the Top,* Cassell, 1968.

A. W. Tedder, *With Prejudice,* Cassell, 1966.

R. W. Thompson, *The Eighty-Five Days,* Hutchinson, 1957.

W. Warlimont, *Inside Hitler's Headquarters,* Weidenfeld & Nicolson, 1962.

S. Westphal, *The German Army in the West,* Cassell, 1951.

F. W. Winterbotham, *The Ultra Secret,* Weidenfeld & Nicolson, 1974.

Examples of Ultra Signals

The letters SH, AG, and so on, at the head of each signal indicate the various army, navy and air headquarters to which it was directed.

The double brackets are a coding device which may be entirely disregarded.

In the body of the text the '£' is used to indicate the repetition of a word. This was done to ensure correct identification of proper names, for instance. For a similar reason, single letters were always represented by 'spellers' and in these examples A, B, C, D, F, J, K, L, N, S, T and X appear as Able, Baker, Charlie, Dog, Fox, Jig, King, Love, Nan, Sugar, Tare and X-ray.

REF.CX/MSS/T208/1.   KV 6735 IN TWO PARTS,

PART ONE.

ZZZZ

((KV 6735 & 6735 PK 89 & 89 IM 21 & 21 SB 99 & 99
coloktho
JY 46 & 46/SH 30 & 30 AG 2 & 2 FU 57 & 57 ON 43 &
43 EF 90 & 90 ST 9 & 9 DL 99 & 99 TA 38 & 38

IN TWO PARTS, PART ONE %

ARRANGEMENTS EVENING SIXTH. SECOND GRUPPE JIG ONE))
ARRIVING FLERS & FLERS (COMMENT, AS IN KV & KV SIX
SIX FOUR SEVEN FOURTHLY). THIRD GRUPPE JIG TWO SEVEN
(COMMENT, SEE KV & KV SIX SEVEN NOUGHT ONE FOR MOVE)
ARRIVING ROMILLY & ROMILLY, FOURTH GRUPPE JIG TWO
SEVEN ARRIVING CHAMPFLEURY & CHAMPFLEURY (COMMENT,
THIS GRUPPE AT SZOMBATHELY & SZOMBATHELY ON THIRTY-
FIRST). SECOND GRUPPE NAN JIG TWO ARRIVING
COULOMMIERS & COULOMMIERS (COMMENT, GRUPPE AT KOELN
BUTZWEILERHOF & KOELN BUTZWEILERHOF ON EIGHTEENTH). STAB

CP/AHW/KH   070813½/6/44

KV 6735 (see p. 66). 6 June. GAF fighters move to France on the evening of
D-Day. By early next morning Ultra reports the airfields at which they will be
based. J stands for Jagd (Fighter) Geschwader, NJ for *Nachtjagd* (night fighter),
NAG for *Nähaufklärung* (short-range reconnaissance), Z for *Zerstörer* (twin-
engined fighters). *Stab* means staff.

((KV 6735 & 6735 PART TWO AND FINAL %

AND ONE NAG & NAG THIRTEEN ARRIVING DINARD & DINARD))
(COMMENT, OTHER ELEMENTS ALREADY THERE SEE KV & KV
SIX SIX THREE NINE). ZEBRA ONE WITH TWO GRUPPEN
ARRIVING LORIENT & LORIENT. (COMMENT, FIRST AND
THIRD GRUPPEN HITHERTO IN WEST AND SECOND GRUPPE
IN AUSTRIA & AUSTRIA). SECOND GRUPPE JIG FIVE
THREE ARRIVING VANNES & VANNES (COMMENT, THIS GRUPPE
AT OETTINGEN-NOERD-LINGEN & OETTINGEN-NOERD-LINGEN
ON TWENTYEIGHTH SEE KV & KV SIX SIX SIX TWO). THREE
ISSUES (COMMENT, OF FUEL, AMMUNITION ETCETERA, ONE
ISSUE FOR ONE OPERATION) TO BE MADE TO EACH UNIT.
%/% SPECIAL ORDERS (COMMENT, NO & NO DETAILS)
REGARDING ISSUE OF TWO ONE CM & CM MORTAR SHELLS
RETAIN VALIDITY

GP/AHW/KH   07081 8&/6/44

ZZ

((XV 6673 & 6673 PK 51 & 51 LM 83 & 83 SB 69 & 69 JY 28 &
28 CO 96 & 96 ~~JY 28 & 28 JY 26~~ 96 SH 95 & 95 AG 70 &
70 FU 26 & 26 EF 57 & 57 ST 80 & 80 DL 78 & 78 TA 8 & 8
XV 76 & 76 IN TWO   PARTS, PART ONE %

FOLLOWING ACCORDING TO OKL & OKL ON FIFTH. AS RESULT OF
DAMAGED INTERFERENCE)) WITH PRODUCTION OF AIRCRAFT FUEL BY
ALLIED ACTION, MOST ESSENTIAL REQUIREMENTS FOR TRAINING AND
CARRYING OUT PRODUCTION PLANS CAN SCARCELY BE COVERED BY
QUANTITIES OF AIRCRAFT FUEL AVAILABLE. BAKER FOUR ALLOCATIONS
ONLY POSSIBLE TO AIR OFFICERS FOR BOMBERS, FIGHTERS AND
GROUND ATTACK AND DIRECTOR GENERAL OF SUPPLY. NO & NO OTHER
QUOTA HOLDERS CAN BE CONSIDERED IN JUNE. TO ASSURE DEFENCE
OF REICH & REICH AND TO PREVENT GRADUAL COLLAPSE OF
READINESS FOR DEFENCE OF GAF & GAF IN EAST, IT HAS BEEN
NECESSARY TO BREAK INTO OKW & OKW STRATEGIC RESERVE.
EXTENDING THEREFORE EXISTING REGULATIONS

MK/RAWB/RFB   0623472/6/44
GB

KV 6673 (see p. 55–6). 5 June. Cheerful news on the evening of D-Day: the
Luftwaffe was critically short of petrol even before the landings. B4 was the
standard grade of aircraft fuel.

ZZ

((KV 6673 & 6673 PART TWO AND FINAL %

(CONTENT NO & NO DETAILS HERE), ORDERED THAT ALL UNITS))
TO ARRANGE OPERATIONS SO AS TO MANAGE /\/ AT LEAST UNTIL THE
BEGINNING OF JULY WITH PRESENT STOCKS OR SMALL ALLOCATIONS
WHICH MAY BE POSSIBLE. DATE OF ARRIVAL AND QUANTITIES OF
JULY QUOTA STILL UNDECIDED. ONLY VERY SMALL QUANTITIES
AVAILABLE FOR ADJUSTMENTS, PROVIDED ALLIED SITUATION REMAINS
UNCHANGED. IN NO & NO CIRCUMSTANCES CAN GREATER ALLOCATIONS
BE MADE. ATTENTION AGAIN DRAWN TO EXISTING ORDERS FOR MOST
EXTREME ECONOMY MEASURES AND STRICT SUPERVISION OF
CONSUMPTION, ESPECIALLY FOR TRANSPORT, PERSONAL AND
COMMUNICATIONS FLIGHTS. SUPPLY OF GOODS WHERE POSSIBLE
AND DUTY JOURNEYS IN GENERAL (IN REICH & REICH AT LEAST)
TO BE BY RAIL. *Above addressed to first Parachute Army.*

061356Z/6/44

--/RAWB/RFB

GB

((KV 6642 £ 6642 BH 81 £ 81 AG 57 £ 57 FU 13 £ 13
       76 £ 76
ON 18 £ 18 YK/EF 43 £ 43 TA 94 £ 94 XF 69 £ 69 %

INTENTIONS NINTH FLIEGERKORPS)) FOR NIGHT SIXTH
TO SEVENTH ACCORDING GERMAN NAVY AT ONE TWO THREE
NOUGHT HOURS SIXTH. TWO ONE TWO FIVE HOURS
CONCENTRATED ATTACK ON LANDING CRAFT SEA AREA
BETWEEN SEINE £ SEINE MOUTH AND BAYEUX £ BAYEUX.
AFTER LANDING, SUCCESSIVE ATTACKS BY GESCHWADERS
IN THE SAME AREA. SECONDLY, AT ONE SEVEN TWO
FIVE HOURS SIXTH GERMAN NAVY GAVE WARNING OF
INTENDED OUTWARD FLIGHT OVER COAST OF STRONG
FORMATIONS AREA PORT EN BESSIN £ PORT EN BESSIN FROM
       NOUGHT   ATTACK
TWO ONE ONE/HOURS TO /ABX SHIPPING IN AREA
ARROMANCHES LES BAINS £ ARROMANCHES LES BAINS. FROM
TWO ONE THREE FIVE INWARD FLIGHT SAME AREA. FROM
NOUGHT NOUGHT THREE NOUGHT HOURS CONTINUOUS OUTWARD
AND INWARD FLIGHTS SAME AREA

                                      061747Z/6/44

KV 6642 (see p. 66). 6 June. A typical air-raid warning, one of many sent out almost every day (often several times a day) throughout the campaign. The German order, issued at midday, called for a raid at 2125 hours the same evening. The Hut 3 signal, timed 1747 hours, gave three and a half hours' warning and facilitated interception by stating the route the raiders would follow.

CX/MSS/T210/177   KV 7225

                    ZZZZ

((KV 7225 £ 7225 SH 23 £ 23 AG 67 £ 67 FU 23 £ 23
ON 56 £ 56 OHA CR YK 12 £ 12 ZE EF 13 £ 13 ST 34 £ 34
DL 77 £ 77 TA 94 £ 94 %

BATTLE HEADQUARTERS PANZER)) GRUPPE WEST EVENING NINTH
AT LA CAINE £ LA CAINE (TARE NINE ONE FIVE TWO)

ARGP/AHW/DC   1004392/6/44.

CX/MSS/T211/14   KV 7267

               ZZZZ

((KV 7267 £ 7267 SH 47 £ 47 AG 91 £ 91
FU 47 £ 47 ON 67 £ 67 CR EF 97 £ 97 ST 52 £ 52
DL 93 £ 93 TA 19 £ 19 %

... (AMMUNITION ISSUING STATION)) SET UP
ONE NOUGHT KILOMETRES SOUTH EAST OF FALAISE
£ FALAISE ALONGSIDE ROAD TO ARGENTAN £
ARGENTAN. THE BRINGING THITHER OF EIGHT
OINT EIGHT CENTIMETRE AMMUNITION
AWAITED ... / ((URGENT ONE EIGHT THREE NOUGHT
HOURS ENTER))

7/AHW/DON   1010352/6/44

KVs 7225, 7267 (see pp. 68–9). 9 June. Two bombing targets. A raid on the first paralysed the armoured counter-attack force. The second is typical of the way in which Ultra regularly located petrol and ammunition dumps.

REF. CX/MSS/T272/8   XL 5490

                    ZZZ

((XL 5490 £ 5490 SH 42 £ 42 SHA 86 £ 86 TG 89 £ 89 BV 17 £
17 ON CR EF 59 £ 59 %

TANK SITUATION ONE TWO SS £ SS)) DIVISION ISSUED LATE EIGHTH.
CHARLIE KING TWO COLON TWO, TWO ABLE COLON ONE, TWO BAKER
COLON ONE. CHARLIE LOVE TWO COLON FIVE NOUGHT, TWO ABLE COLON
THREE FOUR, TWO BAKER COLON NINE, TWO CHARLIE COLON SEVEN,
THREE BAKER COLON ONE. DOG TWO COLON THREE FOUR, TWO ABLE COLON
TWO NOUGHT, TWO BAKER COLON ONE SEVEN, TWO CHARLIE COLON TWO,
THREE CHARLIE COLON THREE. FOX TWO COLON EIGHT, TWO ABLE
COLON SIX, TWO BAKER COLON ONE, TWO CHARLIE COLON (ST ONE
INDICATIONS ONE). COMMENT INTERPRETATION ON BASIS SIMILAR
PRO-FORMA USED BYØ CHARLIE IN CHARLIE SOUTH WEST COLON CHARLIE
KING, TANKS (ROMAN) THREE SEVEN POINT FIVE SHORT. CHARLIE LOVE,
TANKS (ROMAN) FOUR SEVEN POINT FIVE LONG. DOG, TANKS (ROMAN) FIVE.
FOX, ACVS £ ACVS. TWO (FAIR INDICATIONS TOTAL STRENGTH), TWO
ABLE (FAIR INDICATIONS SERVICEABLE), THREE BAKER (FAIR
INDICATIONS TOTAL LOSS). TWO BAKER AND TWO CHARLIE NOT £ NOT
KNOWN
                    101039Z/8/44
CAX/ANW
LDF

XL 5490 (see p. 116). 12 SS Panzer Division's tank strength after the Mont
Pinçon action. An example of the pro-formas by which such returns were always
made. Most returns covered several divisions and were in consequence much
longer.

REF. CX/MSS/T286/123.   XL 5027

ZZZZZ

((XL 5027 £ 5027 SH 32 £ 32 SHA 77 £ 77 TG 29 £ 29 BV 56
£ 56 ON 22/£/22 YK ZB EF 70 £ 70 ST 15 £ 15 DL 97 £ 97 AD
71 £ 71 %

ACCORDING (FAIR INDICATIONS JAGDKORPS TWO) AT ONE SEVEN
HOURS SIXTH, SEVEN ARMY TO)) ATTACK FROM ONE EIGHT THREE
NOUGHT HOURS SIXTH WITH STRONG FORCES OF FIVE PANZER
DIVISIONS FROM AREA SOURDEVAL - MORTAIN £ SOURDEVAL -
MORTAIN 2££££££/£££/££££///£££££/££££££££/££/£££ TOWARDS
THE WEST.   FIRST OBJECTIVE OF ATTACK ROAD BRECEY -
MONTIGNY £ BRECEY - MONTIGNY.   JAGDKORPS TWO TO SUPPORT
ATTACK WITH ALL FORCES EXCEPT ((JIG TWO))

D/AIM/III   Ø£ 070011Z/8/44.

XL 5027 (see p. 115). 1700 hours, 6 August. First news of the Mortain attack.

Ref. CX/MSS/T271/132   XL 5461   IN TWO
                              PARTS PART ONE.
                    ZZZZZ

((XL 5461 £ 5461 SH 20 £ 20 SHA 64 £ 64 TG 67 £ 67 BV 94

94 OH CR YK ZE EF 40 £ 40 ST 49 £ 49 DL 4 £ 4 MI 10

£ 10 XF 75 £ 75 IN   TWO   PARTS PART ONE %

ORDERS TO SEVENTH ARMY)) AND GENERAL DER PANZER TRUPPEN

EBERBACH £ EBERBACH ONE EIGHT HOURS NINTH. ATTACK ON

SOUTHERN WING OF SEVENTH ARMY WILL BE CONDUCTED BY

PANZER GRUPPE EBERBACH £ EBERBACH AFTER REGROUPING AND

BRINGING UP OF DECISIVE OFFENSIVE ARMS. ON ITS SUCCESS

DEPENDS THE FATE OF BATTLE OF FRANCE £ FRANCE. QUOTE

I ORDER UNQUOTE COLON (ONE) COMMAND OF ATTACK COLON

GENERAL EBERBACH £ EBERBACH TO WHOM A NEWLY FORMED

FUEHRUNGSSTAB IS BEING BROUGHT UP WITH OBERSTLEUTNANT

VON KLUGE £ VON KLUGE AS CHIEF OF STAFF. FOR REASONS

OF UNIFIED COMMAND (LATER PARTICIPATION OF SEVENTH ARMY)

AND SUPPLY, EBERBACH £ EBERBACH IS BEING SUBORDINATED

TO GOC £ GOC SEVENTH ARMY. (TWO) OBJECTIVE OF ATTACK

% COLON THE SEA AT AVRANCHES £ AVRANCHES

AFGP/EFB/DG   100349Z/8/44.,

XL 5461 (see p. 118). 1800 hours, 9 August. Hitler personally orders the renewal of the Mortain attack. Ultra gives a day's warning—the signal is timed 0349 hours, 10 August, the attack will go in 'probably on [the] eleventh'.

ZZZZZ

((XL 5461 & 5461 PART TWO AND FINAL &
TO WHICH A BOLD AND UNHESITATING THRUST THROUGH IS
TO BE MADE,)) REAR ATTACKING WAVES SWINGING NORTH AS
AND WHEN OPPORTUNITY OCCURS. (THREE) ASSEMBLY AREA
AND CONDUCT OF ATTACK IN ACCORDANCE WITH QUOTE MY
MY UNQUOTE VERBAL INSTRUCTIONS. THERE IS TO BE A
REGROUPING WITH OBJECT OF CONDUCTING THE THRUST FROM
REA MORTAIN & MORTAIN - DOMFRONT & DOMFRONT. SPECIAL
ATTENTION IS DRAWN TO NECESSITY OF CAMOUFLAGE MEASURES.
(FOUR) TIME OF ATTACK COLON PROBABLY ON ELEVENTH. BE
/////////// PREPARED FOR A POSTPONEMENT AT SHORT
NOTICE OF ONE TWO TO TWO FOUR HOURS. (FIVE) ATTACKING
TROOPS (COMMENT. DETAILS NOT & NOT AVAILABLE)

AFGP/RFB/DC   100358Z/8/44.

REF. OX/MSS/T208/182

ZZZZ

((KV 6893 & 6893 SH 21 & 21 AG 82 & 82 FU 38 & 38
ON 6 & 6 CR EF 77 & 77 ST 77 & 77 DL 52 & 52 TA 17 &
17 IN TWO PARTS, PART ONE %

INTENTIONS ACCORDING UNSPECIFIED FLIVO AT NOUGHT
EIGHT HOURS SEVENTH COLON FIRSTLY, ATTACK)) WITH TWELVE
SUGAR SUGAR PANZER DIVISION AND PANZER LEHR DIVISION
FROM THE AREA SOUTH WEST OF PLACE UNSPECIFIED IN
(COMMENT, EITHER NORTH WESTERN OR NORTHEASTERN). DIRECTION.
SECONDLY, LINKING UP IN BLOCKING POSITION (STRONG
INDICATIONS RIGHT WING) OF THREE FIVE TWO INFANTRY
DIVISION ON LINE LUZELLES & LUZELLES (COMMENT, PROBABLY
LOUCELLES & LOUCELLES TARE EIGHT SEVEN SEVEN THREE) -
CANCAGNY & CANCAGNY - NONANT & NONANT - SOMMERVIEU &
SOMMERVIEU - CHAMVIEUX & CHAMVIEUX (COMMENT, LATTER NOT
& NOT TRACED, POSSIBLY HANVIEUX & MANVIEUX). THIRDLY,
ATTACK FROM LINE FRESVILLE & FRESVILLE $

0807162/6/44

COP/AH/KH

KV 6893 (see p. 67). 7 June. Plans for an early counter-attack on the beach-
head. Though subject to almost twenty-four hours' delay (0800/7–0716/8 June)
this signal commanded high priority because it showed that Hitler had released
Panzer Lehr and 12 SS Panzer Divisions from reserve and revealed the tactical use
Rundstedt would make of them. T 8773, O 3502, etc., are map grid-references.

ZZZZ

((KV 6893 £. 6893 PART TWO AND FINAL %

AZEVILLE £ AZEVILLE (COMMENT, OBOE THREE ¥ FIVE NOUGHT
TWO - TARE THREE TWO NINE NINE))) TO SOUTH EAST WITH
AT THE SAME TIME DEFENCE ON LINE ANGOVILLE £ ANGOVILLE
- HOUESVILLE £ HOUESVILLE (COMMENT TARE THREE NINE
EIGHT NINE - THREE SIX EIGHT NINE) - WEST BANK OF
CHERDERETTE £ CHERDERETTE (COMMENT, LATTER NOT £ NOT
TRACED, POSSIBLY RIVER MERDERET £ MERDERET)

JCP/AIT./KH   080723"/6/44

REF. CX/MSS/T298/79

XL 9245

ZZZ

((XL 9245 & 9245 ZE YK ON CR GU 62 & 62 TGA TG 31 & 31
WH 96 & 96 NX 25 & 25 EM 11 & 11 DL 48 & 48
ST 7 & 7 MI 35 & 35 MIA 66 & 66 SH 92 & 92

ARMY GROUP BAKER ORDER QUOTED BY FLIVO ONE SEVEN THREE:
NOUGHT HOURS FIFTH. ONE. STAB PANZER ARMY FIVE)) WITH
SUBORDINATED HQ & HQ FIVE EIGHT PANZER CORPS TO TRANSFER
BEGINNING SIXTH TO AREA KOBLENZ & KOBLENZ FOR REST AND
REFIT BY CHARLIE IN CHARLIE WEST. TWO. HQ & HQ TWO SS & SS
PANZER CORPS SUBORDINATED ARMY GROUP BAKER, TO TRANSFER
TO EINDHOVEN & EINDHOVEN TO REST AND REFIT IN
COOPERATION WITH GENERAL OF PANZER TROOPS WEST AND DIRECT
REST AND REFIT // OF TWO AND ONE ONE SIX PANZER DIVISIONS,
NINE SS & SS PANZER DIVISION AND HEAVY ASSAULT GUN
ABTEILUNG TWO ONE SEVEN. COMBAT ELEMENTS THREE DIVISIONS
AND TEN SS & SS PANZER DIVISION NOT & NOT OPERATING
ORDERED FOURTH TO AREA VENLOO & VENLOO-ARNHEIM & ARNHEIM-
HERTOGENBOSCH & HERTOGENBOSCH ~~IN~~ FOR REFIT IN XRAY LOVE
NINE ONE EIGHT EIGHT NOT & NOT TO MISS ITEM

POI/RFB/LED   060103Z/9/44

XL 9245 (see p. 153). 5 September. Tanks at Arnhem. Twelve days before
'Market Garden', Ultra reports that II SS Panzer Corps, 9 and 10 SS Panzer
Divisions and other armour are ordered to south Holland.

ZZZ

KO 1444 C 1444

KG HS SB 47 C 47 R^J 32 C 32 JY 10 C 10 PK 89 C 89

CR ONA ON QXA GX YKA YK UC ZSA ZS FZ OU 77 C 77 TOA

TO 68 C 68 WM 36 C 36 NX 44 C 44 LP 30 C 30 DL 72 C 72

STR 30 C 30 STA 59 C 59 ST 54 C 54 MI 72 C 72 XF 91 C 91

SHR 55 C 55 FOR WILD SH 23 C 23
IN TWO PARTS, PART ONE %

WA 472 C 472

HITLER C HITLER AT NOUGHT FIVE HOURS TWENTYFIFTH COLON
(ONE) OKW C OKW RESPONSIBLE TO HITLER C HITLER FOR FURTHER
CONDUCT OF OPERATIONS AS A WHOLE. (TWO) THE FOLLOWING TO
DIRECT OPERATIONS IN ACCORDANCE WITH INSTRUCTIONS TO BE
ISSUED THROUGH ARMY CHIEF OF STAFF GENERAL KREBSC KREBS
WHO IS WITH HITLER C HITLER. (ABLE) IN SOUTHERN AREA WITH
HELP OF OPERATIONS STAFF BAKER (GENERAL-LEUTNANT WINTER
C WINTER) COLON ARMY GROUPS SOUTH AND CENTRE, CHARLIES IN
CHARLIE SOUTHWEST C SOUTHWEST, SOUTHEAST C SOUTHEAST, AND
WEST C WEST. (BAKER) IN NORTHERN AREA, DIRECTLY COLON
CHARLIES IN CHARLIE ARMED FORCES NORWAY C NORWAY AND

JB/CAZ/XH   2614522/4/45

KO 1444 (see p. 262). 25 April 1945. Isolated in the Berlin bunker and out of touch with reality, Hitler re-organized the high command. An example of the kind of intelligence Ultra was producing right down to the end of the war. 'Heer' means 'army' in the wide sense (as in 'General Staff of the Army'). Because 'Armee' also means 'army' (in the narrow sense—e.g. '12 Army') it was sometimes necessary to use the German words for the sake of clarity.

ZZZ

KO 1444 & 1444

PART TWO AND FINAL *

DENMARK & DENMARK, NORTHWEST & NORTHWEST, TWELVE ARMY,
ARMY GROUP VISTULA & VISTULA WITH NINE ARMY, ARMY EAST
. RUSSIA & EAST PRUSSIA, AND ARMY GROUP COURLAND & COURLAND.
THREE) OPERATIONAL DUTIES OF OPERATIONS STAFF ABLE UNDER
GROSSADMIRAL DOENITZ & DOENITZ NOT & NOT TO COME INTO FORCE
FOR TIME BEING. (FOUR) PRINCIPLE TASK OF OKW & OKW REMAINED
THE REESTABLISHMENT OF CONTACT ON BROAD FRONT WITH BERLIN &
BERLIN BY ATTACKING WITH ALL FORCES AND MEANS AND GREATEST
POSSIBLE SPEED FROM NORTHWEST & NORTHWEST, SOUTHWEST &
SOUTHWEST, AND SOUTH AND THEREBY BRING THE BATTLE OF BERLIN
& BERLIN TO A VICTORIOUS DECISION. (FIVE) OPERATIONS GRUPPE
OF THE GENERAL STAFF AND INSPECTOR GENERAL OF PANZER TROOPS
TO COME UNDER COMMAND OF CHIEF OF ARMED FORCES OPERATIONS
STAFF. CMG & CMG OF HEER & HEER AS ARMED FORCES CMG & CMG
DIRECTLY UNDER CHIEF OF OKW & OKW. (SIX) ORDER FOR COMMAND
OF GAF & GAF WERE TO FOLLOW

KW/GAZ/KH   261457ᵃ/4/45

Notes

Chapter 1

p. 3   *50,000 men in 1944:* Speidel 64.

p. 7   *U-boats and so on:* Beesly 64–5.

p. 9   *responsible for their activities:* Winterbotham 21–4, 88–9, etc.

p. 17   *fact never have existed:* Schramm 1764. After reading 'mountains of records' for his book *The Siegfried Line Campaign,* Macdonald concluded: 'Yet one major element often is missing: the "why" behind a commander's decision. Indeed, it is difficult in many instances to determine even who made the decision' (Macdonald 629).

p. 18   *not support the claim:* made, for instance, by Winterbotham 47, 116, 145, 150.

p. 23   n.   *Charybdis of the recipient':* PRO 31/20/3, 17.

Chapter 2

p. 29   *to Hitler on them:* Schramm 256, *Rommel Papers* 453.
           Rommel' via OB West: VL 9032.

p. 30   *charge of coastal defence:* Schramm 263–7.
           come until mid-March: VLS 8693, 8846.
           the St Quentin area: VL 9037.
           section on 6 March: VL 8758.
           envied Germany her OKW: Schramm 1636.

p. 34   *a highly paid NCO':* Schramm 37.

p. 36   *fighting in the bridgehead:* Schramm 1593.
           conference of 29 June: Ellis i. 323, Schramm 1594, Irving 362–4.

     'Make peace, you fools': Lewin, *Montgomery* 208.

p. 37 *the Rhine (2 September):* Pogue 253.

p. 38 *perhaps in some combination:* Ellis i. 54.

     the spring' would fall: Schramm 1530–34.

     became known through Ultra: Winterbotham 190, Cave Brown 356.

     blood of its soldiers': vLs 5160, 5309.

     Rome in great detail: vL 5449.

p. 39 *or another of them:* Schramm 1798.

     central or southern Norway: vL 9126, not decoded until 22 March.

     opinion well into May: vL 5426.

     France!) on 20 March: kv 773, decoded 12 April.

     types of landing-craft: vL 9183.

     OB West next day: kv 353, decoded 6 April.

     concluded a week later: kvs 628, 727, decoded 10 April.

     in shame and ignominy': kv 1705.

  n. *with preparations for invasion:* Ellis i. 133.

p. 40 *Rundstedt on 8 May:* kv 3763.

     between Le Havre and Cherbourg: kv 3242.

     far east as Dieppe: kv 5446.

     this over other areas: kvs 3434, 4728.

     decoded for ten days: kv 7502.

p. 41 *transport) after 10 June:* kv 5689, signalled 29 May.

p. 43 *on 9 January 1944:* vL 4834, decode and signal 26 January.

     again on 23 March: kv 190 of 4 April.

     context in late March: vL 9732.

     persisted until late July: xL 5226, decode and signal 8 August.

p. 45 *the Côtentin in March:* Schramm 271.

     under OB West's command: vL 6997.

     to locate 352 Division: Pogue 171, Bradley 272, Ellis i. 138–9, Churchill vi. 4, Strong 139, Harrison 319 among many others.

     711 Division on 23 May: kv 5399.

     3 and 4 May: kvs 3990, 3183.

p. 46 *a defensive role only:* kv 3185.

     to remain in Strasbourg: kv 828, decode 12 April.

     along with 77 Division: kv 3183.

     7 Army next day: kv 3892 of 15 May.

     the Cherbourg peninsula: kvs 5320, 5437, 5416, all of 26 and 27 May.

particular importance to Normandy: Ellis i. 128, Schramm 302.

6 Parachute Regiment (Périers–Lessay): KV 5416 of 27 May; see also KV 5081 of 24 May.

n. OKW reserve for Reich defence: KV 2388.

p. 47 in the Reims area: VL 5892.

Melun on 6 April: KV 456.

Brest a month earlier: VL 7992 of 8 March.

various locations in Brittany: KVs 3763, 5320, 5437, 4917, 5416, 5554 of various dates in May; KV 5050 gave details of their battle-readiness.

reserve on 30 May: KV 6888 of 8 June.

context in late March: KV 2189.

Amiens on 20 April: KVs 2624, 2721.

the late summer months: KVs 353, 3070, 5193.

new location in March: VLs 8955, 9363, 9644.

April to be Brittany: KV 353 of 6 April.

Rennes a month later: KV 2624 of 2 May.

in two later signals: KVs 3892, 6348 of 15 May and 4 June.

positions on 22 March: KV 131.

p. 48 a workshop in Versailles: KV 218.

Côtentin on 15 May: KV 5081 of 24 May.

without his prior permission: Schramm 302, Ellis i. 119. The latter unaccountably omits 17 SS Division.

just three days later: KV 2388.

middle of December 1943: e.g. VL 6626 of 19 February.

Paris later in May: KV 6131 of 2 June.

still to be delivered: KV 7583 of 11 June.

April and early May: KVs 2760, 4608, 4723.

in Belgium in February: VLs 7347, 7430.

south Normandy in April: KVs 1333, 2624, 2721.

right up to D-Day: KVs 6240, 6377 of 3 and 6 June.

spring and early summer: e.g. VL 7384, KVs 2624, 2721.

from February to May: VL 7576, KV 4723.

refit was duly noted: KVs 3070, 5193.

Italy in December 1943: VL 6626.

in March and April: KVs 181, 325, 485.

p. 49 ruling to the contrary: Schramm 275.

the OKW War Diary: Schramm 116.

n. Normandy dated 15 May: KV 5081 of 24 May.

n. known from other sources: Ellis i. 128.

116 Pz on 8 May: KVs 2624, 2721 of 2 May.

from March to May): VL 8703, KVs 771, 3840.

his way to Paris: KV 3763.

p. 50   *divisions on 20 April:* KV 2295.

but 8000 sick horses: KVS 2002, 2649.

around 8000 men each: KVS 1171, 3185, 4371, 6160.

well provided with guns: KV 8866, not available until 20 June.

decoded 6 and 7 June: KVS 6705, 6799.

p. 51   *said on 21 March:* KV 353 of 6 April.

report of 8 May: KV 3763.

a serious fuel shortage: KV 5689.

lack of trained troops: VL 8072.

still complaining in May: KV 3482.

warning on 19 April: KVS 2612, 2678 of 2 May.

strength of fighting units: KV 5588 of 28 May.

France a week later: Schramm 300, Ellis i. 120.

p. 52   *ago as 6 January:* KV 4819 of 26 January.

main cross-channel attack: KVS 628, 727; see also VL 9689.

days before the landings: KV 5555.

and two fighter Gruppen: KVS 6540, 6476, 7102.

in case of emergency': VL 9471 of 26 March.

the middle of May: KVS 3616, 3684.

p. 54   *required on 16 March:* VL 9024.

the need for volunteers: VL 9356, 9463.

had already been stopped: KV 3606.

tense aircrew replacement position: KV 3353.

n.   *mounting Allied air attacks:* KV 5335 of 26 May.

late as 27 May: KV 5762.

n.   *the beginning of June:* KV 6257.

p. 55   *to mouth in future:* VL 9724.

and front repair workshops: KV 3423 of 10 May.

instruction of 28 April: KV 2555.

p. 56   *considerably below previous quotas:* KV 4762.

if at all possible: KV 6673.

industry was having effect: cf. Ehrman v. 293–7, 396.

to speed up repairs: KV 3015.

prisoners on repair work: KV 5314.

Italy a little earlier: KV 2405.

p. 57   *at or near Dieppe:* KV 5446.

Two signals in June: KVS 8562, 8818.

than two days later: KV 6943.

land-lines on 17 May: KV 5554.

contact for that period: KV 6618.

which was working intermittently: KV 7075.

Chapter 3

p. 65   *in the immediate future:* Schramm 299; Ellis i. 129.
         same 'parachutists' were dropped: KVs 8950, 8997.
         not be ruled out: KV 6724.
         coast were believed threatened: KVs 6859, 6978, 6992,
            7071, 7305, all of 7 and 8 June.
p. 66   *ferry over the Seine:* KV 6822.
         far upstream as Paris: KV 7546.
         hours on 5 June: KVs 6548, 6581.
         I SS Pz Corps: KVs 6854, 7035.
         out its planned operations: KV 7383.
         four hours to spare: KVs 6638, 6642, 6671.
         A comprehensive list: KV 6735.
p. 67   *front by 10 June:* Ellis i. 567; compare Tedder 550.
         to be left untried': KVs 6788, 6801.
         central and northern Brittany: Ellis i. 237–8; Schramm
            313.
         the American right wing: KVs 6893, 6933, 7002, 7112.
         a thrust into Belgium: KV 6834.
p. 68   *command it had just left:* KVs 7415, 7587, 7638, 7645,
            7798, 7978, 8376, 8589.
         directly under 7 Army: KVs 6958, 7002.
         and received his orders: KV 7435.
         Geyr's staff were killed: KV 7681.
         more than a fortnight: Speidel 100.
         cancelled before it started: KV 7450.
         speaks of a 'crisis': Schramm 313, cf. Harrison 373,
            Pogue 194.
pp. 68-9 *target before the raid:* Cave Brown 690.
p. 69   *decisively to the Allies:* Lewin, *Montgomery* 201, Speidel
            99.
         was very serious indeed: Ellis i. 258.
         shells the day before: KVs 6682, 7715.
         to deliver it in: KV 7260.
         army units near Caen: KVs 7468, 7292.
         be forced into action': KV 7134.
         early as 8 June: KV 7497.
p. 70   *attack his tanks attempted:* KV 7998.
         its men and equipment: KV 7382.
         in much better heart: KV 7371.
         made by 8 June: KVs 6978, 6992.
         support thus asked for: KV 7236.

would have on morale: KV 7555.
available two days late: KVs 7518, 7539.

p. 71   Isigny at all costs: KV 7213.
19 Pz (very ill-equipped): KV 7767.
north-east France and Belgium: KVs 7986, 7987, 8024.

p. 72   off the Côtentin peninsula: KV 7864.
fight to the last: KV 7845.
operation on the 9th: KV 7383.
to support the troops: KV 7713.
morning of 13 June: KV 7779.
Hut 3's series of signals: Bradley 293.
them on 14 June: KV 8008.
day by LXXXIV Corps: KVs 8303, 8334.
Corps appealed to Goering: KVs 7976, 8465.
to meet its needs: KV 8393.
in an air-raid: KV 8240, 7743, 7830.

p. 73   Cherbourg on 16 June: KV 8450.
forty-eight hours later: KV 8776.
ability to hold on: KV 8606.
running out of ammunition: KV 8800.
3 Para suffered 'heavy losses': KV 8695.
Americans on 17 June: KV 8618.
by the American thrust: KV 8234.
latest 'no withdrawal' order: Ellis i. 262.
as long as possible: KV 8760.
landings on the coast: KV 8899.
Commander of LXXXIV Corps: KV 8790.

n.   Corps on 20 June: KV 9097.
to demolish Cherbourg harbour: KV 8774.
Divisions were in Cherbourg: KV 8952.
are too mixed up: KV 8986.
were also too old: KV 9461.
exhausted for their task: KV 9001.
to be carried out: KV 9167.
grenadier regiment by sea: KV 9382.

pp. 73-4   the harbour was closed: KV 9366.
p. 74   will do my duty': KV 9173.
all his reserves committed: KV 9255.
for the eastern front: KV 9319.
meant guns or ammunition: KV 9274.
man, last round' message: KV 9409.
Cherbourg ten days earlier: KVs 9384, 9443.
by refusing to surrender: KV 9501.

the Epsom battle began: KVs 9422, 9563.

the south was over: KV 8707.

La Haye du Puits: KV 8741.

to II Para Corps: KV 9144.

p. 75   St Lô on 23 June: KVs 9313, 9351.

to cover that area: KVs 9492, 9559.

on the American front: Rommel Papers 476.

in Belgium and Holland: KVs 7986, 7987, 8024.

first identified in action: Ellis i. 254, 260–61 and notes 24
    and 43 from unpublished sources; cf. Montgomery,
    Normandy 221; Pogue 181.

filled the awkward gap: KV 7975.

remarks about a 'crisis': Ellis i. 266, Tedder 552.

order of 11 June: KV 7912.

review at this time: e.g. KVs 7705, 8192, 8849.

116 Pz farther east: e.g. KVs 8250, 8393, 8527.

p. 77   due to take place: cf. KVs 8392, 8401.

Caen still more tightly: KVs 8499, 8680, 9205.

it could be signalled: KV 8884.

made an earlier return: KV 7853.

rate of motor transport: KVs 9454, 9999.

according to Speidel: Ellis i. 118.

them Panthers) from Belgium: KVs 8881, 9058.

n.   on the main routes: KV 8885.

little eastwards to conform: KVs 9200, 9241.

pp. 77-8   attack on I SS Pz Corps: KVs 9275, 9308.

p. 78   2000 men, in each case: KV 9518.

been, on 11 June: KV 7593.

on the north bank: KV 7982.

arrived' near Le Tréport: KV 8250.

inland and nearer Dieppe: KV 8373.

Schwerin, on the 19th: KV 8903.

on the Normandy fighting: KV 9337.

Seine by 25 June: KV 9635.

imposition of wireless silence: XL 1430.

p. 79   first few days' fighting: Schramm 314, Ellis i. 118, 258–9.

n.   Allied air superiority: KVs 9485, 9493, 9793.

locations west of Paris: KV 9378.

of the same message: KV 9395.

were detected at Lille: XL 897.

p. 81   he made of it: on this paragraph see Ellis i. 279, 282
    (and note 36), 284, 311, 318, Pogue 182, Harrison
    445. Lewin, *Montgomery* 210, has 16 GAF identified
    on 3 July.

on the first day: KV 9563.

vehicles since the landings: XL 786.

repair-shops by nightfall: XLs 771, 939.

dangerously low at once: KV 9976.

day' on the 27th: XL 430.

the fighting died down: XL 252.

p. 82   morning of 1 July: XL 362.

ye who enter here': Ellis i. 285.

from coming too close: KV 9635.

destroyed from the air: XLs 27, 152.

the direction of Caen: XLs 328, 332, 349.

II SS Pz Corps: XL 1346.

p. 83   I and II SS, XLVII and LXXXVI: XL 426.

edged a little eastward: XL 232.

railway south of Angers: XL 786.

be unable to cope: XL 644 of 4 July.

in the published accounts: Ellis i. 319, Montgomery, Normandy 241.

p. 84   corner of his front: Ellis i. 286, 319–21, Schramm 322–3, 1594, Lewin, *Montgomery* 207–8, Irving 292–4.

seen from the air: XL 821.

controlled all three divisions: XL 882.

in the expected position: XL 1005.

Corps by the 10th: XLs 1283, 1447.

p. 85   seven on long repair: XL 1190.

it into the fighting: XL 1430.

of much operational value: XLs 1479, 1490, 1518, 1561, 1570.

job the next day: XLs 1583, 1644.

p. 86   raid a week later: KVs 7976, 9114.

p. 87   returns, dated 27 June: KVs 9454, 9976, 9999, XLs 212, 430.

of these were empty: KV 8502, XLs 1059, 1649.

consumption induced by battle: KVs 8495, 8851, 9156.

superiority in the air: KV 9793.

n.   army and the GAF: KV 7814.

in place of petrol: XL 789.

n.   transport for supply journeys: XL 754 of 3 July.

travel on 7 July: XL 1260.

p. 88   shortage of spare parts: KV 7965, XL 1688.

against an airlanding': KV 7767, XL 393.

division at the battle-front': XL 332.

and a static role: XLs 799, 889, 1003, 1079, 1115, dated 5–7 July.

below its planned strength: Ellis i. 274.
by an ammunition shortage: Ellis i. 302, Bradley 302–4.

p. 89   *were few experienced leaders:* KV 9416.
for pilots and aircraft: XL 681; cf. KV 9085.
forty-five for day fighters): XL 1671.

p. 90   *D-Day had been noticed:* KVs 7535, 8427.
augur a landing 'anywhere': KVs 7364, 8287, 8667, XLs 355, 502.
as identical with it: XLs 103, 130.
the end of July: KV 8251.

p. 91   *landed from the sea:* XLs 242, 355, 356 of 30 June and 1 July.
utilized in late July: XLs 687, 688.

p. 92   *fortify the troops psychologically':* XL 1509.

Chapter 4

p. 98   *directed from the air:* XL 552.
casualties, from this cause: XL 1248.
mortar and artillery ammunition: XLs 453, 552.
repeated almost at once: XLs 701, 742.
the previous month's gale: Bradley 304–6, Ellis ii. 141.
before an expected attack: XLs 557, 597.
danger if attacks continued: XLs 639, 686.
it was too weak: XL 711.

p. 99   *use up all reserves:* XLs 750, 850, 899, 1792.
both claimed defensive successes: XL 768.
out of Army reserve: XL 723.
more as Army reserve: XL 1511.
coast to La Haye: XL 1328.
corps had expected it: XL 1594.
the Carentan–Périers road: XL 1717.
reserves' on 11 July: XL 1700.
ammunition for several days: XLs 1634, 1795, 1964, 2477, 3301.
guns and seven lorries: XL 2513.
on the same scale: XL 1948.
in 3 Para Division: XL 1987.
of its proper strength: XL 3131. As the serial numbers indicate, several of the signals in this paragraph were late decodes; the latest of them, XL 3301, was not sent until 24 July.
Vire–Taute canal action: XLs 1638, 1641.

p. 100 *killed, wounded and missing:* XL 1792.

St Lô on the 13th: xLs 1863, 1952.
by gunfire and bombs: xL 2030.
6 June–14 July: xL 2772.
expected new attack came: xLs 2201, 2256.
including 2360 officers: xL 4989 of 6 August; Schramm
    326.

p. 101   *St Lô–river Taute sector:* xL 3307.
Army on its front: xL 3135.
entrenching-tools and camouflage: xL 3000.
allow standards to fall: xL 3252.

p. 102   *be unable to block:* xL 2986.
of its fighting strength: xL 3375.
broke von Kluge's nerve: cf. Ellis i. 383–4 and Lewin,
    Montgomery 221.
received more regular supplies: xLs 3491, 3494.
dawn on 26 July: xLs 3566, 3568, 3709.
south-west of St Lô: xL 3572.

p. 103   *my otherwise annihilated formation':* Rommel Papers
    489–90.
Ultra for several days: e.g. xLs 3576, 3615.
battle until 28 July: xL 3815.
line until the 31st: xL 4233.
late as 2 August: xL 4476.
value 'hardly even IV': xLs 5543, 5601.
in the Caen area: xL 3642.
was the priority reversed: xL 3702.

p. 104   *the Allies be prevented:* xL 4068.
halt the American advance: xLs 3717, 3798, 3818.
of only 3400 men: xL 3933.
there was none available: xL 3810.
Corps to co-ordinate them: Ellis i. 384.
Caen the previous evening: xLs 3213, 3336.
it ten days earlier: Schramm 326, Pogue 193–4.
first gone to Falaise: Ellis i. 348.
had finally been laid': Irving 383.
Masterman on the other hand: Masterman 158, cf. Strong
    142.
brought to bear elsewhere': HP 3119. This confirmation of
    Fortitude's endurance was not decoded until October.

p. 105   *Allies a strategic success:* xL 4068.
of ammunition and fuel: xLs 4160, 4407, 4638.
of only 200 men: xL 4396.
was not yet over: xL 4152.

of 7 Army himself: Ellis i. 385, Blumenson 323.

to carry them out: XL 4376.

to get mixed up: XLs 4448, 4638, 4639.

strength of 1500 men: XL 4662.

south-east of Avranches: XL 4429.

in the Channel Islands: XL 4434.

p. 106   *the division was holding:* XL 1693.

to break them up: XL 2353.

by the operational orders: XL 2300.

alongside 10 SS Pz: XLs 1753, 1864, 2247.

276 Division in its rear: XL 1762.

withdrawn on 15 July: XL 2162.

pp. 106-7   *near Gavrus next day:* XL 2354.

p. 107   *early on the 16th:* XL 2161, 2416.

did not move far: XL 2306.

line on 11 July: XL 1639.

south-eastern outskirts of Caen: XL 1518.

Lisieux, twenty miles back: XL 2392.

part of the front: XLs 1783, 1914.

for support recently received: XL 1982.

losses of motor transport: XL 2277.

quiet for twenty minutes: XLs 2607, 2608.

pp. 107-8   *just south of Caen:* XL 2613.

p. 108   *over by 21 Pz:* XL 2729.

with a counter-attack: XLs 2620, 2663.

was likely to fall: XLs 2684, 2918, 3037, 3377, 3960, 4022.

from here towards Falaise: XLs 3102, 2878.

towards Paris was imminent: Ellis i. 378, Lewin, *Montgomery* 221.

air effort outside Caen: XLs 3541, 3642.

p. 109   *this for several days:* XL 4599.

relieved by 272 Division: XL 3891.

reached him on the 30th: Ellis i. 392 and note 33.

p. 110   *in place of Fromm:* This appears to be the signal which, according to Mr Lewin (*Ultra* 190), Sir Edgar Williams saw Churchill reading at Montgomery's headquarters on 20 July, but there is something odd about the story. Keitel's instructions were not issued until the small hours of 21 July. Churchill flew to Normandy on 20 July, but visited the American sector first. He did not reach Montgomery's headquarters until the 23rd, and flew home that night (Churchill vi. 22–4)—almost

twenty-four hours before xl 3329 left Hut 3! See also
c 280, 282.

plot failed in Berlin: c 286, 289.

its own immediate superior: xls 3415, 3546.

of Goering or Himmler: xl 3433.

Search for Oberbürgermeister continues': c 294.

to a neutral country: xl 4310.

p. 111   *just after midnight:* Schramm 336, Ellis i. 405.

headquarters on the 3rd: Warlimont 448, Schramm 464.

XLVII Corps when it attacked: xls 5053, 5133.

out of 7 Army: xl 4605 implied that this interpretation
was current at the front by the night of 2–3 August.

to the army immediately: xl 4062.

p. 113   *to the plotters' treason:* Ellis i. 397.

strike down towards Falaise: Ellis i. 407, Pogue 206.

Panzer Army on 6 August: xl 5725.

German attack had begun: Ellis i. 416, Pogue 208.

of the Normandy front': Blumenson 465.

already an accomplished fact: xl 6059.

p. 114   *and 17 SS PzGr:* Ellis i. 406.

to free the armour: e.g. xl 4545.

sector for several days: e.g. xls 4611, 4667, 4682, 4788,
4842, 4854, 4877.

in the Sourdeval area: xls 4577, 4799, 4852.

night of 5–6 August: xl 4881.

had not yet arrived: xls 4804, 4847.

Americans had just captured: Blumenson 466.

p. 115   *Falaise the previous night:* xl 4873.

begin until after midnight: Ellis i. 413.

German command that day: Ellis i. 412.

dawn on 7 August: xl 5125.

withdraw for the night: xls 5125, 5156.

in mid-afternoon: xl 5119.

drive on to Avranches: xl 5248.

p. 116   *light and medium howitzers:* xl 5600.

2 SS Pz during the morning: xls 5285, 5289.

the slightest Allied pressure: xl 5476.

east as Blois 'obscure': xl 5333.

defence line behind Mortain: xl 5341.

10 SS Pz's difficulties: xls 5023, 5039.

Panthers out of thirty-four: xl 5490.

tools and excavating equipment: xls 5501, 5533.

the neighbourhood of Poitiers: xl 5050.

p. 117   *Nantes, Angers and Tours:* XL 5273.
         without waiting for replacements: XL 6188.
         command of 2 SS Pz: XL 5396.
         southern flank around Domfront: XLs 5398, 5406.
         started out that morning: XL 5433.
         to Blois and Chartres: XL 5438.

p. 118   *to complete the envelopment:* Bradley 375–6.

p. 119   *and the last round:* This is clearly the signal mentioned in Ellis i. 425 and Pogue 211. Something corresponding much more closely to the attack 'SW from Domfront, subsequently turning NW' and the strike into the northern flank of the US XV Corps referred to in Schramm 340, 464 and elsewhere was a late decode signalled on 15 August as XL 6435. Hitler's order for it, dated 11 August, went out still later as XL 6856, which also listed reinforcements to be brought up. Most of these were already known by that time; they included 338 Division from the Rhône valley—although the German Admiralty had just predicted a landing in the south 'any day'! (XL 5589). It is also worth noting that by the time the attack in the text was due to begin, we knew the weapon-strength of one of the two rocket brigades and the unhappy ammunition supply state of XLVII Corps (XLs 5701, 5708).

p. 120   *from seventeen to thirteen:* XLs 5521, 5680.
         to reinforce 7 Army: XLs 5525, 5577.
         through a little later): XLs 5489, 5492, 5532, 5539, 5540, 5550, 5551, 5552, 5687, 5691, 5715, 5792.
         before the earlier message: XLs 5780, 5834, 5835, 5860, 5887, 5898, 6128, 6136.
         at the army's request: XLs 5845, 5849, 5865, 5896.
         south-west of Paris: XL 6138.

p. 121   *Falaise, Flers and Domfront:* XL 6334.
         which was signalled currently: XL 6121.
         to 5 Panzer Army: XL 6434.
         about by French civilians: XLs 6167, 6272.

p. 122   *it by air supply:* XLs 6312, 6333.
         a great deal sooner: XLs 6312, 6324, 6325, 6337.
         he regarded as essential: XL 6330.
         Trun, to the north: XL 6342.
         evening of 15 August: XL 6588.

p. 123   *and Pz Lehr Divisions:* XLs 6720, 6734, 6803, 6938.
         not far from collapse: XL 6495.

and eleven guns left: xLs 6521, 6685, 6708.
control his strike force: xL 6534.

n. the withdrawal had begun: Ellis i. 432–4, evidently using the originals upon which the Enigma messages and the Ultra signals were based.

p. 124 others for the retreat: xL 6791.
ferries in working order: xL 6809.
get out that night: xL 7066.
the method of operation: xL 7058.

p. 125 could be made good: xL 2797.
for further emergency measures: xLs 4989, 5534.
of sixty-year-olds: xL 6376.
smaller units already disbanded: xL 4914.
to be broken up: Ellis i. 453.
up to the front: xL 7115.
soldiers for the 'fortresses': xL 4319.

p. 126 within twenty-four hours: xL 6262.
Luftflotte 3 on 15 August: xL 8202.

n. OKH, OKL and OKM: xL 4904.
were on the way: xL 8904.
capture Paris in October: Ehrman v. 284.
end of the month: Pogue 244.

p. 127 cannot last much longer': Bryant 263.
capacity in the field': Ehrman v. 398.

Chapter 5

p. 129 which nothing could stem': Speidel 151.
by its own success: Ryan 75.
have time to recover': Horrocks 69.

p. 130 the war in 1944: Pogue 246, Ryan 50, Lewin, *Montgomery* 231, Schramm 367, 386.

p. 133 Army Groups B and G: Westphal 172.
Ultra revealed him saying: HP 3936.

n. complaints by demanding improvements: HP 4514.

p. 134 n. over in September 1944': Lewin, *Ultra* 345–6.

p. 135 still being worked on: xLs 6450, 6721, 6881, 7104, 8253, 8528.
Bourgogne) on 17 August: xL 6753.
was already being negotiated: cf. Ellis i. 457.
2 Army crossed the Somme: xL 8698.

p. 136 into a defensible condition: xLs 9090, 9100.
it was made defensible: xL 9174.
fortifications by 12 September: xL 9460, HPs 20, 689.

position was not ready: HP 530.

is no second position': XL 9597, HPs 188, 1891.

positions or be annihilated': HP 744.

p. 137   be held 'until annihilation': HP 188.

p. 138   at Dijon in time: XL 7753.

12 September at the earliest: XL 7448.

1 Army could protect it: XLs 7901, 7915.

up with 1 Army: XL 8412.

p. 139   on Verdun and Metz: XLs 7964, 8778, 8802, 8809.

refitting' three Panzer divisions: XLs 8815, 8874, 8987, 8994, 9089.

their repair workshops behind): XLs 8841, 8891.

mean its own destruction: XLs 9143, 9248.

n.   loss of irreplaceable equipment: XLs 8117, 8580.

an officer in Kaiserslautern!): XLs 9104, 9174.

p. 140   area of Army Group G: XLs 9219, 9248.

p. 142   before the retreat began: XLs 7052, 7296.

149 aircraft by 18 August: XL 7031.

337 on the 7th: XLs 7880, 8095, 8918, 9010, 9516.

as a possible target: XLs 8194, 8266.

any of these officers: XL 8173.

Fliegerkorps IX's recent history: XLs 8570, 8632, 8905.

p. 143   target for precision bombing: XL 9020.

n.   Trier road on 4 September: XL 9415.

than the fighting troops: XLs 8662, 8829.

attack five minutes afterwards: XL 8041.

command of Luftflotte 3: XL 7693.

for an immediate decision: XLs 7217, 7218.

could not operate properly: XL 7352.

p. 144   whole of his command: XLs 7920, 8220, 8543, 8929, 9146, HPs 83, 144.

in quite small quantities: XL 9805, HPs 385, 860, 1155.

p. 145   put down civil disturbances: XLs 9481, 9881, HPs 99, 1802.

in the Channel Islands: XLs 8162, 9095, 9245, HPs 49, 133, 183, 203, 230, 236, 512, 751.

n.   the control of operations: Belchem 212.

n.   Montgomery for four days: Ellis ii. 16–17.

p. 147   halted at the dockside: Ellis ii. 5.

midde of the month: Ellis ii. 349.

for lack of supplies: For criticism of the mistake, see, for instance, R. W. Thompson, *The Eighty-Five Days,* and Lewin, *Montgomery* 233. The orders of 10 and 14

September are in Ellis ii. 17–18, 26–7 and 50, and
Ehrman v. 526–7. Bradley 414–15 complains about
supply.

harbour on 28 August: XL 8751.

p. 148   *4 and 5 September:* XLs 9162, 9165, 9192, 9260.

his views next day: XL 9381.

on the adjoining mainland: e.g. XLs 9308, 9370, 9466.

corps and divisional locations: XLs 9441, 9814, HPs 24,
          38, 120, 261.

p. 149   *raised against facile optimism:* Pogue 245, Strong 145.

Holland on 17 September: Ellis ii. 31, Ryan 574.

of the fighting formations': Schramm 377.

p. 150   *hole in SHAEF's pocket':* Macdonald 119.

1 December or even sooner: Ellis ii. 142, Ehrman v.
          395–9.

will collapse before then': Churchill vi. 170–71.

refusal to weigh evidence': Lewin, *Ultra* 351.

p. 151   *by Eisenhower and Montgomery:* Strong 149, Ryan 139–
          41 and see 103–43 generally.

level in disguised form: Horrocks 79, 82, 100, 104.

Summary until 16 September: Pogue 283.

attack on 20 August: XL 7397.

p. 153   *men the previous day:* XL 7324.

from Germany to Beauvais: XLs 7534, 8091.

tanks on the 26th: XL 8076.

Having rallied near Evreux: XL 7457.

to Soissons and Laon: XL 8463.

under 5 Pz Army: XL 8746.

the west of Liège: XL 8994.

south-east at Maastricht: XL 9857.

the Allies' chief objective: HP 9.

p. 154   *there were only twenty:* Ryan 133.

as far as Arnhem: HPs 175, 242.

p. 155   *XXX Corps' first thrust:* LXVII Corps: XLs 8186, 8455,
          9098, 9353, HPs 24, 38, 120, 393; LXXXVIII Corps:
          XLs 9192, 9384, 9534.

frontier east of Nijmegen: XLs 8086, 8105, 9070, 9084.

from the central front: XLs 9001, 9260.

located at s'Hertogenbosch: HP 294.

p. 156   *via Flushing and Breda:* XL 9192.

Terneuzen the same evening: XL 9308.

were hastily improvising more: XL 9345.

protection was being arranged: XLs 9370, 9376, 9397.

had crossed so far: XL 9466.
ferries was regularly reported: e.g. HP 344.
make this intention explicit: HP 624.
Amsterdam and Rotterdam harbours: HPs 541, 557, 629,
   722, 723.
pp. 156-7   Nijmegen on the 18th: HP 606.
p. 157   the batteries reported it: HPs 752, 830, 1071, 1458.
            horses and much equipment: HP 1010. Ellis ii. 69 quotes
               the same figures from Army Group B's War Diary.
               Ryan 397 gives some reason for doubting their ac-
               curacy.
            after the action began: cf. Ellis ii. 42, Ryan 476.
            the partially successful operation: HPs 1551, 1578.
            behind the West Wall: HPs 2134, 2188.
            the very near future': HPs 4082, 6374.
p. 158   in a month's time: HPs 7092, 9288.
            Ligurian coast after all: XLs 2512, 4192, 5589, 5786,
               5988, 6013, 6230, 6339, 6435.
            only parts of each: XL 7268.
p. 159   loss of 338 Division: XLs 5438, 5956, 6162, 6435.
            raids on radar installations: XLs 5431, 5945, 6164, 6204.
            Orange on 12 August: XL 6265.
            reports from 19 Army: XLs 6532, 6557.
            element in 19 Army': XL 8437.
            Avignon to remedy this): XLs 6849, 7148.
            assemble for this purpose: XLs 7001, 7051, 7159.
            and then to Dijon: XLs 7168, 7825.
pp. 159-60 rocket and grenade launchers: XL 7283.
p. 160   19 Army to make haste: XL 7915.
        n. with 7 US Army: PRO 31/20/9.
            defence of this position': XL 6919.
            was being carried out: e.g. XLs 9122, 9484.
            after it was issued: XLs 7480, 7827.
            American after-action report: quoted in Bell 41.
            trouble on 25 August: XL 7830.
            Blumentritt on 25 August: XL 8240.
            to Besançon and Belfort: XL 8281.
            through Châlons to Dôle: XL 8356.
p. 161   to be almost useless: XLs 8437, 8788.
            116 Pz on 30 August: XL 8796.
            as a precautionary measure: XLs 8992, 9089.
            within sight of home: XLs 9352, 9617.
            reported Army Group G: XL 9863.

400 rounds between them: HPs 1309, 1516.
out to the last: XL 6919.
belt of 'scorched earth': XL 5272.

p. 162   *army keys with them:* XLs 4736, 4798, 5102.
Allies at the door': XLs 5540, 5664, 5699.

n.   *of his family estates:* C 333, 340.
a heap of ruins: XL 9598.
fight the American tanks: XLs 4883, 5143, 5519, 8855.
to prolong the siege: XLs 5206, 5485, 5921.

p. 163   *night of 12–13 September:* XL 5856, HP 147.
had not been penetrated: e.g. XLs 5732, 5972, 6154.
was to be informed: HPs 52, 141, 300, 424.

Chapter 6

p. 167   *and well into November:* e.g. HPs 2242, 2296, 3151, 3226,
5642, 6264, 6556.
this, and its failure: HPs 2835, 3226, 4621.
about to be evacuated: HPs 3479, 5019.
and 1 Parachute Army: HPs 5519, 6077, 6261, 6537.
to the Saar front: HP 7667.

p. 169   *and other small craft:* HPs 5702, 6075, 6091.
before the Ardennes offensive: HP 8540.
in the top category: HPs 3171, 5094.
could be sent up: HPs 4620, 4767.
be considered as disbanded: HP 8012.
were to move out: HPs 1976, 2082, 2329, 2845, 2929,
3029, 3810, 3974.

p. 170   *1 Para Army on 14 October:* HPs 3464, 3676, 3822.
the next four days: HPs 4704, 4759, 4810, 4893, 4899,
4928, 4957, 5155.
east of the Maas: HP 8011.
Emmerich on the Rhine: HPs 2310, 2675.

n.   *modified the plan accordingly:* HPs 5557, 6988, 7217.

p. 171   *confirmed on 5 October:* HPs 2274, 2483.
between Aachen and Cologne: HP 2815.
20 October at the latest: HP 3102.
line north of Aachen: HP 3810.
almost down to Aachen: HPs 3230, 3794, 3810, 4254.
shifted from the Saar: HP 1661.
7 Army south of Aachen: HPs 3734, 4672.
Aachen on 21 October: HPs 4672, 5012.
about an airlanding: HPs 5247, 5673, 7092.

p. 172   *XII SS Corps complained):* HPs 6398, 6811, 7098.

to be speeded up: HPS 7278, 7814, 7890, 7296.

his misgivings to Hitler: Schramm 441.

of the river Roer: e.g. HPS 8375, 8535.

Cologne, Bonn or Koblenz: e.g. HPS 7735, 7740, 7925, 8064, 8095, 8939, 9170.

available for the task: HPS 2118, 2208, 2311.

p. 173   *Pont-à-Mousson and Château Salins:* HPS 3062, 3294.

the Metz–Nancy area: HP 4601.

put out of action: HP 6087.

danger-point to another: e.g. HPS 6083, 6087, 6293, 6417, 6615, 6732, 6968, 7185, 7218.

416 Division next day: HPS 7757, 8175, 8188.

used in the offensive: HPS 9200, 9411.

in about four days: HP 8821.

p. 174   *shut up in Metz:* HPS 7940, 8597, 8736, 8464, 8465.

some types of ammunition: HP 8937.

were reported six times: HPS 1661, 2145, 4334, 7940, 8435, 9577.

on many other occasions: e.g. HPS 6615, 6853, 7505, 7589, 7873, 8388, 8537, 8538.

out of the question): HPS 1660, 4508.

p. 175   *three or four weeks:* HPS 2082, 2337, 4601.

361 Volksgrenadier Division: HPS 4656, 4666, 4711, 4786.

conduct the Meijel attack: HPS 3676, 4459, 4656, 4814.

Alsace by early November: HPS 5324, 5368, 5455, 5587, 7505.

been smashed at Saverne: HP 8465.

to strengthen the defence: HP 8455.

perimeter) were already expected: HP 8340.

transferred to 1 Army: HPS 8239, 8754.

after it was made: HP 8758, dated 1 December. Himmler took over on 30 November (Schramm 420).

p. 176   *in the northern sector:* HPS 2226, 2286, 2296, 2552.

the defence of Germany: HP 2737.

in case of emergency: HP 3733.

being very severely hit: Jones 466–9 demonstrates this graphically.

the output of fighters: Speer 406–9.

p. 177   *because of air attacks:* HPS 4627, 4397.

Cologne to discuss details: HPS 6054, 6064, 6084, 6130.

the customary unit badges: HPS 6524, 6778.

runways and parking-places: HPS 6790, 6887.

p. 178 *were still coming in:* HPs 6997, 7084, 7168, 7176, 7177, 7237, 7277, 7283, 7285, 7360, 7374, 7421.
raid north-west Germany: HPs 7653, 7664, 8259.
10 December was announced: Schramm 437, 443, Ellis ii. 178, Cole 63–9.
the disposal of OKL: HPs 5996, 7837.

p. 179 *Koblenz on 5 December:* HP 8624.
and almost unopposed attacks: HP 8333.

p. 180 *third weeks of December:* e.g. HPs 8509, 8837, 9016, 9138, 9223, 9333, 9423, 9520; other contemporary strength returns in HPs 9001, 9003, 9016, 9019, 9107.

p. 181 *on a small scale:* HP 4689.
no longer training pilots: HP 6333.
base south of Stuttgart: HPs 1983, 2570.
circulated three weeks later: HP 4644.

p. 182 *attack on 27 October:* HPs 2692, 3114, 4646, 4660, 4765, 7197.
included for that reason: Some items are identical with some in a contemporary American intelligence summary, based on Ultra and other sources, parts of which Bell was able to reprint as his pp. 88–110. Lewin, *Ultra* 351–4, reproduces part of this.

p. 183 *from west to east:* HPs 5270, 8022.
suffering on 2 October: HP 2045. At the same time II SS Corps was consuming twice as much petrol as it received: HP 2074.
trains of supply vehicles: HP 2674.
the end of November: HP 3307.
motorized transport altogether: HP 7790.
by the fuel shortage: e.g. HPs 4689, 5147.
subject in mid-November: HPs 7111, 7214.

p. 184 *establishing horse-transport columns:* HP 4546. One of the ten-day allocations was intercepted soon afterwards, and signalled as HP 5501.
identified in that area: HPs 4168, 4814.
up at Hitler's order: HPs 6762, 7364; cf. Beesly 234.

p. 185 *Prussia, Czechoslovakia and Norway:* HPs 4677, 6538, 7325, 7674, BTs 759, 1199, 1387, 1535.
officers from other units: HP 4806.
be in full swing: HPs 4685, 6381.
mind almost at once: HPs 4780, 4951.
commanders on 10 January: BT 2778.
value on its own: BT 4210.

Chapter 7

p. 189	*off at the base':* This paragraph is based chiefly on Ellis ii. 170–75, Pogue 303, 306, 361–74, Bradley 374, 442–7, Horrocks 158, and Cole 58; Ellis and Pogue draw heavily on the weekly SHAEF, 12 Army Group and 21 Army Group Intelligence Summaries.

His own account: Strong 154–5.

as Pogue points out: Pogue 371.

reputation as an alarmist: Pogue 366–9, Strong 178.

p. 191   *of the formations involved':* Tedder 623, Belchem 243.

he claims were destroyed: Strong 175–6.

n.   *by Group Captain Winterbotham:* Winterbotham 177–9.

n.   *tell-tale intercepts from Ultra':* Lewin, *Ultra* 356.

n.   *through it all again" ':* Lewin, *Ultra* 357.

p. 192   *created 6 Pz Army:* Pogue 309, Warlimont 476, Schramm 372.

also somewhere near Osnabrück: HP 2274.

12 SS near Hanover: HPs 2670, 2845.

than the SS divisions: HPs 3621, 3622, 3678.

p. 193   *complement of heavy weapons:* HPs 3935, 3971, 4086.

the end of October: HPs 2815, 3123, 3810, 3102, 4342.

Paderborn early in November: HPs 4357, 5867.

6 Pz Army area: HP 6611.

end of the month: HPs 7278, 7814, 8092.

was on the move: HPs 7403, 7549.

and intended no operations: HPs 7587, 7687.

p. 194   *'SS Panzer Army 6':* HP 4341.

batteries as army troops: HPs 4807, 5476, 6982.

purpose was still obscure: HP 6523.

was positively established: HP 7157.

dawn on the 3rd: HPs 5400, 5437.

signals every three days: HPs 5484, 5599, 5690, 5820, 6042, 6165, 6256, 6792, 6876, 7221, 7291, 7390, 7436, 7516, 7614, 7875, 8210, 8324, 8427, 8480, 8519, 8609, 8707, 8777, 8816, 9053, 9224, 9283, 9508.

p. 195   *of the large number:* e.g. HPs 2987, 3224, 4058, 4521, 6208, 7444, and many more in a series covering October and the first part of November.

and 5 Panzer Army: HPs 7061, 7357, 6939.

p. 196   *extremities of the front:* HPs 6964, 7630, 7578, 6497.

were destined for Alsace: HPs 8449, 8459.

as could be ascertained: Schramm 438 dates these delays only a day or two earlier.

p. 197   *tanks on 1 December:* HPs 7735, 7740, 7706, 7925, 8095, 8163, 8718, 8880, 8939.

Kesselring's command in Italy: HPs 7311, 8243, 8551.

p. 198   *road-junction at Ciney:* HPs 7508, 7710, 7822, 7910, 8017, 8093, 8161, 8419, 8472, 8536, 8847, 9041, 9049, 9214, 9374.

Fw 190s out of 108: HPs 8624, 8837.

half as many more: HPs 9138, 8520.

p. 199   *though sometimes hinted:* for instance by Winterbotham 178.

p. 200   *the resources to sustain:* Ellis ii. 171–2.

p. 203   *and recurred frequently thereafter:* HPs 5400, 5437, 5484, 5820, 6042, 6165, etc.

stirring within the sepulchre': SHAEF Weekly Intelligence Summary No. 37, Ellis ii. 170.

p. 204   *were observing wireless silence:* HP 9198.

p. 208   *until shortly before midnight:* HP 9588.

    n.   *return of 6 January:* BTs 2151, 2191.

    n.   *882,560:* BT 2506.

p. 209   *days of the offensive:* e.g. Cole, *Ardennes* 332, Liddell Hart 672, Horrocks 161.

LXVI Corps near Prüm: HP 9586.

news of the battle: HP 9670.

on the Saar front: HP 9411.

from the Roermond area: HP 9585.

1 SS nearing Malmédy: HPs 9642, 9648.

p. 210 n.   *decoded until 8 January:* BT 1635.

the direction of Luxembourg: HPs 9631, 9707, 9720, 9722, 9778.

of all three services: HP 9808.

orders of 6 Army: HP 9880.

between Wiltz and Clerf: HP 9791.

    n.   *to the Meuse quickly:* Cole, *Ardennes* 292–3, Schramm 1343.

and five other divisions: HP 9818.

taken by 25 Army: BT 50.

command structure tolerably clear: HP 9800.

from Givet to Prüm: Ellis ii. 182–4, Pogue 378, Strong 162–6.

of the divisions engaged: Strong 161 says that on the previous evening he thought that as many as twenty-

five divisions might be involved. The map in Ellis ii.
186 locates twenty-two in the salient.

p. 211   *by the previous night:* Eisenhower 382.
which is sometimes made: e.g. Ellis ii. 183, Horrocks 161.
across the river Sauer: HP 9897.
come from the north: HP 9913.
leaving Alsace for Bitburg: HPs 9795, 9841.
area south of Bastogne: HP 9828.

p. 212   *'supply Battle Group Heydte':* HPs 9836, 9917.
without accomplishing much: Cole, *Ardennes* 271.
the end of November: HP 8074. The other references, all
during October and November, are HPs 2032, 2360,
2534, 7004.
St Vith on 26 December: BT 478; cf. Cole, *Ardennes* 270.

p. 213   *away from the Ardennes:* Cole, *Ardennes* 443, 671,
Schramm 1343–7, Ellis ii. 185, Belchem 251.

n.   *war on 17 December:* Cole, *Ardennes* 261, Horrocks 165.
their capture of Houffalize: HP 9959.
11 Pz following behind it: HPs 9929, 9930, 9967, 9927.
beaten by the weather: BTs 20, 31, 33, 46.
12 SS Pz Division: BTs 86, 39.

p. 214   *because of decoding difficulties:* BT 389.
only other comparable document: BT 981.

p. 215   *order to economize fuel:* BT 452.
brigades remaining fully motorised': Schramm 981–6.
to their commands too?: BT 2594.

n.   *out of current production:* BTs 4008, 4119.
the Meuse at Liège: BTs 85, 117, 158, 162.
its eventual break-out: BTs 115, 480.
their place in Ultra: BTs 115, 116, 146, 147.

p. 216   *on the grand scale':* BT 160.
intentions for the 24th: BT 208.
the river next morning: BT 259. The route traced by 2 SS
in its Enigma messages differs substantially from that
marked on the map in Ellis ii. 186; see, for instance,
also BT 628.
reached on Christmas Day: BTs 396, 491.
day at this period: e.g. BTs 190, 199, 258.
flown and serviceability rates: e.g. BTs 393, 467, 524.
them single-engined fighters: PRO AIR 37/111. 374.

n.   *St Vith to all traffic:* BT 475.

p. 217   *days of the offensive:* HP 9990; cf. BT 165.

did so in future: BTS 311, 356.

wood north of Bastogne: In his *Crusade in Europe* (395) Eisenhower wrote 'During the 27th it became clear that the German was throwing his principal effort towards Bastogne', perhaps a reflection of this signal.

3 PzGr Divisions having failed: BT 578.

p. 218   *Saarbrücken only a few:* BTS 479, 913, 942, 975, 1040, 1104, 1281, 1313, 2008, 2116, 2351, 2725. In BT 942 1 SS Pz also reported its experience that a single direct hit on a Panther tank by a rocket fired from a Typhoon aircraft meant a total loss. Albert Speer gives a vivid description of the hazards of movement by road in the salient in *Inside the Third Reich* 417–18. It took him twenty-two hours to travel the 200 miles from Houffalize to Hitler's headquarters outside Bad Nauheim on 31 December.

in Holland and Belgium': BTS 958, 1211, 1235. Slightly differing figures are given in modern accounts: Schramm 977 has 1035 aircraft operating and 300 missing afterwards, Ellis ii. 190 'over 900' and 270, with 150 Allied machines destroyed and 111 damaged.

p. 219   *fortnight of the offensive:* BTS 847, 1061, 1121, 1378, 1546, 1604, 1989.

their front-line units: e.g. BTS 736, 745, 765, 1181.

be concentrated on Bastogne: e.g. BTS 965, 1249, 1337, 1370, 1468, 1568.

began on 3 January: BTS 801, 923, 1030, 1098, 1103, 1167, 1183, 1203, 1214.

the Sauer near Wiltz: BT 1129.

soon still farther back: BT 1770.

the sector of attack': BT 1724.

plan' on the 10th: BT 1933. The next stage of its retreat was covered in BT 2139.

whole force, 216 aircraft: BT 2323.

p. 220   *early hours of 8 January:* Schramm 1346, 1353.

pressure in the Ardennes: Churchill vi. 243.

division they could muster: Macdonald 41, Strong 173–4.

pp. 221-2   *it had been fighting:* BT 2314.

p. 222   *companies the same day:* BT 2470.

10 SS was in Baden: BTS 2588, 2750.

the Saar and Alsace: BTS 3581, 3699.

as already forecast: BTS 1673, 1756, 1759, 1778, 1916, 1960.

midday on 22 January: BT 2998.

with tanks and petrol: BT 3067.

another three more days: BTs 3005, 3059, 3161, 3233 and 3318 meanwhile added useful detail, but did not elucidate the main problem.

p. 223 *forces on their own:* BT 3333.

and materials 'for O': BT 3449.

n. *to the Russian front:* Schramm 1353–4.

p. 224 *6 Panzer Army eastwards:* BTs 3561, 3571.

constructed chain of reasoning: BTs 3596, 3965. Further confirmation arrived later in the shape of BTs 3618, 3619, 3685, 4045.

p. 225 *were more generally informative:* They were combined into one signal, BT 1585.

A set of instructions: BT 3245.

p. 226 *blocked by halted vehicles:* BTs 1557, 2351, 2415; cf. p. 218 above.

the rate of replenishment: BTs 2295, 2396, 2496, 2230; several other quartermaster returns from 5 Panzer Army were seen in January: BTs 2495, 2434, 4206, 4249.

Panthers and four Tigers: BTs 2151, 2190.

mixed types undergoing repair: BT 2579.

fit for defensive action: BT 4087.

accuracy of this figure: BT 2493.

16 and 31 December: Schramm 1359.

ten days of January: BT 2340.

p. 227 *kind of a reserve:* BTs 2635, 2879; cf. Speer 560.

intensification of submarine warfare: BTs 2777, 3985.

Chapter 8

p. 230 *the next few days:* Schramm 1347–8.

battle a trifle confused): BTs 436, 446, 534, 575, 844.

salient on 23 December: BT 288.

the attackers' start line: BT 782. The value of the information summarized in the second half of this paragraph was emphasized by the Ultra Intelligence Officer with 7 US Army in his post-war report: PRO 31/20/9.

pp. 230-2 *between Saargemuend and Bitsch:* BT 977.

p. 232 *north of the town:* BT 1044.

striking results were claimed: BT 1275.

might be abandoning Alsace: BT 1355.
direct from the front: BT 2017.
move south by rail: BTs 1756, 1759, 2186.
416 Division on 18 January: BT 2686.
engaged in the struggle: Macdonald, *Last Offensive* 117–18.

p. 233   front—not much greater): BTs 2263, 2687, 2901, 2983, 3074, 3230.
After 'vehement disagreements': Ehrman vi. 89.
at a SHAEF conference: Tedder 658.
21 Army Group's intentions): BTs 4268, 4359, 4859.
Army round München-Gladbach: BT 4269.
only seventy-three tanks: BT 4243.
in the coming battle: Ellis ii. 259, Macdonald, *Last Offensive* 137.

n.   week after Veritable began: BT 5408.
p. 234   the usual four weeks: BT 4584.
before the battle started: BTs 4288, 4424.
including its last reserves: BT 4763.
end of the month: BT 6351.
the next three weeks: BTs 4974, 5339, 5773, 6191, 6742, 6842; BTs 6058, 6657 are similar returns from OB West and Army Group H respectively.
the water-level dropped: BT 4859.
as Goch and Gennep: BT 4805.
the likely target area: BTs 4738, 4759, 4851, 5085, 5702, 5856.
descent on the Ruhr: BT 5830.
between Emmerich and Königswinter: BT 5264.

p. 235   tanks and assault guns: BT 4963.
Dinslaken on 3 February: BTs 5002, 5303, 5369, 5777, 5854, 6089, 6255.
had eroded German strength: BTs 6119, 6222.
between Euskirchen and Brühl: BTs 4989, 4990, 5060.
sector had been traced: BTs 4849, 5064.
opened on 23 February: BTs 5301, 5369; BT 5777 gave further confirmation three days later.
the east of Jülich: BT 5677.
to prevent a breakthrough: BTs 5868, 5902.
in the Black Forest: BT 5849.

p. 236   signalled on 1 March: BT 6050.
avert if he could: Schramm 1374.

the chain of command: BT 6913, which was signalled the
next afternoon, was accordingly sent only to SHAEF
and Army Groups, marked 'Strictly Personal' for the
Senior Intelligence Officers.

more highly than life': BT 9340.

of the whole war: BT 6661.

Ardennes salient) were 'exhausted': BT 4779.

p. 237   listed among their equipment: BTs 5031, 6082.

transport was very short: BT 6189.

fuel and ammunition stocks: BTs 6666, 6705, 6721, 7011.

morning of 7 March: BT 6655.

it received enough petrol: BT 6766.

as at 3 February: BT 4498.

drafted in as reinforcements: BTs 4441, 4635.

in Army Group G: BT 4636; further details in BTs 5323,
5369, 5412.

pp. 237-8   guns on 21 February: BT 6112.

p. 238   reported Army Group G: BT 5988.

day before it began: BT 6194.

of the western war': Bradley 509.

Patton reached the Rhine: BT 6661.

am the new V3': Mellenthin 349.

p. 239   inside a few days: BTs 7383, 7670, 7683.

which it eventually occurred: BTs 6805, 6879, 7024,
7952.

cries of 'Wolf, wolf': BTs 6901, 7132, 7662, 7869 and
many others.

in the Ems estuary: BTs 8032, 8041.

both dated 13 March: BTs 7178, 7696, 7784, 7902. See
also BT 7097.

given a month earlier: BT 5264.

from the same source: BT 7900.

issued four days earlier: BT 7017.

p. 240   which had just arrived: BTs 7807, 7935.

collection scheme' round Cologne: BT 7705.

day was therefore unavoidable: Bradley 514, Macdonald,
Last Offensive 220.

the neglect of duty': The court-martial and execution of
Major Scheller were reported in C 430. Scheller's part
in the loss of the bridge is described in Macdonald,
Last Offensive 212–17.

level on 10 March: See also BTs 6785, 6818, 6876.

p. 241   *for their human torpedoes:* BT 7336.
    to the wrong place: BTs 7363, 7423.
    much chance of success: BT 7794.
    between army and navy: BT 8042.
    fuel for another attempt: BT 8123.
    Bayerlein of Panzer Lehr: BT 7536.
    anywhere and committed piecemeal: BTs 6779, 6816, 7258.
    be employed as well: BT 7584.
    was only 5000 strong: BT 7651.
    out by flank attacks: BTs 7535, 7599.
    further reinforcements were reported: BTs 7841, 8254.
    Tigers and eleven Jagdtiger: BTs 8331, 8344, 8356.
    become the Ruhr pocket: BTs 8631, 8646, 8538, 8542, 9122.
    between Koblenz and Boppard: BT 6782.

p. 242   *to deal with it:* BTs 7750, 7809 also refer to the Bad Kreuznach–Alzey situation on 19–20 February.
    gave Patton the 'intuition': Bradley 519.
    of them by bombers: BT 7425.
    at points of danger: BT 5510.
    measures for jet fuel: BT 5321.
    the Air Ministry comment: BT 6019.
    forty serviceable Me 262s: BT 4845.
    were dissolved in March: BT 7777.
    destined for the army: BT 5815.
    weapons as ordinary infantry: BT 6509.

pp. 242-3   *Parachute Divisions in Holland:* BT 8182.

p. 243   *bombs for the rest':* BTs 8328, 8460.
    in a Hitler order: BT 7964.
    the next three weeks: BTs 7956, 8029.
    of the promised allocation: BT 9204.
    to be demonstrated shortly: Speer 445.
    bridgehead in mid-March: BT 7451.
    the end of March: BT 9122.
    attack on 28 April: KO 1609.

p. 244   *Frankfurt early in February:* BT 4439.
    of blocking the roads: BT 4666.
    executions had worked wonders: BTs 6642, 7126.
    the bridge at Mannheim: BT 8160.
    momentum farther than intended: BTs 8268, 8336, 8863.
    was to be suppressed: BT 5705.
    for General Staff careers: BT 7828.

Chapter 9

p. 247 n.   *on the western front:* PRO 31/20.
p. 248   *plight of the Dutch:* BT 1735.
            in Munich and Prague: BTs 1636, 2042.
            the western Allies' advance: e.g. BTs 1310 (Dresden),
                1887 (Bohemia), 910 (Himmler), 1241 (Doenitz),
                9508, KOs 674, 732, 1017, 1018 and a number more
                in April (prisoners-of-war).
            Hut 3's last signals: KO 2084.
            people had already collapsed': BT 9588.
            north-east from Hanau: BTs 8753, 8764.
            had already been made: BTs 8421, 8457, 9778.
p. 250   *to Student's own flank:* BTs 9492, 9532, 9573; see also
                BTs 9096, 9111.
            through wherever they chose: BT 8970.
            far south as Würzburg: BTs 9075, 9077, 9108, 9175,
                9584, 9655.
            had already been photographed: SHAEF Weekly Intelli-
                gence Summary No. 50.
            if necessary be sacrificed: BTs 9737, 9801.
            but too few weapons: KOs 302, 864.
            Hitler ordered extensive flooding: KOs 430, 765.
            moved to The Hague: KOs 1453, 1465, cf. KO 1735.
            at the meeting itself: compare Ellis ii. 419.
            reports and supply returns: e.g. BTs 9427, 9950, KOs 190,
                282, 311, 367.
            point of being surrounded: BT 9122.
p. 251   *defences to reinforce Bayerlein:* BT 9176.
            thrust from Kassel westwards: BT 9143.
            was 'small arms ammunition': BTs 9373, 9662, 9678.
            between the two commanders: BTs 9199, 9339, 9846.
            petrol inside a week: KO 146.
            him that were intercepted: KOs 376, 377, 503, 504.
            night of 24–5 March: BTs 8631, 8646.
            from Worms and Darmstadt: BTs 8509, 8590, 8606,
                8650, 8898.
            horses and two carts: BTs 8590, 8655.
        n. *the Salzburg–Berchtesgaden area:* e.g. BTs 9021, 9118,
                KOs 733, 1762, 2059.
p. 253   *the Halle–Nürnberg railway:* BTs 9806, 9867.
            'industrial installations' at Nordhausen: BT 9713.

underground V2 rocket factory: see Jones 454.
ball-bearing manufacture at Schweinfurt: BTs 9817, 9846.
from the Russian front: KO 337.
Zeiss works at Jena: BT 9991.

n. *a change of plan:* PRO 31/20/5.
headquarters was at Coburg: BT 9555.
supply route through Ohrdruf: BTs 9627, 9687.
ten Jagdtiger under command: KO 237.
with Bayerlein through Korbach: BTs 9534, 9538, 9745.
time for 'new measures': BTs 9894, 9943.
85 Division in mind: KO 356.

p. 254   *Circumstantial evidence suggests:* KO 218.
Dresden to face west: KO 359.
in case of need: KO 978.
Leipzig on 16 April: KO 670.
threat five days later: KO 1134.
Regensburg on the 23rd: KO 1329.
Group G in Bavaria: KOs 799, 891.

p. 255   *self-propelled anti-tank guns:* KO 1497.
petrol for its tanks: KO 1215.
across the Czech border: KO 1371.
consisted mainly of stragglers: KO 1512.
stocks to the division: KOs 1334, 1339, 1340.
increase its striking power: KOs 1609, 1612.
petrol could be provided: KO 1610.
command of General Wenck: KO 1267.
Mulde for the purpose: KOs 1327, 1328.
miles to the west: KOs 1422, 1449.
word from 12 Army: KO 1443.

p. 256   *to 'do its duty':* KO 1654.
before coming into effect: KO 1695.
Berlin by 15 June: KO 1546.
of the Ultra signal: KO 1846.
the OKW War Diary: Schramm 1466.
Doenitz as his successor: KO 1846.
pieces of confirmatory evidence: BTs 3753, 6077, 6848.

p. 257   Inside the Third Reich: p. 435.
Ruhr bridges for demolition: BT 7628.
by Keitel and Hitler: Speer 435–6.
than two days later: BT 7849. The German text of the decree is in Schramm 1580–81, translation in Speer 562.

issued in nineteen days: Speer 460.
of a 'transport wilderness': BT 9387; cf. Speer 453.
to be left alone: KO 717.

p. 258   *the prospect in mid-April:* SHAEF Weekly Intelligence Summary No. 56.

seriously in mid-March: Ellis ii. 302–3 reproduces a passage from Intelligence Summary No. 51.

the bases of strategy: Ellis ii. 298, Churchill vi. 401–2.

attention in late April: Intelligence Summary No. 57.

issued on 15 April: Schramm 1587–9.

in an 'inner fortress': Ellis ii. 429–30.

p. 260   *of Munich was suggested:* BT 5959.

as was another: BT 7796.

of them at Weimar: BTs 8465, 8569, 8788, 9458.

several departments of OKL: KO 69, BTs 9843, 9871.

miles of one another): KO 796. See also KO 1246.

p. 261   *both Potsdam and Traunstein:* KO 887.

part to Wasserburg: KO 1078.

take no more chances: Pogue 456, Strong 188.

district by 19 April: KO 1361.

the south-bound group: KO 1381.

to go to Berlin: KO 1373.

his headquarters near Salzburg: KO 1509.

were causing some alarm: KO 1380.

in the Reich Chancellery: Schramm 1755–6, Ellis ii. 432.

p. 262   *on the previous day:* KO 1338.

close by at Fuerstenberg: KOs 1450, 1531.

the outskirts of Flensburg: KOs 1826, 1980.

n.   *the order in Berlin:* Schramm 1590–91.

Kiel on the 22nd: KO 1241.

the north of Salzburg: KO 1858.

Hitler's 24 April order: It is reproduced in the British Official History: Ellis ii. 429–30.

p. 263   *Berchtesgaden and Zell-am-See:* KOs 1879, 1886, 1944, 2059; see also KOs 1829, 1914, 1932.

under tactical conditions': Macdonald, *Last Offensive* 441.

its intention was delivered: KO 2030, Schramm 1756.

Index